Pub-16.00

Commerce and Social Standing
in Ancient Rome

COMMERCE AND SOCIAL STANDING IN ANCIENT ROME

JOHN H. D'ARMS

Harvard University Press

Cambridge, Massachusetts, and London, England

1981

Copyright © 1981 by John H. D'Arms
All rights reserved
Printed in the United States of America

Library of Congress Cataloging in Publication Data

D'Arms, John H. 1934–
    Commerce and social standing in ancient Rome.
    Bibliography: p.
    Includes index.
    1. Rome—Commerce—History.   2. Social classes—
Rome—History.   I. Title.
HF377.D37   306'.3   80-25956
ISBN 0-674-14475-9

To Teresa

Preface

Attitudes and behavior and the relationship between them are the chief subjects of this book. My aim is to achieve a better understanding of Roman social structures by offering a response to two questions: what were the predominant Roman attitudes toward commerce and trade in the late Republic and first two centuries of the Empire, and how did Roman conduct relate to them? The chief focus is upon men, rather than upon markets; on the traders of articles rather than on articles of trade; on senators, *equites*, municipal notables, and freedmen, and their respective roles and functions in Roman commercial operations.

In a number of recent works, Roman social and economic historians have been exploiting the considerable ancient evidence for sizes, prices, numbers; ingenious use is being made of models, tables, and coordinates. It will be obvious how much the following pages owe, directly and indirectly, to these and other works, and very especially to M. I. Finley's *The Ancient Economy*, which stimulated me to try to formulate new questions and to seek at least the outlines of answers. I envy the precision and clarity with which the authors of quantitative studies have been able to express their results. My topics—attitudes, behavior, social standing—are far more subjective, more difficult to conceptualize and to define. The ancient literature is so often tendentious or merely conventional that it seems to impose a barrier between the historian and the sensibilities of the Romans, whereas inscriptional and archaeological materials, less "ideological" in character, present difficulties of their own.

If the nature of the evidence has presented one set of problems, the proper form and organization of the discussion has presented another. When an argument is conducted at too general a level, or over too wide a time span, or is too free with analogies drawn from other periods and

places, one opens oneself to the charges of oversimplification, super-
ficiality, or even distortion. On the other hand, too narrow a focus may
altogether prevent from emerging such conclusions as may be of general
interest and validity. All historians seek to strike some reasonable
balance between the excessively general and the excessively particular, and I am not so sanguine as to suppose that my own solution is
above criticism.

The first chapter attempts to provide an intellectual framework for
the book as a whole. Examples of aristocratic attitudes toward commerce and toward professional traders are drawn from a number of
preindustrial societies, and compared and contrasted with those of
ancient Rome. For Rome, the thought of M. I. Rostovtzeff and of
M. I. Finley serves as the point of departure; it leads to the formulation
of fresh questions about the ways in which Roman upper-class attitudes
actually affected Roman commercial structures. Chapter 2 examines
Roman attitudes and conduct in depth, and in historical context, over
a period which ranges from the middle Republic to the Ciceronian
Age; I attempt to show how thought and action remained integrated,
and more than formally compatible.

There follows a succession of studies of certain social groupings.
Chronologically, geographically, and textually, these next four chapters
are more sharply focused, ranging in date from the Ciceronian Age
through the second century of the Empire. The first two are devoted
largely to senators. In Chapter 3, the combining of literary with archaeological evidence throws new light both upon the commercial interests of certain late Republican aristocrats, and upon the highly
conventional character of certain passages in Roman literature. In
Chapter 4, I attempt a fresh analysis of the villa society on the Bay of
Naples, stressing linkages and points of interconnection between the
pleasure palaces of the Roman rich and the economic forces of the
Campanian region.

The next two chapters are devoted largely to freedmen. In Chapter
5 Trimalchio, his sources of wealth, and his attitudes are subjected to
fresh scrutiny. I attempt here to combat recent centrifugal tendencies
in literary criticism and historical writing, and to offer a different
interpretation, one which seems to me to be more compatible with what
the author of the *Satyricon* actually wrote. Chapter 6 turns to actual
wealthy freedmen (Augustales) in actual urban centers (the ports of

Puteoli and Ostia); analysis of the various types of information which can be gleaned from their gravestones leads to new conclusions about their function, and their importance, in early imperial economy and society.

Although each of the studies in these four chapters is intended to have some independent value as a piece of historical analysis, there are thematic links between them, and they form, I believe, an increasingly coherent sequence. In Chapter 7, a general discussion of personal attitudes and of private commercial initiatives, across the social spectrum and under the changing conditions of the principate, I attempt to tie together the major themes of the book, and to convey an overall impression of the relative importance which social standing played in the pursuit of commercial wealth in the early Roman Empire.

This book, though short, has been in gestation for more than five years, and along the way generous assistance from institutions and from individuals has placed me heavily in debt. It is a pleasure now to offer my warmest thanks, recognizing that to acknowledge such obligations is not necessarily to discharge them adequately, and that to name persons is not to imply their endorsement of the book's contents—for these I alone remain responsible.

My working plans were clarified, and early drafts of four chapters were written, as a result of the award of a John S. Guggenheim Fellowship for 1975–76, which I spent as Visiting Member of the School of Historical Studies at the Institute for Advanced Study, Princeton. I am grateful to J. F. Gilliam for frequent and sympathetic counsel throughout that year, and to other historians in the Princeton environment for stimulating conversations: T. R. S. Broughton, E. Champlin, W. R. Connor, C. Habicht, T. J. Luce among classicists, but also historians of later epochs, especially R. Darnton, R. Forster, J. H. Hexter, Lawrence Stone, and Avrom L. Udovitch. At the University of Michigan my departmental colleagues B. W. Frier, L. Koenen, D. O. Ross, and the late Herbert C. Youtie, as well as the historians Raymond Grew and Sylvia Thrupp, had a salutary influence on parts of my text; so also have the students who participated in my graduate classes and seminars, and V. Fiscus, whose collaboration improved Chapter 1.

The writing was completed in Italy. Three years at the American Academy in Rome offered only occasional interludes for sustained research and writing, but those interludes would have been fewer still and less productive had it not been for the steady encouragement of my wife, Teresa. Residence at the Academy assisted my work in important ways. Above all, it meant proximity to archaeological material and inscriptions, both published and unpublished, to which Italian authorities in the ministry of Beni Culturali courteously facilitated access; it meant proximity as well to many Italian friends from whose conversation and criticism I profited greatly—to name them all is not feasible, but I must express appreciation and gratitude to E. Gabba, S. Panciera, M. Torelli, and F. Zevi. Moreover, the Academy's Roman situation and institutional character attract a steady stream of visiting scholars, to many of whom I have been able to turn for bibliographical suggestions, appraisal of portions of this book, and other kinds of practical assistance. I have been thus helped, in Rome and elsewhere, by J. S. Ackerman, G. W. Bowersock, F. E. Brown, Daniel Cecil (who drew the maps), W. V. Clausen, E. F. D'Arms, Sir Moses Finley, Peter Garnsey, Karin Einaudi (director of the Fototeca Unione), W. V. Harris, Keith Hopkins, the late Milton J. Lewine, R. Meiggs, R. E. A. Palmer, L. Richardson, Jr., D. R. Shackleton Bailey, J. B. Ward-Perkins, E. L. Will, and T. P. Wiseman; in addition, I learned much from all the participants at the Academy's year-long symposium on Roman Seaborne Commerce during 1978–79. Finally, the staff of the Library of the American Academy, under the direction of Rogers Scudder and Lucilla Marino, responded promptly, resourcefully, and cheerfully to my many urgent calls for help, and thereby spared me countless hours of searching.

The influence, direct and indirect, of the late M. W. Frederiksen upon these pages stands in a class apart. Since my interests in Roman Campania led me to him in 1965, we had been in frequent contact, and there was no scholar whose reactions to my ideas and written drafts I sought so eagerly or prized so highly. His erudition, so lightly carried and so openly shared, was astonishing; yet I found still more remarkable the independence and equilibrium of his scholarly judgment, based upon an unostentatious command of half a dozen specialized fields, and an ability to put them all to work in the service of broader historical understanding. In Roman studies, he constituted an unusually effective link between archaeologists and historians, as well as between Italy and the world of Anglo-Saxon scholarship; his premature and tragic death has left his many friends and admirers in a state of shock. I count myself fortunate to have had his comments on these chapters shortly before he died.

Ann Arbor
September 1980

Contents

Figures

Maps

Abbreviations

Most abbreviations used in this book are those employed in *L'Année Philologique* or are otherwise well known. Attention should be called to the abbreviations of the following works, some of which are frequently cited and some of which may be unfamiliar to readers.

ANRW	H. Temporini, ed., *Aufstieg und Niedergang der römischen Welt*
Broughton, *MRR*	T. R. S. Broughton, *The Magistrates of the Roman Republic*, 2 vols.
Brunt, *Equites*	P. A. Brunt, "The *Equites* in the Late Republic," *Second International Conference of Economic History: Aix 1962*
CIL	*Corpus Inscriptionum Latinarum*
D'Arms, *RBN*	J. H. D'Arms, *Romans on the Bay of Naples*
DdArch.	*Dialoghi di Archeologia*
Dubois, *PA*	C. Dubois, *Pouzzoles antique*
Duff, *Freedmen*	A. M. Duff, *Freedmen in the Early Roman Empire*
Duncan-Jones, *ERE*	R. Duncan-Jones, *The Economy of the Roman Empire: Quantitative Studies*
FA	*Fasti Archeologici*
Finley, *Economy*	M. I. Finley, *The Ancient Economy*
Finley, *Property*	M. I. Finley, ed., *Studies in Roman Property*
Frank, *ESAR*	T. Frank et al., *An Economic Survey of Ancient Rome*
ILLRP	A. Degrassi, *Inscriptiones Latinae Liberae Rei Publicae*
ILS	H. Dessau, *Inscriptiones Latinae Selectae*
MacMullen, *RSR*	R. MacMullen, *Roman Social Relations*
Meiggs, *RO²*	R. Meiggs, *Roman Ostia*, second edition
NdSc.	*Notizie degli Scavi di Antichità*
PIR	*Prosopographia Imperii Romani* (*PIR²* refers to available volumes of the second edition)
RE	Pauly-Wissowa-Kroll, eds., *Realencyclopädie der klassischen Altertumswissenschaft*
Rostovtzeff, *SEHRE²*	M. I. Rostovtzeff, *The Social and Economic History of the Roman Empire*, second edition
Rougé, *OCM*	J. Rougé, *Recherches sur l'organisation du commerce maritime en méditerranée sous l'empire romain*
Seaborne Commerce	J. H. D'Arms and E. C. Kopff, eds., *Roman Seaborne Commerce: Studies in Archaeology and History* (= Memoirs of the American Academy in Rome 36)

SB, *Att.*	D. R. Shackleton Bailey, *Cicero's Letters to Atticus*, 7 vols.
SB, *Fam.*	D. R. Shackleton Bailey, *Cicero: Epistulae ad familiares*, 2 vols.
Shatzman, *SWRP*	I. Shatzman, *Senatorial Wealth and Roman Politics*
Treggiari, *RFLR*	S. Treggiari, *Roman Freedmen during the Late Republic*
Wiseman, *NMRS*	T. P. Wiseman, *New Men in the Roman Senate 139 B.C.–14 A.D.*

Commerce and Social Standing
in Ancient Rome

Traders in Roman Society:
Two Approaches

I

An archive consisting largely of personal correspondence was discovered some years ago in the port of La Rochelle by Robert Forster; it forms the basis of a monograph entitled *Merchants, Landlords, Magistrates: The Depont Family in Eighteenth Century France*. Grandfather Paul Depont was a commercial shipper, whose profits from the slave trade enabled him to invest in land near La Rochelle in the first decades of the eighteenth century: he was the founder of the family fortunes. His son, Paul François Depont, was made one of 609 *trésoriers de France* in 1723, thereby becoming a member of the lower fringes of the French nobility; his wealth was entirely in land and in capital investments; and he continued to live in La Rochelle, participating actively in local politics. Upward social mobility was more marked in the next generation: the son of Paul François, Jean Samuel, attained the rank of *intendant* (there were but thirty in all of France), and lived almost all his adult life not in La Rochelle but among the *haute société* of Paris. Relations between the father and his son the *intendant* could be stormy, as we learn from Paul François' letters to Jean Samuel in Paris; a principal cause was that Jean Samuel, the *grand Parisien*, was embarrassed by the commercial base of the family fortune; he confessed that he was scandalized to learn that his grandfather was formally designated as "merchant" and "shipper" in official state contracts.

It would not do for a member of the French nobility to have a background in commerce or trade, for such activities had long before acquired socially negative connotations. Early in the seventeenth century in France "they holde a base and sordid kind of profession for a gentleman to trade by merchandise, and by the lawes of England, France and

Germany hee loseth the qualitie of a nobleman that doth trafficke."[1] When two impoverished but respectably connected young men arrived in Charleston in 1764 to seek their fortune in trade, Henry Laurens would not hear of it: they must become Planters first, for the sake of appearances; retail trade "would be mean, would lessen them in the esteem of people whose respect they must endeavor to attract."[2]

Indeed, for a nobleman, even indirect participation in commercial enterprises provoked negative reactions. When, in the 1480s, Filippo Strozzi disingenuously pretended to desire a Florentine palace which was "useful and not pretentious," and so made provisions for a series of revenue-producing shops and stalls along the street flanking the entrance, Lorenzo the Magnificent had little difficulty in dissuading him. Such "utility" was servile and degrading, full of ugliness, Lorenzo admonished; moreover, the palace's noble inhabitants would be greatly inconvenienced. A century later a Frescobaldi heiress closed up the loggia of her Florentine palace in order to make space for four shops; she was promptly accused of avarice, of preferring "utility" to honor and to respect for tradition.[3] Within aristocratic systems of values such as these, the form of wealth preeminently considered socially respectable was the possession and cultivation of one's own landed estates, and even there it was the civilized style of life, rather than the reaping of agricultural profits, that stamped these pursuits as appropriate for the nobility.

How comparable, *mutatis mutandis*, were the attitudes to trade and traders which find expression in the works of upper-class authors in the Roman world of the late Republic and early Empire? At first sight, the parallels appear to be close indeed: in fact, a Renaissance historian has argued recently that the revival of classical studies and values at the beginning of the Renaissance had direct and important bearing on the process whereby, in northern Italy, mercantile and craft activities

1. R. Dallington, *The View of France* (1604), ed. W. P. Barrett (Oxford 1936).

2. G. C. Rogers, ed., *The Papers of Henry Laurens*, vol. 4 (Columbia, S. C., 1974), p. 338; cf. F. P. Bowes, *The Culture of Early Charleston* (Chapel Hill 1942), p. 118.

3. The palazzo Strozzi: G. Gaye, *Carteggio inedito d'artisti*, vol. 1 (Florence 1839), pp. 354ff, discussed also by E. H. Gombrich, "The Early Medici as Patrons of Art," first published in 1960, and reprinted in E. H. Gombrich, *Norm and Form: Studies in the Art of the Renaissance* (London 1966), pp. 54–55. The Frescobaldi palace: R. A. Goldthwaite, "The Florentine Palace as Domestic Architecture," *The American Historical Review* 77 (1972), p. 989.

came to acquire their socially negative connotations.[4] The early church
fathers provide a direct link between antiquity and the early Renaissance; St. Ambrose, condemning the insatiable greed of merchants,
enjoined them to use the sea for purposes of food, not for purposes of
commerce: "God did not make the sea to be sailed over."[5] Concerning
the buying and selling of merchandise (*mercatura*), concerning the
"professional" men who sailed the seas and earned their living thereby
(*mercatores*), concerning the shippers of wares who went on board
themselves (*navicularii*), Romans of the senatorial class could be contemptuous and disparaging. Cicero once described *mercatores* as *homines tenues, obscuro loco nati*. When Verres had the audacity to claim
that he had purchased, rather than appropriated, the statues and paintings, silver and gold, ivory and precious stones, which belonged to the
inhabitants of his province, Cicero's response was both pointed and
impolite: "A sterling defense, by heaven! We have sent a trader to a
province with the insignia of a governor"; he is equally scornful of the

4. C. M. Cipolla, "The Italian 'Failure,' " in F. Krantz and P. M. Hohenberg, eds.,
*Failed Transitions to Modern Industrial Society: Renaissance Italy and Seventeenth
Century Holland* (Quebec 1975), pp. 9–10.

5. Ambros. *De Elia*. 70: *Mare non ad navigandum deus fecit, sed propter elementi
pulchritudinem*; for a discussion of this and other Ambrosian texts condemning commerce and *mercatores*, see F. Homes Dudden, *The Life and Times of St. Ambrose*, vol.
2 (Oxford 1935), pp. 548–549. The common medieval aphorism that "a man who
trades can never or only rarely be pleasing in God's sight" (*homo mercator aut numquam
aut vix deo placere potest*) may in fact derive from the verses of Ecclesiasticus (chaps.
26–27) which begin "A merchant shall hardly keep himself from doing wrong / And
a huckster shall not be freed from sin. / As a nail sticketh fast between the joining of
the stones, / So doth sin stick close between the buying and the selling." Cf. J. Melitz
and D. Winch, eds., Jacob Viner, *Religious Thought and Economic Society: Four
Chapters of an Unfinished Work* (Durham, N. C. 1978), p. 36–37 (to be used with
caution: see the review by J. T. Noonan, Jr., *The Economic Journal* 89 (1979), pp.
482–484). For a general discussion of the attitudes towards commerce and traders
among medieval thinkers, see P. Jones, "Storia economica," in *Storia d'Italia* 2
(Einaudi, Turin 1974), pp. 1469 ff.; and note also R. S. Lopez, *The Commercial
Revolution of the Middle Ages, 950–1350* (Cambridge 1976), p. 60: "Paupers were
more acceptable than merchants: they would inherit the Kingdom of Heaven and help
the alms-giving rich to earn entrance. Merchants were gold-hungry, said Rathier, the
Belgian bishop of Verona: they were less useful than farmers who fed the entire population, said Aelfric, the English abbot of Eynsham; they did not know what honor
means, said Ramon Muntaner, the Catalan soldier adventurer." For similarly negative
attitudes toward merchants in China during the Han dynasty (206 B.C.–A.D. 220), see
now M. G. Raschke, "New Studies in Roman Commerce with the East," in *ANRW*,
II (Principat) 9.2 (Berlin, 1978), p. 637 with refs. in nn 601–608.

notion that Verres acquired a ship so as to "go into shipping."[6] When, in a much quoted passage of *De Officiis* (1.151), Cicero states that *mercatura* is not so very discreditable (*non est admodum vituperanda*), he immediately adds the important qualification that it must be engaged in on a grand scale (*magna et copiosa*). On one occasion, concerned for the health of his favorite freedman, who was about to embark upon a long sea voyage, Cicero urged Tiro not to go on board a commercial ship, "for sailors are inclined to hurry things for their own profit"; if travel he must, let him embark with some reputable person (*cum honesto aliquo homine*) who could be expected to exert influence on the *navicularius*.[7]

The tone of disparagement continues into the Empire. C. Sempronius Gracchus, scion of a noble late Republican house, eked out a miserable existence as a shipper in the age of Tiberius: according to Tacitus, "he supported himself by petty trading (*sordidas merces*) between Africa and Sicily."[8] *Sordida merces*: it is a recurring phrase, and is employed exclusively in contexts where the scale of commercial operations is small,[9] or the respectability of the practitioner is suspect (witness the motives which Tacitus ascribes to the freedman Atilius, who undertook to build an amphitheater at Fidenae).[10] Philostratus introduces the sophist Proclus of Naukratis, who, while living at Athens, maintained close relations with his native place, whence he arranged to receive regular shipments of incense, ivory, myrrh, papyrus and books, which he then sold to dealers in such wares in Athens. Philostratus takes pains to add the information which sets the behavior, and the attitude, of Proclus firmly apart from the mentality of the trader: "On no occasion did he show himself avid of profits, mean-spirited (ἀνελεύθερος) or acquisitive"[11]—his readers would have been certain to associate such lowly instincts with persons "that do trafficke."

6. *Homines tenues*: Cic. II *Verr.* 5.167 (the significance of which is discussed below in Chapter 2, section I. Verres as *mercator*: II *Verr.* 4.8: *Di immortales, praeclaram defensionem! Mercatorem in provinciam cum imperio ac securibus misimus*. Verres as shipper: II *Verr.* 5.46 (*naviculariam facere*).

7. Cic. *Ad Fam.* 16.9.4.

8. Tac. *Ann.* 4.13.2: *Per Africam ac Siciliam mutando sordidas merces sustentabatur.*

9. Cic. *De Off.* 1.151; *Mercatura . . . si tenuis est, sordida putanda est*; cf. *In Pis.* frag. 9.

10. Tac. *Ann.* 4.62.2; cf. Quint. *Inst.* 1.12.17: *dum sit locupletior aliquis sordidae mercis negotiator.*

11. Philos. *Vit. Soph.* 2.21.

The ideas remained current in the late Empire, as is shown by a phrase of Sidonius Apollinaris: "He ekes out a miserable existence by mere trading."[12]

"What mattered . . . was the scale of the transaction, and the practitioner's attitude to it."[13] The writings of our Roman upper-class spokesmen well illustrate the social sanctions against trading operations which were petty and mean, but there were also legal sanctions prohibiting men of senatorial rank from direct involvement in shipping enterprises which were copious and grand. According to the *plebiscitum Claudianum* of 219–218 B.C., no senator, or senator's son, might own an ocean-going ship (*maritimam navem*), which the law defined in terms of capacity of more than three hundred jars; Livy comments that "every form of profit seeking was thought unsuitable for senators."[14] Previously, though, he had introduced an important qualification. It was clearly considered legitimate to ship the surplus produce from one's estates along the rivers to the coast—Cato had in fact recommended that estates be situated near a river, precisely to facilitate the marketing of produce.[15] But large-scale exportation to distant markets, elsewhere in Italy or overseas, was on a different order of magnitude, and this was what was being prohibited. The law, moreover, was no mere temporary measure. Cicero's words prove that it was technically still in force in 70 B.C.,[16] its terms were restated in Caesar's *lex de repetundis* in 59 B.C.; and it was apparently formally binding still in the third century of the Empire, if that is the correct inference from *sententiae* of the jurist Paul.[17]

The upper-class expressions of contempt for *mercatura* and *mercatores* (*negotiatores* under the Empire), and the legal sanctions against senatorial engagement in seaborne commerce, imply the existence of

---

12. Sid. Apoll. *Ep.* 6.8.1: *Pauperem vitam sola mercandi actione sustentat.*
13. Wiseman, *NMRS*, p. 79.
14. Liv. 21.63.4: *Quaestus omnis patribus indecorus visus.*
15. Cat. *De Agr.* 1.3; cf. Strab. 5.235.
16. Cic. II *Verr.* 5.45. On the significance of the passage, see below, Chapter 2, section II.
17. Scaev. *Dig.* 50.5.3, a restatement, in Caesar's extortion law, of the terms of the *lex Claudia.* Paul's *Sententiae*; G. G. Archi et al., *Pauli Sententiarum Fragmentum Leidense* (Leiden 1956), sent. 2, p. 5: *Senatores parentesve eorum, in quorum potestate sunt, vectigalia publica conducere, navem in quaestum habere, equosve curules praebendos suscipere prohibentur: idque factum repetundarum lege vindicatur.* See further Rougé, *OCM*, p. 12n2; pp. 311–312.

another and related attitude: that the economic pursuits becoming to a man of *dignitas* were preeminently agricultural. The relationship might be expressed more broadly, and applied to cities, as when in the *De Re Publica* Cicero blames the final overthrow of Carthage and Corinth on the fact that *mercandi cupiditas et navigandi* had caused them to abandon agriculture and warefare.[18] After all, since censorial assessments of Roman citizens were implicitly based upon the extent of their landed possessions, senators were landowners by definition; and authors like Cicero or the Younger Pliny, and doubtless most wealthy *equites* as well, might seem to have characteristics in common with "gentlemen" of later ages, or at least with the well-known *gentiluomini* of Machiavelli's definition: "those who live in idleness on the abundant revenues of their estates, without having anything to do either with their cultivation or with other forms of labor essential to life."[19] In Cicero's famous classification of trades and professions according to moral criteria, grandness of scale, as we have seen, helped to render *mercatura honesta*, but it is the investment of trading profits in agriculture that places trade more firmly in the category of *artes liberales*: "Of all the ways of acquiring wealth, none is better than agriculture, none more pleasant or fruitful, none more fitting for a free man."[20] The various Italian properties in which the Younger Pliny passed days of civilized leisure were all either agricultural estates or had complements of productive lands, and as for his assets, "I am nearly entirely in land" he once remarks;[21] he derived particular satisfaction from acquiring adjacent properties (*pulchritudo iungendi*).[22] Neither Pliny nor other aristocrats would have regarded this interest in increasing their properties as "acquisitive": indeed, members of the Roman nobility are found adopting an attitude of lofty indifference to financial gain of any kind.[23]

18. Cic. *De Re Pub.* 2.7–10; on which see below, Chapter 2, section II.

19. Machiavelli, *Discorsi* 1.55.7, trans. L. J. Walker (London 1950), cited also by Wiseman, *NMRS*, p. 68.

20. Cic. *De Off.* 1.151. But cf. below, Chapter 2, section I.

21. Pliny *Ep.* 3.19.8: *sum quidem prope totus in praediis.* On Pliny's estates, the main base of his wealth, see Duncan-Jones, *ERE*, pp. 17–32. Pliny's remark is further discussed below in Chapter 5, section II; for his attitudes, see Chapter 7, section I.

22. Pliny *Ep.* 3.19.2.

23. In 91 B.C. L. Licinius Crassus argued that increasing the size of one's patrimony was not a mark of *nobilitas* (Cic. *De Or.* 2.225–226 = *ORF*³ fr. 45, p. 255) "*Quid te agere? Cui rei, cui gloriae, cui virtuti studere? Patrimonione augendo: at id non est*

Jean Samuel Depont, Cicero, Tacitus, and Pliny have this in common, that they exhibit an attitude which might be described as one of moral disdain for traders and men of commerce, and attach high value to agriculture, above all as a nonoccupation, a gentlemanly pursuit. Here are spokesmen from two sophisticated and complex civilizations, eighteen centuries apart but comparable in that both were preindustrial economies and stratified societies—which is to say, differences of status were marked and keenly noticed, frequently commented upon by the wealthy few, the persons who comprised the political and social elite. But the Roman evidence fails us in one particular in which the French is explicit: we do not have even one example of a Roman senator who, like Depont, deprecated traders but can be shown nevertheless to have trade in his own background: that is, condemns the very source of his family's wealth. And yet, if there were senators whose fortunes derived from *mercatura*, their adoption of a disdainful attitude is precisely what we might expect, owing to the familiar tendency for new members of any elite to assimilate and espouse the values and attitudes characteristic of their new station: it is difficult to conceive of a more eloquent spokesman for and dedicated defender of traditional senatorial values than M. Tullius Cicero, a *novus homo*.

The immense wealth of many late Republican senators is well documented, and has now been made the subject of a lengthy monograph;[24] for the early Empire, a recent list of the sizes of known private fortunes numbers twenty-nine entries, with assets ranging from HS 1,800,000 to HS 400,000,000.[25] Abundant also are the signs of wealth, many of them archaeological, reflecting that tendency towards conspicuous consumption which the Romans knew as *luxuria*:[26] elaborate and ostentatious building in the cities of the Empire, vast and magnificent villas and palaces on the coasts and in the hinterland. The numbers of Roman senators never fell below four hundred; the property qualification for membership in the senatorial *ordo* remained at one million sesterces for at least the first two centuries of the Empire; it has been calculated that Roman imperial senators enjoyed annual incomes which were two thousand times higher than the levels of min-

nobilitatis." Cf. Cicero's contention that *nobiles* had always preferred popularity and glory to money, which they despised (*Phil.* 1.29).

24. Shatzman, *SWRP.*
25. Duncan-Jones, *ERE*, pp. 343–344.
26. Brunt, *Equites*, p. 136.

imum subsistence of a family of peasants.[27] Studies of the composition of the ruling class reveal clearly that as old senatorial families died out, new men from Italy and, increasingly, from the provinces appeared to take their place: wealth remained concentrated within the hands of a small group of individuals, but the social composition of that group itself changed radically between the years 100 B.C. and A.D. 180.[28]

Furthermore, with the restoration of peace in Italy after the civil wars, the seas were safe for shipping and economic exploitation of the provinces could resume—indeed, could proceed at rates previously unprecedented. The prosperity and intensity of building programs, and improved harbor facilities, at the great Italian ports (figures 1, 16, 17, 19)—Puteoli, Aquileia, Ostia[29]—provide a tangible context for the Younger Seneca's listing overseas trade first among the ways in which a would-be *dives* might expect to acquire a fortune,[30] for the elder Pliny's assertion that a huge number (*universa multitudo*) was sailing the seas in his day in hopes of profit,[31] and for Juvenal's remark that more men were on the sea than on the land, such was their eagerness to be rich.[32] We now know of a late Republican vessel with a cargo of nearly 7,000 wine jars and a capacity of 325–425 metric tons; we know that merchant ships carrying up to 200 tons of cargo could be towed up the Tiber from Ostia to Rome; we know that by the end of the second century the standard size of the ocean-going vessels used for the transport of grain was between 340 and 400 tons.[33] The volume

27. K. Hopkins, "Economic Growth and Towns in Classical Antiquity", in P. Abrams and E. A. Wrigley, ed., *Towns in Societies* (Cambridge 1978), p. 49.

28. On this subject the literature is vast; I cite only selected studies. For the late Republican senate, see Wiseman (*NMRS*); for the changing composition of the senate under the Empire, see the bibliographical conspectus of A. N. Sherwin-White, *The Letters of Pliny: A Historical and Social Commentary* (Oxford 1966), pp. 377–378; for the hellenized East, cf. G. W. Bowersock, *Augustus and the Greek World* (Oxford 1965), pp. 141–145; C. Habicht, *Istanbuler Mitteilungen* 9–10 (1959–60), pp. 122–123.

29. Puteoli: M. W. Frederiksen, *RE* 23 (1959) 2044–54, J. H. D'Arms, *JRS* 64 (1974), pp. 104–124; Aquileia: A. Calderini, *Aquileia romana* (Milan 1930); Ostia: Meiggs, *RO*[2].

30. Sen. *Ep.* 119.5: *circumspiciebam, in quod me mare negotiaturus immitterem*.

31. Plin. *NH* 2.118; cf. his further observation that first pirates and later *avaritia* drove men to risk death by sailing on winter seas (2.125).

32. Juv. 14.276–277.

33. Republican ship: A. Tchernia, P. Pomey, A. Hesnard, *L'épave romaine de la Madrague de Giens, Gallia*, suppl. 34, (Paris 1978), pp. 105–106; the Tiber, Ostia, and grain transport: H. T. Wallinga, "Nautika I: The Units of Capacity for Ancient

of Roman commercial shipping was substantial, the profits great, and men were not significantly deterred by the risks involved.

Here we are presented with a composite picture of the upper echelons of Roman society which seems coherent and consistent, but is nonetheless disturbing. A world in which the senatorial elite possessed wealth in abundance, concentrated primarily in landed estates. A world in which tradition, convention, and the laws appeared to perpetuate upper-class values and attitudes that glorified agricultural pursuits and deprecated the pursuits of commercial gain. But a world, at the same time, which witnessed accelerated rates of change in the composition of Rome's governing class, and in which the ports throughout the Mediterranean (map 1) were bustling and the sea itself full of commercial traffic, conveying the articles of Italian and, increasingly, provincial trade and manufacture to and from the major harbors (figure 1). Are we to accept the negative remarks of our predominantly senatorial authors essentially as they stand, and to conclude that commercial wealth was never, or to a degree so small as to be statistically insignificant, the source—near or remote—of senatorial fortunes? Is it legitimate to consider Machiavelli's description of a *gentiluomo*, cited above, as properly illustrative of Roman attitudes? Machiavelli himself was compelled to recognize major differences between most European aristocracies and the patriciate of Venice. "The gentlemen of that Republic," he wrote, ". . . do not have great incomes from landed possessions, but their great riches are based on trade and movable property."[34] Were there, in fact, no Jean Samuel Deponts in ancient Rome?

Ships," *Mn.* 17 (1964), pp. 1–40; cf. L. Casson, "Harbour and River Boats of Ancient Rome," *JRS* 55 (1965), pp. 31–39; G. Rickman, *Roman Granaries and Store Buildings* (Cambridge 1971), pp. 6–7. As early as the Augustan Age, the emperor could mobilize resources, in exceptional circumstances, to produce prodigious maritime giants: the vessels which transported the Flaminian and Vatican obelisks to Italy had a capacity of more than 3000 tons, and the latter was at least 104 meters in length: Plin. *NH* 36.70; 16.201–202, on which see R. P. Duncan-Jones, "Giant Cargo-Ships in Antiquity," *CQ* n.s. 27 (1977), pp. 331–332; see further O. Testaguzza, *Portus* (Rome 1970), p. 110. For the phases of growth, and substantial remains, of port installations in Rome, see now F. Castagnoli, "Installazioni portuali a Roma," in *Seaborne Commerce*, pp. 35–42; evidence demonstrates that the early second century B.C., the Augustan Age, and the reign of Trajan were all notable periods of development.

34. *Discorsi* #1. 55. He continues: "Thus the name of gentlemen among them [the Venetians] is a name of dignity and reputation, without being founded on any of those

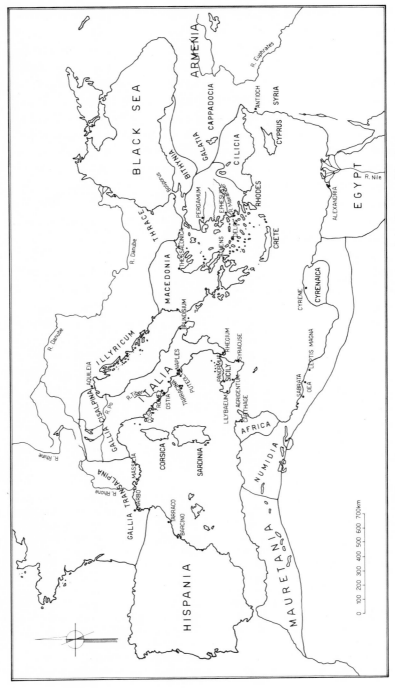

1. Italy and the Mediterranean in the first two centuries of the Roman Empire.

While I know of no previous attempts to formulate these questions in just this way, two distinguished social and economic historians of the past and present generation have given us original and comprehensive syntheses in which they treat the general problem of the importance of commerce and trade in the Roman world. The syntheses were written from different conceptual and methodological perspectives and are of different scope and scale. And they offer, either explicitly or by implication, very different answers to the questions raised above. It will be useful to review briefly that portion of the work of M. I. Rostovtzeff and of M. I. Finley which bears directly upon the matter of concern to us here.

II

Rostovtzeff approached the issue with characteristic confidence and verve. In a now famous passage of his *Social and Economic History of the Roman Empire* he wrote: "No scholar has endeavored to collect the evidence about the rich men of the second century, about the sources of their income, and about the character of their economic activity. A careful investigation of this subject promises good results . . . As far as I can judge from the evidence I have got together, the main source of large fortunes . . . was commerce. Money acquired by commerce was increased by lending it out mostly on mortgage, and it was invested in land."[35]

It must be noted, first of all, that Rostovtzeff produced very little tangible evidence of senatorial involvement in shipping enterprises. His "classical example of a shrewd and successful . . . merchant" (figure 2) is non-Roman and nonsenatorial,[36] his "rich men of the commercial class," whom he associates both with Italy and the provinces, are the inhabitants of the cities throughout the Empire.[37] As

---

things in other cities signified by the word *"gentleman."* Cf. W. J. Bouwsma, *Venice and the Defense of Republican Liberty: Renaissance Values in the Age of the Counter-Reformation* (Berkeley and Los Angeles 1968), p. 58.

35. *SEHRE*[2], p. 153, cited also by MacMullen, *RSR*, pp. 48–49.

36. Ibid., p. 613n31.

37. Ibid., p. xiv: "The representatives of this form of capitalism [i.e., capitalism based upon commerce, industry and scientific agriculture] were the city *bourgeoisie*, which steadily increased in numbers . . . The result was an unprecedentedly rapid and striking development of commerce, industry, and agriculture, and the constant growth of the capital accumulated in the cities gave a fresh impetus to the brilliant efflorescence of city life throughout the Empire."

was demonstrated long ago in an excellent critique of his main writings, Rostovtzeff was here proceeding largely on an intuitive basis, following his deep conviction that, in respect to their economic activities, differences only of scale distinguished Roman antiquity from the modern world.[38] Now that the shaping of the social ideology of Rostovtzeff, and the importance of his personal experience in pre-Soviet Russian society, have been brilliantly and convincingly elucidated by Momigliano,[39] the background of his historical intuition is much clearer. From his fundamental assumption, that "modern capitalistic development . . . differs from the ancient only in quantity and not in quality," it follows logically that the economic categories and conceptions of the present can fairly be applied to Roman economic behavior. This is why, in the pages of Rostovtzeff's work, terms such as "capitalism," "bourgeoisie," "middle class," "proletariat," "factories," and "mass production" appear so often and are so often loosely defined.[40]

The two most telling criticisms of Rostovtzeff's thesis are familiar, and must stand. First, his descriptions and analyses of ancient social and economic behavior depended too closely on assumptions which are appropriate only to an industrial, highly specialized age. Second, he either failed to recognize, or at any rate did not sufficiently emphasize, the fact that throughout most of antiquity, including the period in question, that of the late Republic and early Empire, the foundation of economic life for all persons was not commerce and industry but agriculture (figure 3). Commercial shipping and manufacturing ventures were at best ancillary, owing in large part to the smallness of units of production, the tendency for production and distribution to remain nonspecialized and in the same hands, the difficulties, costs, and risks of distant transport, the geographically restricted nature of most markets, and the negligible progress of technological innovation and improvements.[41] Rostovtzeff's magnificent celebration of the ur-

38. M. Reinhold, "Historian of the Classic World: A Critique of Rostovtzeff," *Science and Society* 10 (1946), pp. 361–391.

39. A. D. Momigliano, "M. I. Rostovtzeff," *Studies in Historiography* (New York 1966), pp. 91–104.

40. Reinhold (above, note 38), pp. 362–363; Momigliano (above, note 39), p. 103; see further G. W. Bowersock, *"The Social and Economic History of the Roman Empire by M. I. Rostovtzeff," Daedalus* 103 (1974), pp. 15–23; MacMullen, *RSR*, pp. 48–52.

41. On all this, see Reinhold (above, note 38) pp. 365–369; MacMullen, *RSR*, pp. 49–51, 97–101; K. Hopkins, *Conquerors and Slaves* (Cambridge 1978), pp. 15–19; for transport costs see Duncan-Jones, *ERE*, pp. 366–369; on ancient technology, cf.

ban bourgeoisie, whose wealth was commercially based, rests on foundations which are, both theoretically and factually, insecure.

We may freely grant the cogency of these criticisms. But it is equally important that they be weighed as exactly as possible, neither underestimated nor exaggerated. Granted that the Roman Empire was a preindustrial economy—it nonetheless exhibits signs of complexity, order, and system in its institutions, to an extent which makes labels like "primitive" inappropriate unless they are carefully qualified. Granted that the definitive modern work on Roman commerce will seem small when placed on the shelves next to the definitive modern work on Roman agriculture—there may be point in seeking to define more closely the actual patterns of social involvement in Roman shipping enterprises, and to try to identify Roman senators with interests in trade. The fact remains that no scholar has actually heeded Rostovtzeff's call to research and investigated the sources of wealth of rich men of the second century.[42]

Would such an investigation in fact yield the kinds of results which Rostovtzeff predicted? Finley would be sceptical. In a preface to a famous discussion of classical Greece he made it clear that between Rostovtzeff's views of the ancient economy and his own there was no comfortable middle ground; that new discoveries, new facts, could never be able to bridge the gap between them, for their conceptions and categories were entirely different.[43] Archaeological evidence merely for the volume of trade, for the wide distribution of the products of Roman manufacture, the kinds of materials which so interested Rostovtzeff, are viewed with fierce—and, be it admitted, at times justified—scepticism: in *The Ancient Economy*, Finley pointed out with obvious relish how the accidental survival of artifacts of stone, metal, and baked clay can lead to unwarranted assumptions about flourishing "industries" and "factories"; he cites the instructive example of the thirty-nine sherds of *terra sigillata* pottery, scattered over an area of 400

---

now H. W. Pleket, "Technology in the Greco-Roman World: A General Report," *Talanta* 5 (1973), pp. 6–47.

42. Observed also by MacMullen, *RSR*, pp. 48–49. Cf. the comment of Shatzman, (*SWRP*, p. 5), that "it is more than forty years since Rostovtzeff called for such an investigation." But Shatzman's own investigation is restricted to the senators of the late Republic, whereas Rostovtzeff was calling for research centered upon the second century of the Empire.

43. M. I. Finley, "Classical Greece," *Second International Conference of Economic History: Aix, 1962* (Paris 1965) p. 12.

square meters, which turned out, after patient examination, to be the fragments of one bowl.[44] He demands "more specification, more qualification, where possible quantification, of such otherwise misleading vague phrases as 'intensive exchange,' 'exceedingly active,' 'examples have been dug up.' "[45] Finley's own method is to concentrate, rather, on certain passages in Roman senatorial writings—the passages from Cicero's *De Officiis* and those from the Younger Pliny, cited above, and passages also from the *Cena Trimalchionis* of Petronius—and to rely heavily upon them as providing "models" for both Roman ideology and behavior. The works of these writers, he argues, faithfully represent upper-class attitudes, and these, in turn, are "not a bad guide" to prevailing Roman social and economic behavior.[46]

In Finley's thinking, as in that of Rostovtzeff, conceptions as to Rome's social structure may be said to provide the key to a proper understanding of Roman economic practices. His emphasis is upon the hierarchical and highly stratified nature of Roman society. This is valuable, in that it enables us to break free from an excessive concentration upon institutions, and to visualize more clearly the huge discrepancies in size between the Roman governing elite, in whose hands power, influence, and wealth were chiefly concentrated, and the rest of the population. If we accept a recent estimate of the population of the Roman Empire at the beginning of the second century A.D. as consisting roughly of fifty million persons, the senatorial stratum amounted to something like 0.002 percent.[47] We are thus forcefully reminded that in studying the canonical works of Roman writers, we ignore the overwhelming mass of the population, the numberless persons at the base of the pyramid which to Finley best represents Roman social structure. But according to Finley, study the writers we must if we are properly to understand Roman economic behavior: for him "status" determines the mentality, the attitudes, and so the economic relations, of the Roman world. In a sense, to know a Roman, to understand his point of view and his economic behavior, is to determine as precisely as

44. Finley, *Economy*, p. 33.
45. Ibid., p. 33.
46. Ibid., p. 57. More recently, Finley has reemphasized some of these ideas in "The Ancient City: From Fustel de Coulanges to Max Weber and Beyond," *Comp. Stud. Soc. Hist.* 19 (1977), pp. 305–327.
47. MacMullen, *RSR*, p. 88.

possible the point which he occupies along what Finley calls "the spectrum of statuses";[48] once we know that, the Roman's economic activities and social attitudes are predictable with a high degree of accuracy.

Finley is therefore not likely to be optimistic about our finding Jean Samuel Deponts in the Roman senate of the late Republic or early Empire; still less is he likely to recommend the subject of research which Rostovtzeff thought, a generation ago, promised "good results." Senators like Cicero and the Younger Pliny are landowners, not traders; they are contemptuous of *mercatores*, *navicularii*, and (under the Empire) *negotiatores*; since they themselves do not admit to commercially based family fortunes, there is probably little point in attempting to identify such cases. Moreover, Finley is sceptical of the modernistic— that is, Rostovtzeffian—inferences often drawn from such evidence. It is more important to inquire who was doing the trading. The answer: small men, *obscuro loco nati*: Trimalchio, a freedman, who immediately ceased to trade after amassing a fortune, who invests in land and henceforth talks and acts like a caricature of a Roman senator.[49] The impression derived from Roman literature, Finley continues, is confirmed by study of the inscriptions:[50] traders are freedmen, *liberti*, or at any rate very small fry "rigorously kept," as one reviewer of *The Ancient Economy* has expressed it, "in the back of the political bus."[51]

In fairness, it should be noted that Finley has simultaneously argued forcibly for "more and better quantification of evidence," and against the view that "only quantification produces 'scientific' (as distinct from 'subjective' or 'ideological') analysis and results."[52] Moreover, in his brief discussion of Roman commerce and manufacturing, he shows himself alert to some of the difficulties of a status-based model: he concedes, first, that "the ancient sources are distorted by incompleteness and partiality"; second, that there was, to a small degree, evasion

48. Finley, *Economy*, pp. 68, 87.

49. Finley, *Economy*, pp. 36, 50, 51. For a different assessment, see Chapter 5 below.

50. Finley, *Economy*, p. 59: Finley was here following A. H. M. Jones, "The Economic Life of the Towns of the Roman Empire," reprinted in *The Roman Economy*, ed. P. A. Brunt (Oxford 1974), pp. 52–55.

51. W. R. Connor, *"Homo Lucrans?" Arion* n.s. 1 (1973–74), p. 736.

52. M. I. Finley, "Archaeology and History," *Daedalus* 100 (1971), pp. 168–186, esp. pp. 173–174.

of what he calls "the Ciceronian code" through silent partnerships and through slave and freedman agents; third, that there were exceptions, "not only exceptional individuals but also exceptional cities," trading centers such as Ostia, Palmyra, Arretium.[53] But the anomalies are not discussed in any detail, arguments from exception are dismissed somewhat peremptorily,[54] and "the decisive point remains that, against the relatively few known instances of [evasion], not a single prominent equestrian can be identified 'who was primarily a merchant' or any *equites* 'who were themselves active in the grain trade or engaged personally in sea-borne commerce'—even *equites*, let alone senators."[55]

Whereas the emphatic insistence in *The Ancient Economy* upon the Roman obsession with status is salutary and surely correct, attempts to convert this true observation into an analytical principle, and to explain thereby the major paths and divagations of the Roman economy, present both difficulties and fresh opportunities. One scholar has concluded a thoughtful review-discussion with the judgment that "in the final reckoning, we may submit that the status-based model is not wholly false, but it is not a substitute for economic history."[56] The emphasis on the fact that lucrative activities, particularly those of seaborne commerce, were concentrated at Rome "in the hands of men of low status," political "outsiders,"[57] has been one of the clear gains of Finley's studies, in that it requires historians to reexamine their assumptions, to bring the terms of discussion up to date, and to seek to determine more precisely the actual role which status did play in the commercial arrangements of the Roman world.

III

As a beginning it may be said that whereas Rostovtzeff's writings have a tendency to leave out of account strong expressions of upper-class

53. Finley, *Economy*, pp. 57–59.

54. Ibid., p. 59.

55. Ibid., p. 58; Finley's quotations are, respectively, from Brunt, *Equites*, and T. R. S. Broughton's comment on that paper in *Second International Conference of Economic History* (above, note 43), pp. 128, 150.

56. M. W. Frederiksen, "Theory, Evidence, and the Ancient Economy," *JRS* 65 (1975), pp. 164–171 (quotation on p. 170). For other discussions of *The Ancient Economy*, see A. D. Momigliano, *Riv. Stor. Ital.* 87 (1975), pp. 167–170; J. Andreau, *Ann. Scuol. Norm. Sup. Pisa*, 3rd ser., 7 (1977), pp. 1129–52 (banking); W. R. Connor (above note 51); and see the comments of C. Nicolet, *Rome et la conquête du monde mediteranéen*[2], 1 (Paris 1979), pp. 177–78.

57. Finley, *Economy*, p. 60.

disdain towards commerce and commercial men, in Finley's work those negative attitudes are assumed to be normative, the decisive determinants of actual conduct and practice. Neither these nor other scholars have probed deeply enough into the actual relationship between upper-class attitudes towards commerce and the realities of behavior. Yet the dynamics of this interrelationship, however ill-charted,[58] are of considerable importance for social historians of any age: attitudes need to be established as precisely as possible, and tested carefully against such evidence as lies beneath the surface of ideology, so as correctly to assess implications for the social framework.

Are there special conditions which, if satisfied, can invalidate negative attitudes towards the involvement of respectable men in retail trading operations? Voltaire approvingly observed that in eighteenth century England, in contrast to France and Germany, no stigma attached to the brothers or younger sons of peers of the realm who "trafficked," or were active as merchants in the city; whereas the protégés of Henry Laurens, introduced above, once they had established themselves "in a creditable manner as Planters . . . [could] carry on the sale of many species of European and West Indian goods to some advantage and with a good grace."[59] How long do negative attitudes prevail, to what extent are they reshaped in the light of changing historical conditions? We have seen that, for St. Ambrose, pleasing God and shipping one's merchandise were incompatible pursuits, but

58. Cf. M. Jahoda and N. Warren, ed., *Attitudes: Selected Readings* (Baltimore 1966), p. 211, commenting on the paucity of empirical studies by social scientists of the relationship between attitudes and behavior, and citing the "need for theoretical models which do justice to the complexities" of this relationship. See further "Attitudes," in D. L. Sills, ed., *International Encyclopedia of the Social Sciences* 1 (New York 1968), pp. 449ff. Also instructive is Leonard Silk's profile of economist Herbert A. Simon, which appeared in the *New York Times* on Nov. 9, 1978. Silk represents Simon as believing that the conception of economic man as a "highly rational, but extremely narrow calculating machine" needs to be revised: Simon would substitute for the highly specialized concept of rationality a broader vision, one which makes allowances for the impact of attitudes on behavior. Adopting a broader concept of rationality would enable economists to "deepen their comprehension of the way human beings behave, how rationality changes over time . . . and what influences upon personal choice are exercised by the institutional structure of society." See also H. Schuman and M. P. Johnson, "Attitudes and Behavior," *Ann. Rev. Sociol.* 2 (Palo Alto 1976), pp. 161–202.

59. France: see Voltaire's English letter on Commerce (1733) in B. R. Redman, ed., *The Portable Voltaire* (New York 1949), pp. 521–524; Charleston: *The Papers of Henry Laurens* (above, note 2), p. 338.

a different perspective is detected in the writings of Libanius, who considered the invention of seaborne commerce, and the improved social relationships which resulted, part of God's providential design.[60] The formula "in the name of God and of profit" is found in a merchant's account book as early as the middle of the thirteenth century; and merchants living in the days of San Bernardino, we know now, had ceased to behave as though religious attitudes and business affairs belonged in separate and unrelated compartments: merchants had more respect for the teaching of the Church, and theologians were more accommodating to the rational conduct of business, than was once supposed.[61] The Frescobaldi heiress whom we encountered earlier might be sharply criticized for converting her palatial loggia into commercial shops, but other noble families were doing the same in late sixteenth century Florence; the attitude of disparagement was largely that of nostalgia for a bygone era and had lost its power to influence conduct significantly.[62]

Furthermore, even when a collection of attitudes may be legitimately said to form an aristocratic ethos, can it be assumed that these enable us to predict behavioral consequences in all or most situations? Not only must we make plentiful allowance for divergences from normal attitudes in individual cases; the shapers of ideology themselves are scarcely disinterested parties. From an historian writing of Tudor-Stuart England there comes a salutary warning: to distrust official idologies of any age, on the grounds that they represent only imperfectly the realities of a social system; prevailing values and attitudes have a tendency "to glorify the existing upper classes and conceal the benefits they derive from their position. They exaggerate the duties and minimize the privileges of the few. They also present a picture of a fully

---

60. St. Ambrose: above, note 5. Cf. J. Viner (above, note 5), p. 37, who quotes from Libanius *Orat.* 3: "God did not bestow all products upon all parts of the earth, but distributed his gifts over different regions, to the end that men might cultivate a social relationship because one would have need of the help of another. And so he called commerce into being, that all men might be able to have common enjoyment of the fruits of earth, no matter where produced."

61. J. Kirshner, ed., *Raymond de Roover: Business, Banking and Economic Thought* (Chicago 1974), p. 345 (first published as "The Scholastic Attitude towards Trade and Entrepreneurship," *Explorations in Entrepreneurial History*, 2nd ser., 1 [1963], pp. 76–87).

62. R. A. Goldthwaite, "The Florentine Palace as Domestic Architecture," (above, note 3), p. 989.

integrated society in which stratification by title, power, wealth, talent, and culture are all in absolute harmony, and in which social mobility is consequently both undesirable and unthinkable. Reality, however, is always somewhat different."[63]

The following chapter is an attempt to analyze the relationship between Roman upper-class attitudes towards seaborne commerce, and the actual conduct of trade for the later Roman Republic. Since the few upper-class pronouncements cited above can hardly be said to have absolute value, attitudes themselves must be examined in greater depth, in their historical contexts, and counterexamples considered. By assembling and exploiting various other kinds of evidence, including that for private partnerships (*societates*), we hope to clarify the prevailing pattern of social organization of Roman seaborne commerce; this requires paying special attention to the manner in which attitudes affected conduct in the changed conditions of the late Republic.

63. L. Stone, *The Crisis of the Aristocracy, 1558–1641* (Oxford 1965), p. 36.

2

Attitudes, Conduct, and Commercial Organization in the Late Republic

It is inherently implausible, on historical grounds, either that Roman attitudes had negligible impact on conduct or, conversely, that attitudes and practice were always and everywhere compatible, coherent, and consistent. We continue to lack a full and proper historical treatment, for the late Republic, of the relationship between attitudes towards money-making activities, and the activities themselves. This chapter is not intended to fill that wide gap, but rather, in its focus on seaborne commerce, on *mercatores*, *negotiatores*, and the Roman upper classes, to illustrate some of the dynamics of a complex interrelationship. Although important evidence from earlier periods is considered, the chronological emphasis here is largely upon the Ciceronian Age—in part because of the abundance of Ciceronian evidence; in part because in the most recent discussion of Republican economic attitudes, Cicero's writings also occupied the foreground. Historians may find that a fuller analysis, from a somewhat different perspective, makes a useful contribution.

I

"Every form of profit seeking was thought unsuitable for senators."[1] As an explanation of the reasons for the passing of the *lex Claudia* in 218 Livy's statement is misleading, as will be seen below; and it will not do either as a guide to late third century aristocratic attitudes towards acquiring wealth. When a funeral eulogy was delivered for L. Caecilius Metellus in 221, we find included in a list of conventional ambitions "acquiring great wealth by good means" (*pecuniam magnam bono modo invenire*).[2] Attention has recently been called to the im-

1. Liv. 21.63.4, quoted above in Chapter 1, note 14.
2. Plin. *NH* 7.140.

portance of this passage, and emphasis rightly placed upon *invenire*, which is hardly the word for inheriting.[3] To acquire a fortune, in appropriate ways, remained, in Roman eyes, praiseworthy achievement for members of the governing class. A Crassus, as we have seen, might criticize the *nobilis* who worked to increase his *patrimonium*, but that was not the view of the Elder Cato, who maintained in a speech that a truly admirable and godlike man was one who, upon his death bed, could show that he had added more to his patrimony than he had inherited.[4] Nor was Cato's an exception to normal Roman attitudes, as has now been clearly established in an important analysis of the period 219–70 B.C.[5] Polybius, a shrewd appraiser, notes the Romans' moneymindedness and acutely observes that "at Rome the most disgraceful things of all are to accept bribes and to show greed for gain from disapproved activities; for no less strong than their admiration for money-making from the proper sources is their disapproval of greed for gain from forbidden sources."[6] Cicero would have found little with which to quarrel in that formulation, and indeed, in *De Officiis*, went so far as actually to single out and describe a kind of person, neither statesman nor philosopher, who lived a *vita otiosa*, concentrating on the management of his own financial interests, "not increasing wealth by any and every means, nor preventing one's relations from enjoyment of it, but rather sharing it also with both friends and with the state, should the need arise."[7]

"What truly matters," Cicero continued, "is first, that such wealth be properly acquired, through no base or contemptible form of gain; next, that it be increased by intelligence, industriousness, and thrift"

3. W. V. Harris, *War and Imperialism in Republican Rome, 327–70 B.C.* (Oxford 1979), p. 67 (hereafter cited as Harris, *WIRR*).

4. Plut, *Cat. Mai.* 21.8 See also Cato's declaration in the Rhodian oration (Gell. 6.3.37): *nos omnia plura habere volumus*.

5. Harris, *WIRR*, pp. 68–104 ("Economic Motives for War and Expansion during the Rise to World Power").

6. Polyb. 6.56.1–3, cited also by Harris, *WIRR*, p. 88. See the later comment by Polybius (31.27.11): "So unusual and extreme is [the Romans'] exactitude about money."

7. Cic. *De Off.* 1.92: *Illud autem sic est iudicandum, maximas geri res et maximi animi ab iis, qui res publicas regant . . . esse autem magni animi et fuisse multos etiam in vita otiosa, qui aut investigarent aut conarentur . . . aut interiecti inter philosophos et eos, qui rem publicam administrarent, delectarentur re sua familiari non eam quidem omni ratione exaggerantes neque excludentes ab eius usu suos potiusque et amicis impertientes et rei publicae, si quando usus esset.*

(*ratio*, *diligentia*, *parsimonia*).[8] The obvious question thus arises: what, in concrete terms, are these "proper means" of acquiring wealth? Do they in fact exclude commerce (*mercatura*), as the various statements reviewed in Chapter 1 might seem to imply?

As a beginning, closer examination of the passage in the *Verrines*, where *mercatores* were described as *homines tenues*, *obscuro loco nati*[9] places these words in a distinctly less pejorative light. Cicero was not emphasizing the lowly status of these men. Traders from the Roman provinces, sailing from distant places to ports where they were unknown, they innocently placed their trust in their possession of Roman citizenship—to no avail, if they were to encounter provincial governors as rapacious and unscrupulous as Verres. Rather, Cicero was highlighting the comprehensiveness of coverage implicit in the concept of *civitas*; he achieved this by revealing that citizenship protected not just the rich, the powerful and the well-known, but also men of modest means, who lacked influential connections. The intent was to elicit his jurors' sympathy and pity, not to denigrate *mercatores* or their occupation.

In fact, Cicero was here implying that *mercatura* is *honesta*—an implication which is confirmed by passages in the philosophical works, where he either juxtaposes commerce and agriculture as equally desirable means of acquiring wealth,[10] or else refers to persons "who seek gain respectably, through commerce."[11] Furthermore, again on Cicero's showing, *mercatores* could be both respectable and affluent: on one occasion, he characterizes merchants from Puteoli as *homines locupletes atque honesti*; on another, he asserts that the wealth of *mercatores* could surpass that of Scipio and Laelius.[12] These *mercatores*

8. Ibid.: *Quae primum bene parta sit nullo neque turpi quaestu neque odioso, deinde augeatur ratione, diligentia, parsimonia, tum quam plurimis, modo dignis, se utilem praebeat nec libidini potius luxuriaeque quam liberalitati et beneficentiae pareat.* Cf. also *De Off.* 2.87. These passages are not discussed in the most recent treatment of Cicero's attitudes towards wealth: M. Raskolnikoff, "La richesse et les riches chez Ciceron," *Ktema* 2 (1977), pp. 357ff. See also the discussion by H. Schneider, *Wirtschaft und Politik: Untersuchungen zur Geschichte der späten römischen Republik* (Erlangen 1974), pp. 252ff.

9. Cic. II *Verr.* 5.167, cited above in Chapter 1, section I. Cf. Finley, *Economy*, p. 60 *et alibi* for the view that literary sources (and legal texts) emphasize "the low status of the professional traders and manufacturers throughout Roman history."

10. Cic. *De Fin.* 5.91; *Tusc.* 5.86.

11. *Parad. Stoic.* 46: *qui honeste rem quaerunt mercaturis faciendis.*

12. *Mercatores* of Puteoli: II *Verr.* 5.154; *divitiae* of *mercatores*: *Orat.* 232, adduced also by F. Coarelli, *DdArch.* 4–5 (1970–71), p. 263. For the distinction in Cicero between *dives* and *locuples*, see Roskolnikoff (above, note 8), pp. 359–360.

might be foreigners constantly on the move, but they might also be permanent residents in a province.[13] If foreigners, they could none-theless expect to find much in common with their resident counterparts; if they were permanent residents in a city, they could form organized groups and act in organized ways, out of common interest.[14] So much so, indeed, that Cicero is twice found asserting that Rome "had on many occasions gone to war on behalf of *mercatores* and *navicularii*."[15] This was exaggeration, for the passages are polemical in tone and unspecific as to particular historical episodes; nevertheless, it estab-lishes that the issue whether Rome should ever act to protect com-mercial interests was a substantive one, and could be seriously debated.[16]

The cumulative force of these Ciceronian statements helps to place his famous discussion in *De Officiis* of livelihoods which are *liberales* and *sordidae*,[17] in clearer perspective. The argument must of course be seen as part of Cicero's philosophical objective in writing the *De Officiis*; at the same time, his ethical pronouncements were intended to be taken seriously by his Roman readers. Even those who believe that Cicero was here doing no more than faithfully reproducing the views of his source (in this case the Rhodian philosopher Panaetius) can characterize Cicero's positive view of *mercatura* as an "oddity."[18] Here, it is not *mercatura* per se which is treated as base, but only commerce which is on a small scale; large scale commerce (*magna et copiosa*) is not only not to be disparaged but actually "seems to deserve the highest respect," providing that, "satiated or rather content with one's commercial gains, one makes one's way from port to landed estates."[19] The language implies that commercial gain needs ulti-mately to be transferred to the land in order to be fully legitimized;

13. *Incolere et mercari consueverant:* Sall. *Jug.* 47.1; cf. Caes. *Bell. Afr.* 75.3.
14. Foreigners: Cic. II *Verr.* 5.167: *Multarum rerum societate iuncti sunt;* permanent residents: II *Verr.* 2.137.
15. Cic. II *Verr.* 5.149; *De Imp. Cn. Pomp.* 11.
16. See Harris, *WIRR*, pp. 100–101.
17. Cic. *De Off.* 1.151; discussed above in Chapter 1, section I.
18. P. A. Brunt, *Proc. Camb. Phil. Soc.* 19 (1973), p. 29. Cicero's words *haec fere accepimus* are a claim to be reproducing his sources (see M. W. Frederiksen, *JRS* 65 [1975], p. 165), but they are also conventional, and hardly inconsistent with the author's shaping the material in a manner compatible with Roman sensibilities.
19. *De Off.* 1.151: [*Mercatura*] *si satiata quaestu vel contenta potius, ut saepe ex alto in portum, ex ipso portu se in agros possessionesque contulit, videtur iure optimo posse laudari.*

that is, in order for the *mercator* to acquire the necessary sanction of moral approval. But Cicero is also significantly unspecific about the length of time a man could devote to trade before becoming "satiated or content," and it might take many voyages to acquire a fortune. The passages examined above, where *mercatura* is presented as wealth-producing, and the practitioners are presented as *honesti*, are entirely consistent with the attitude adopted in *De Officiis*. If Panaetius actually held those views, we must conclude that Roman and Rhodian aristocrats here found themselves in close agreement.

Traders could be rich and *honesti*: the facts remain that men of *dignitas* never describe themselves as *mercatores* and could be scathingly derisive about members of their own class who themselves embarked on ships for gainful purposes: it was precisely such trafficking back and forth between Africa and Sicily which prompted Tacitus' disparaging comments about C. Sempronius Gracchus under Tiberius.[20] Instead, in order to document the involvement of the Roman elite in trading and commercial enterprises, it is necessary to focus upon different Latin vocabularly: *negotium exercere* and cognate terms.

Mercatores and *negotiatores* were assuredly different people.[21] Early in this century a French scholar elegantly expressed the distinction in social terms: "Le *mercator* est un marchand, avec la légère nuance de défaveur et comme le parfum de boutique qui s'attache à ce mot: le *negotiator* est 'un homme qui est dans les affaires.' "[22] The distinction is helpful, for whereas in Latin usage men of equestrian rank are spoken of as conducting business (*negotiari*) in a manner consonant with their *dignitas*,[23] *mercatura* and its cognates are never associated with men of comparable or superior standing. It is hence often correct to view the professional *mercatores* or *navicularii* as small men (*viri municipales*, provincials, freedmen, other subequestrians), backed and supported—in ways which will be clarified below—by larger men. Respectability, however, does not tell all, for *mercatura* could certainly

20. Tac. *Ann.* 4.13.2, cited above in Chapter 1, section I.

21. Cic. *Planc.* 64: *negotiatoribus comis, mercatoribus iustus.*

22. J. Hatzfeld, *Les trafiquants italiens dans l'orient hellénique* (Paris 1919), p. 196; on which see, more recently, C. Nicolet, *L'ordre équestre a l'époque républicaine*, vol. 1 (Paris 1966), pp. 358–362 (hereafter cited as Nicolet, *Ord. éq.*).

23. Cic. II *Verr.* 2.73: [Q. Minucius] *qui Syracusis sic negotiaretur ut sui iuris dignitatisque meminisset.* See further Nicolet, *Ord. éq.*, vol. 2 (Paris 1974), pp. 953–954 (no. 235).

be a part of the activities of a *negotiator*.[24] The crucial element of difference, rather, lies in the multiplicity of a *negotiator*'s lucrative pursuits and interests; the scale and the sphere of his action also mattered.[25] To what precise degree, then, were shipping and commercial ventures included among a man's *negotia*? The answer is complicated by the imprecision inherent in *negotiari* and its cognates, and by the tendency of some scholars, in consequence, to associate commercial pursuits with the *equites*, who were widely believed to constitute the Roman equivalent of a commercial "middle class."[26] This tendency was exaggerated, anachronistic, and required a corrective; Brunt made a major contribution by emphasizing the similarity of interests, including economic, between *equites* and senators; he, and now others, have argued that most *equites* must have been, like the senators, landowners, and as for *negotiatores* "they were not all traders; the term . . . includes men whose business was in land, and bankers and money lenders."[27] The observation is a necessary corollary to Brunt's main thesis that "the *equites* . . . did not constitute a united pressure group with economic interests opposed to those of the senate."[28]

Brunt himself recognized, however, that "commerce in the strict sense was not a matter of indifference" even to senators, and that the actual evidence for the business of *negotiatores* relating to land is very meager and exceptional.[29] One respondent to Brunt opined "that the Roman *equites* were not so completely uninterested in trade,"[30] whereas a recent analysis of the place of economic motives in Roman imperi-

---

24. *CIL* X, 1797 (Augustan Age): *mercatores qui Alexandr. Asiai Syriai negotiantur*.

25. On the wide range of activities encompassed in the concept of *negotia*, see A. J. N. Wilson, *Emigration from Italy in the Republican Age of Rome* (Manchester 1966), pp. 4ff, 156ff; see further P. Baldacci, *Rend. Ist. Lombardo* 101 (1967), p. 275: "La differenze tra i due termini non riguarda dunque tanto la natura dell'attivitá commerciale quanto la sua entitá e la sua sfera d'azione."

26. See, e.g., H. Hill, *The Roman Middle Class in the Republican Period* (Oxford 1952).

27. Brunt, *Equites*, pp. 122–123; 126; cf. Nicolet, *Ord. eq.*1, pp. 249–269, 470–471; Shatzman, *SWRP*, pp. 99ff.

28. Brunt, *Equites*, p. 118.

29. Ibid., p. 126, and n. 2.

30. T. R. S. Broughton, in *Second International Conference of Economic History*: Aix 1962 (Paris 1965), p. 150; cf. Shatzman, *SWRP*, p. 100n4: "It is one thing to admit that petty traders were not Equites, and another one to say that Equites were not engaged in commerce at all."

alism stresses senatorial interest in the affairs of *negotiatores* during the second century, and the increasing influence of the monied but non-senatorial classes in Roman external policy over the fifty year period beginning in the 120s.[31] Since Brunt's study is sometimes regarded as definitive,[32] and with it, at least by implication, the notion that commerce and trade were peripheral to the activities of the *negotiatores*, a brief review of the evidence is appropriate here; what is at issue is not the overall preponderance of landed to commercial wealth in Rome's upper classes, but the relative importance, the degree, of the latter, particularly as regards *negotiatores*.

Cicero once refers to *omnes illius provinciae publicani, agricolae, pecuarii, ceteri negotiatores*.[33] The force of *ceteri* in this passage has been correctly interpreted as showing that the first three activities in the series fell within the range of activities of the *negotiator*; but viewed from a different perspective the passage confirms that businessmen engaged also in trade: for what are the activities of the *ceteri negotiatores* if not those of *mercatura*? Other references distinguish sharply between *negotiatores* and *aratores*;[34] another shows that by *negotiator* the activities of a trader are exclusively intended.[35] There are certainly contexts in which *negotiator* must mean banker or moneylender, but *argentarii* (the acknowledged experts at making and investing money) and *faeneratores* are more often designated as such;[36] and it may at any rate be questioned whether "it is of such people that Cicero is *mainly* thinking"[37] (my italics) when he mentions *negotiatores* in Sicily, Africa, or Gaul. More typically, when *mercatores, negotiatores, aratores*, and *pecuarii* are mentioned in a series, as for example in a famous passage in which Cicero extols the wealth of the province of Sicily, all of these activities are subsumed under the imprecise and general rubric *negotium gerere*.[38] That the concept *negotium gerere* or *negotiari* was

---

31. Harris, *WIRR*, pp. 98ff.
32. Finley, *Economy*, p. 186n33.
33. Cic. *Font.* 46; cf. 12: *unum ex toto negotiatorum, colonorum, publicanorum, aratorum, pecuariorum numero*. See G. Clemente, *I Romani nella Gallia meridionale* (Bologna 1974), pp. 114–115.
34. Cic. II *Verr.* 2.153, 168; *Font.* 12.
35. Cic. *Ad Att.* 2.16.4.
36. *Argentarii*: Cic. *De Off.* 2.87. *Faeneratores*: see, e.g., Cic *De Off.* 1.150; Liv. 6.14.3., Suet. *Tib.* 48.1; Firm. *Math.* 3.7.4.
37. Brunt, *Equites*, p. 126.
38. Cic. II *Verr.* 2.6.

comprehensive enough to include the activities of *mercatores*, and that this is in many instances its primary meaning, helps to explain how and why *negotiator* came to be the normal word for trader or merchant under the Empire.[39]

Again, to view the *negotiator* essentially as a banker or moneylender with investments in land, rather than as a man with multiple interests, including commerce and the financing of seaborne trade, is to ignore an arresting feature of our evidence for late Republican *negotiatores*: their geographical concentration in and near the major commercial centers, the port cities. Cicero, characterizing Sicily as "an island which has outlets everywhere,"[40] names the ports of Syracuse, Agrigentum, Lilybaeum, Panhormus, and others; the list places the activities of the *negotiatores*—explicitly distinguished from *aratores*—"who do business in Syracuse, Agrigentum, Panhormus, Lilybaeum," in a firmly commercial context.[41] L. Raecius and Q. Minucius were *equites Romani* and *negotiatores* at Panhormus and Syracuse, respectively; that their interests included involvement in trade is prima facie likely since they were based in the ports, and the likelihood is strengthened by their interests in and beyond the Aegean: Raecius is a name attested among the Roman *negotiatores* at Delos, whereas Q. Minucius once entertained King Antiochus of Syria.[42]

It would of course be natural for bankers and moneylenders, as well as for traders, to congregate in and near the chief commercial centers, and in fact we know that *homines negotii gerentes* as well as *mercatores* were very much a part of the social fabric in such cities as Puteoli.[43] The essential point is that *negotiatores* must normally have had multiple interests, and in port cities shipping and commercial commitments would have assumed an important place among them. Like C. Rabirius Curtius Postumus, the well-known *negotiator* of the Cic-

39. Observed by M. W. Frederiksen, *JRS* 65 (1975), p. 166; for discussion, see Rougé, *OCM*, pp. 279ff; Wilson, *Emigration from Italy* (above, note 25), pp. 6, 182. On the importance of trade among the activities of the *negotiatores* in the East, see F. Cassola, "Romani e Italici in Oriente", *DdArch*. 4–5 (1970–71), pp. 307–308.

40. II *Verr.* 2.185: *insula quae undique exitus maritimos habeat.*

41. II *Verr.* 2.153: *qui Syracusis, qui Agrigenti, qui Panhormi, qui Lilybaei negotiantur.* For a recent attempt to exploit local prosopographical profiles as indices of a town's commercial character, see R. C. Knapp, "The Origins of Provincial Prosopography in the West," *Ancient Society* 9 (1978), pp. 203–204.

42. L. Raecius: Nicolet, *Ord. eq.* 2, p. 1003 (no. 299): Q. Minucius: ibid., pp. 953–954 (no. 235).

43. Cic. *In Vat.* 12.

eronian Age, or like a character in Petronius' *Satyricon*, they might combine owning ships with landed possessions and a *familia negotians*.[44]

An example will help. The late Republican Avianii, well acquainted with Cicero, provide excellent illustration both of the diversity of a trading family's *negotia*, and of that family's geographical diffusion in the major commercial centers. Although based for at least three generations in Puteoli, where C. Avianius C. f. C. n. Flaccus held the chief magistracy early in the Augustan Age, one of them was engaged by Pompey in the sale and transport of grain for the state; the family must have owned ships to further their *negotia* in Sicily.[45] Furthermore, collateral members of the *gens* were established at Sicyon near Corinth, engaged in the trading of works of art. Cicero, by the end of 46, had purchased Greek statues from M. Aemilius Avianianus, himself the patron of C. Avianius Evander, a notable and widely traveled sculptor whom M. Antonius transported from Sicyon in Greece to Alexandria and who then settled, after Actium, in Rome, where he restored a statue in the temple of Apollo Palatinus.[46] C. Avianius was IIvir at Ostia in A.D. 20.[47] While we cannot determine precisely the nature of his connections with the sculptor active in Rome, the Puteolan grain traders, and the Sicyonian members of the *gens*, it is certainly legitimate to presume that connections existed and were important. Puteoli, Sicily, Sicyon, Rome and Ostia: the Avianii and their various trading and commercial interests formed an intertwining network, and the geographical *foci* of their activities are the major ports.[48]

44. For the multiple *negotia* of C. Rabirius Curtius Postumus—amphorae in Germany, South Italy and Sicily (*CIL* I², 2340a, c = *ILLRP* 1184), production of tiles (*CIL* I², 2340b), ships conveying Egyptian merchandise to Puteoli (Cic. *Rab. Post.* 40)—see Wiseman, *NMRS*, p. 199; Nicolet, *Ord. éq.* 2, pp. 1000–1002 (no. 297), q.v. also for his identification with Curtius Postumus; Shatzman, *SWRP*, p. 100n4; pp. 395–396 (no. 192). For the character in the *Satyricon*, see below, Chapter 5, section II.

45. Pompey's *cura annonae* from 57: Cic. *Ad Fam.* 13.75, 13.79; cf. C. Nicolet, "Institutions politiques de Rome," *Annuaire, École pratique des hautes études* (4th section), 1976–77 (Paris 1977), pp. 333–334. For the Avianii of Puteoli, see J. H. D'Arms, *HSCP* 76 (1972), pp. 207–216.

46. See S. Treggiari, *RFLR*, pp. 136–138, for references and discussion. For the date of Cicero's purchase, see SB, *Fam.* 2, p. 370 (no. 209).

47. Meiggs, *RO²*, p. 511.

48. The Avianii are not an isolated example, and the prominence, among their attested enterprises, of the production and sale of works of art may not be fortuitous.

Towns could, moreover, without being situated on the sea, be magnets for men with multiple business interests. In this regard the famous cult centers of Latium have an interest which extends beyond the religious sphere. Before the beginning of the first century B.C. the sanctuaries of Fortuna Primigenia at Praeneste (figure 4) and of Hercules Victor at Tibur had been reconstructed on a mammoth scale. Ex-votos of precious metals and terracotta figurines were sold in *tabernae* attached to the sanctuaries; money was changed, cash deposits lodged in temple treasuries, and pilgrims housed and fed in the vicinity. *Mercatores*, *negotiatores*, *argentarii*, *nummularii*, many of them active in overseas markets, were at the center of this society; the traditional sylvan and military aspects of the cults themselves were giving way, in a world of expanded geographical horizons and economic opportunities, to emphasis upon risk, gain, and adventure. Since it was nonetheless the ports which served as the nodes of communication with the East, it is important to note that the Cossinii of Tibur had connections at Puteoli, as well as with Greece and the Orient.[49]

Since *negotium gerere* and its cognates in Latin denote a wide range of economic activities, difficult to fix within precise categorical boundaries, supplementary evidence such as that discussed above should be brought to bear when possible: it creates a general presumption in favor of including trading and commercial activities among a man's *negotia* even when those are unspecified, and geographically localized no more precisely than by country. P. Sittius of Nuceria contracted debts *negotii gerendi studio*, and large sums were owed him *in provinciis et in regnis*; Cn. Calidius carried on *negotia* for many years in Sicily; Sex. Aufidius had *negotia* in Africa.[50] What exactly is implied, as regards proportionate interests in agriculture or trade—or the types of trade—by such

---

A recent study of the Cossutii shows them engaged principally in the respectable professions of architecture and sculpture, over a wide time span, with their activities attested in Athens, the Aegean, and Aphrodisias; in Puteoli, Luna, and Rome (E. Rawson, *PBSR* n.s. 43 [1975], pp. 36–47). Rawson believes (p. 41) that a M. Cossutius, active around 50, was the key figure in the sculptural "firm," patron of a number of freedmen *marmorarii*. For criticism and additions cf. M. Torelli, in *Seaborne Commerce*, pp. 313–321.

49. On all this, see G. Bodei Giglioni, "Pecunia fanatica: L'incidenza economica dei templi laziali," *Riv. Stor. Ital.* 89 (1977), pp. 33–76.

50. P. Sittius: Cic. *Sull.* 58, *Ad Fam.* 5.17; Sall. *Cat.* 21.3; cf. Shatzman, *SWRP*, pp. 312, 336. Cn. Calidius: Cic. II *Verr.* 4.42; Nicolet, *Ord. éq.* 2, pp. 823–824 (no. 77). Sex. Aufidius: Cic. *Ad Fam.* 12.27.1; Nicolet, *Ord. éq.* 2, p. 794 (no. 43).

assertions? The equestrian Calidius was father of a senator, and the *splendor* of Sex. Aufidius was the equal of that of any Roman knight. But if we rely upon their superior *dignitas* as a guide to the nature of their *negotia*, and presume that agricultural or financial activities must primarily be meant, how are we to explain other evidence, which reveals men of standing carrying on *negotia* in a manner inconsistent with their *dignitas*,[51] or which proves that mere possession of equestrian rank is no necessary guarantee of respectability?[52]

And what of freedmen, whom Cicero, in some moods, appears to associate with humble positions in commerce or manufacturing?[53] They are in fact attested among the *negotiatores* and could even be highly respected: P. Umbrenus the Catilinarian, for example, *in Gallia negotiatus erat, plerisque principibus civitatium notus erat, atque eos noverat*.[54] Indeed, the further a town's distance from Rome, the less prone were her citizens to make fine distinctions between a rich and powerful freedman and a freeborn Roman: this has now been strikingly confirmed at Naxos by the honors paid to C. Curtius Mithres, who had multiple interests in the Greek East and was a *libertus* of C. Rabirius Curtius Postumus.[55]

In short, imperfections have begun to show up in the apparently solid and coherent edifice of late Republican upper-class attitudes towards trade and traders reviewed Chapter 1. First, whereas a Roman senator such as Cicero might speak with lofty aristocratic disdain about *mercatores*, in other contexts he could display a different attitude: *mercatores* may in fact be rich and *honesti*. Second, the *negotia* which preoccupied men of higher social standing cannot typically be supposed, merely on grounds of their status, to exclude commercial and trading enterprises. Multiplicity of economic activities is the general rule, and the concentration of personnel in the major distribution cen-

51. Cic. II *Verr.* 2.73 (cited above, note 23).

52. Cic. *Ad Q. Fr.* 1.2.6: *homo levis ac sordidus sed tamen equestri censu*. On the distinction between *equites equo publico* and men whose wealth alone qualified them for the order, see Wiseman, *Historia* 19 (1970), pp. 67–83; *NMRS*, pp. 68–69.

53. E.g., Cic. *De Off.* 1.150: *Opificesque omnes in sordida arte versantur; nec enim quicquam ingenuum habere potest officina*. Cf. MacMullen, *RSR*, pp. 100ff.

54. Cic. *Cat.* 3.14; Sall. *Cat.* 40; see further Treggiari, *RFLR*, p. 103.

55. *Bulletin Epigraphique* (1970), no. 438, on which see J. Reynolds, *JRS* 66 (1976), p. 197. Cicero was well treated by Mithres at Ephesus and elsewhere: *Ad Fam.* 13.69. For the identity of the patron of Mithres, see Nicolet, *Ord. éq.* 2, pp. 1001–1002.

ters, the Italian and Mediterranean ports, is indicative of trading *negotia*. But what of senators, who were legally prohibited from owning ocean-going ships; what was the relationship between legal sanction, convention, and actual practice among the members of Rome's governing class? Answers to these questions must begin with a closer examination of the *plebiscitum Claudianum* of 219–218 B.C.[56]

II

Little is known of the specific context out of which emerged the prohibition of senators and senators' sons from possession of *maritimae naves*. Since Livy's account,[57] which leaves no doubt as to the resentment of the law among the *patres*, reflects a tradition biased against the people, the differing modern interpretations of the *plebiscitum Claudianum* have focused, understandably, upon the motives of C. Flaminius, the only senator—if Livy is to be believed—who supported the proposal introduced by the *tribunus plebis* Q. Claudius. Flaminius has appeared as a champion of traditional senatorial values, the *mos maiorum*, reflected by Livy in the familiar phrase *quaestus omnis patribus indecorus visus*.[58] The *plebiscitum* itself, on this view, has been interpreted as part of a more general expression of popular dissatisfaction with senatorial management of the war with Hannibal, and as intended to restrict the activities of members of the governing class to the proper and principal *officia* of public life: war, politics, and legislation.[59] But since the terms of the law did not exclude senators from all forms of money-making, only from that which derived from owning ships of a certain size, Livy's description is hardly a satisfactory explanation of a law which was in any case enacted nearly two centuries before his own day.[60] In a more recent assessment, Flaminius appears as an independent and realistic politician, seeking support from persons in the state (including newer plebeian families) who had acquired wealth in the wake of Rome's previous wars, were striving now to expand their interests in Italian and foreign markets, and who resented

56. For the date of Q. Claudius' tribunate, see Broughton, *MRR* 1, p. 238.
57. Liv. 21.63.3–4.
58. Liv. 21.63.4, cited above, note 1, and cf. above, Chapter 1, note 14.
59. Frank, *ESAR* 1, p. 74; for a full review of scholarly opinion on the purpose of the *lex Claudia*, see F. Cassola, *I gruppi politici romani nel III secolo a.C.* (Trieste 1962), pp. 216–217.
60. Rightly emphasized by Harris, *WIRR*, pp. 66–67; cf. also Shatzman, *SWRP*, p. 100.

the intrusion of senators into what they will have increasingly regarded as their own proper spheres of activity.[61] This view assumes not only the existence of a large and influential group of traders among the voters; it further requires these presumed supporters of Flaminius to have entertained no political aspirations themselves, for a legal barrier now effectively blocked such persons' paths to magistracies and to the senate.[62]

Given our lack of contemporary evidence, further speculation as to Flaminius' motives is hazardous. What we know is that the *plebiscitum Claudianum* was carried, despite general senatorial resistance; we also know that when the Elder Cato, that staunch defender of traditional senatorial values, came to write *De Agricultura*, he said nothing whatever about the disreputability of *mercatura*, emphasizing, rather, both its profitability and its risks.[63] It may have been precisely this perception of the riskiness of seaborne commerce which was widely shared, which Flaminius exploited in debate with his senatorial colleagues, and which led some of them ultimately, if grudgingly, to adopt his point of view. After all, in a society structured according to *ordines*, with the orders themselves determined by the census, the stability of the *patrimonia* of senators was essential for the stability of the ruling class itself. Better the gradual but steady returns and market surpluses from farming and pasturage than the swift but unpredictable profits from *mercatura* which one disastrous sea-voyage might erase.[64] It is

61. Z. Yavetz, "The Policy of C. Flaminius and the *Plebiscitum Claudianum*," *Athenaeum* 40 (1962), pp. 325–344, esp. 340–341.

62. Cf. Cassola, *Gruppi politici* (above, note 59), p. 217.

63. Cat. *De Agr.* 3 (*praefatio*): *Mercatorem autem strenuum studiosumque rei quaerendae existimo, verum ut supra dixi, periculosum et calamitosum.* For an equivocal view of the value of Cato's preface as a guide to his general attitudes towards money-making, see A. E. Astin, *Cato the Censor* (Oxford 1978), pp. 250ff; he concludes that the preface cannot be "assumed to be a carefully considered statement of Cato's judgements and principles"; but this "does not mean that it lacks value as evidence for Cato's attitudes and preconceptions" (pp. 253–254).

64. For a suggestive study of the relationship between commercial risk and senatorial mentality, see now E. Gabba, "Riflessioni antiche e moderne sulle attività commerciali a Roma nei secoli II e I a.C.," in *Seaborne Commerce*, pp. 91–102. It will be clear that I cannot accept the view—presented without arguments—of M. H. Crawford, who prefers to regard the *lex Claudia* "simply as an attempt by the community as a whole to define its aristocracy as a landed aristocracy, untainted by wordly cares, an attempt resisted by that aristocracy as lèse majesté" ("The Early Roman Economy, 753–280 B.C.," in *L'Italie préromaine et la Rome républicaine, Mélanges offerts à J. Heurgon* [Rome 1976], p. 203n28.

in this sense that the *plebiscitum Claudianum* can be seen as a reaf-
firmation of traditional values (*patria instituta ac mores*), and specifically of the landed aristocratic ideal, at a time when the realities of
senatorial behavior had begun seriously to challenge their validity.

For if some Roman senators were not deeply and directly involved
in commercial shipping by 219, there would clearly have been neither
need for restrictive legislation nor senatorial opposition to its precise
terms. Furthermore, unless the Romans had become accustomed to
launching ships for commercial purposes in the period before the law
was passed, the legislation itself is unintelligible—which is not to say
that mercantile interests were a fundamental or even a major factor in
propelling Rome onward towards the conquest of Italy.[65] On the Mediterranean by 219–18 coastal colonies at Antium, Terracina, and—
most significantly—Ostia had been in existence for more than a century: part of the purpose of these *propugnacula imperii* must already
have been to expedite the distribution of the products of trade—within
Italy, predominantly wine and oil, and grain from overseas; but some
manufactured products must also have been shipped.[66] Even though
Rome had first assembled her own fleet for military purposes at the
outset of the First Punic War, acquisitiveness contributed to her de-
termination to continue fighting until all of Sicily was conquered: new
sources of income were soon arriving from her new province, *praedia
populi Romani*.[67] Rome's offer of assistance to Egypt in war against
Syria, and her annexation of Corsica and Sardinia in defiance of the
peace treaty of 241, are suggestive of increased overseas interests,
including economic; and commercial contacts between Rome and the
East had been established in the third century B.C.[68] The embassy to
Carthage on behalf of some five hundred traders, imprisoned there
after "sailing from Italy" and supplying rebels in the Mercenary War,
proves that the senate was prepared to go to some lengths to protect

65. See now Harris, *WIRR*, pp. 58ff, who emphasizes Rome's desire for plunder
and the drive to acquire land; cf. pp. 62ff, a critical reappraisal (though not a refutation)
of the arguments of Cassola, *Gruppi politici* (above, note 59), chap. 4 (pp. 121–198).

66. See in general J. H. Thiel, *A History of Roman Sea-Power before the Second
Punic War* (Amsterdam 1954), pp. 8ff; Broughton (above, note 30), p. 151. Ostia:
Meiggs, *RO*², p. 25.

67. Cic. II *Verr.* 2.2; Harris, *WIRR*, pp. 63–64.

68. Egypt: Z. Yavetz, *Athenaeum* 40 (1962), p. 333f; Rome and the East: F. Cassola,
DdArch. 4–5 (1970–71), pp. 305ff.

Romans who engaged in foreign trade.[69] On the Adriatic, Brundisium was planted in 244, and in 230 Roman envoys to Queen Teuta warned the Illyrians who had "robbed or killed *many* Italian traders, capturing and carrying off *no small numbers* of prisoners" (my italics).[70]

Thus, Roman commercial ships were on the seas and putting into Italian and foreign ports in the period between the first two Punic Wars; third century aristocrats were eager, as we have seen, to acquire wealth in ways which were morally approved; finally, they appear to have found nothing reprehensible about engaging in seaborne commerce. This was the historical setting in which Q. Claudius' *plebiscitum* was proposed and promulgated. Did senators comply?

It would seem implausible on general grounds that senators remained uninterested in exploiting the greatly expanded economic opportunities in the decades which followed the defeat of Hannibal, an age which one historian has now characterized as generally charged with a "spirito affaristico."[71] There is Cato, whose views on increasing one's patrimony and on the profits to be gleaned from *mercatura* have already been cited; his biographer writes that he came to apply himself more and more strenuously to money-making, concluding that agriculture was more entertaining than profitable.[72] Other forms of business commended themselves: ponds, hot springs, fuller's earth, pitchworks, land with natural pasturage and forests, "all of which brought him large profits."[73] There is contemporary construction in Rome, attesting to rapid growth of seaborne commerce, and to sophisticated arrangement for the hauling, storing, and distributing of imports up the Tiber: a new complex consisting of rebuilt port (*emporium*) and an immense connected storage place (*porticus Aemilia*) was begun in 192, systemmatically developed, and completed by 174 in the region south of the Aventine.[74] Measuring 1900 by 300 feet, the Aemilian

69. Polyb. 1.83.7–8; on which see Harris, *WIRR*, p. 65.

70. Polyb. 2.8.2–4; cf. Liv. 40.42.1–5; on the First Illyrian war see Harris, *WIRR*, pp. 195–197.

71. E. Gabba, "Riflessioni" (above, note 64), pp. 92–93.

72. Plut. *Cat. Mai.* 21.5

73. Ibid., 21.5. Even if Plutarch may have taken literally some Catonic "overstatement for immediate effect" (Astin, *Cato* [above, note 63], p. 250), the general purport of the passage is unmistakable, and not to be impugned.

74. On the date, size, and significance of the *porticus Aemilia*, see F. Coarelli, "Architettura e arti figurative in Roma, 150–50 a.C.," in P. Zanker, ed., *Hellenismus*

warehouses (figure 5) were conceived on a grandness of scale which allowed them to remain virtually unaltered to the end of antiquity. There is the emphasis of Polybius, around 150, on the numerous public contracts let out by the censors for building and repairing of Italian public works, rivers, harbors, parks, mines, and lands, and his assertion "that there is hardly anyone who is not involved either in the sale of these contracts or in the kinds of business (ἐργασία) to which they give rise."[75]

There are, furthermore, the resident Italian *negotiatores* at the free port of Delos, which assumed increasing importance in the decades after 167; with the destruction of Carthage and of Corinth (146) came new riches, and a Mediterranean still more open to commercial shipping.[76] Puteoli was designated "a second Delos"[77]—striking illustration of the way in which strong commercial links shortened wide overseas distances. Different ancient authors preferred different dates for the introduction of *luxuria* to Rome.[78] Precise chronology matters less than the fact that the rapid growth of wealth after Pydna, reflected in part by the sizes of the fortunes of individual aristocrats, provoked debate in high places as to the ways in which wealth ought to be disbursed, and in the interests of whom. The various manifestations of public munificence and private luxury were countered, in the minds of some, by an emphasis upon saving, accumulation, and thrift.[79]

---

in Mittelitalien, Abh. Akad. Wiss. 97 (Göttingen 1976), pp. 22–23; cf. more recently Coarelli, "Public Building in Rome between the Second Punic War and Sulla", *PBSR* 45 (1977), pp. 1ff.

75. Polyb. 6.17; on which see E. Badian, *Publicans and Sinners* (Cornell 1972), pp. 45–46; for the meaning of ἐργασία, cf. p. 129n61.

76. Delos: Strab. 486, with A. J. N. Wilson, *Emigration from Italy* (above, note 25), pp. 102ff. According to the same author (Strab. 14.668), the island could import, sell, and re-export ten thousand slaves in a single day; Strabo links the market with Rome's increasing use of slaves after the destruction of Carthage and Corinth. The figure ought not to be taken literally, but the statement ought not to be discarded—as Harris has rightly emphasized (*WIRR*, p. 82).

77. Lucil., in *ROL* 3, p. 38 frag. 118 (= Paulus, ex Fest. 88.4): *inde Dicarchitum populos Delumque minorem*; for the probable date (the 140s), see D'Arms, *RBN*, p. 8.

78. Vell. Pat. 2.1.1–2; cf. Polyb. 31.25.6–8.

79. See Gabba, "Riflessioni" (above, note 64), p. 93. For the growth of luxury, including the *villa expolita* on the coast, see D'Arms, *RBN* pp. 1–17; for the sizes of individual fortunes, see Harris, *WIRR*, pp. 86–87.

Against this background the private economic interests, including commercial, of Roman senators appear in sharper focus. To be sure, it still seems that aristocrats were long willing to forego the very large profits to be made from the public contracts;[80] it may be, particularly as regards the leading senators, that much of their regular and new income came, in one form or another, from their lands.[81] But land and sea were now more closely linked than ever before, and sources of private wealth during the second century are notoriously ill-documented. Cato is one of the few personalities whose financial affairs are known in any detail, and in addition to the investments already described, he found a way to make large profits through maritime loans.[82] The conduct of other contemporary notables, too, is worthy of scrutiny. In 179 there was public outcry when M. Aemilius Lepidus, in whose aedileship both *porticus Aemilia* and the Tiber *emporium* were begun, constructed a breakwater near his *praedia* at Terracina.[83] That these new harbor and docking facilities were designed to expedite the shipment of the products of Lepidus' estates, especially wine, to northern markets cannot be doubted; wine from this area could now be marketed from the new complex on the Tiber at Rome—a complex which Lepidus had supervised as it grew—and wine from Terracina was reaching Gallia Narbonensis in a slightly later period. Furthermore, a manufacturing center for first century amphoras carrying Caecuban wine has now been identified at Canneto, near Terracina; this was certainly not the first local atelier.[84]

Would Cato have denied that the terms of the law which forbade senators to own ships influenced the means which he employed to secure his maritime profits? Would Lepidus have denied that he had a financial interest in the cargo ships which his breakwater protected

---

80. Ascon, 93C, Cass. Dio 55.10; on which see E. Badian, *Publicans and Sinners* (above, note 75), pp. 50, 120n16; Harris, *WIRR*, p. 80n2.

81. See Harris, *WIRR*, pp. 79–80, admitting, however, "a large penumbra of uncertainty."

82. Plut. *Cat. Mai.* 21.6, discussed below, section III. See also Astin, *Cato* (above, note 63), pp. 252–253, 320.

83. Liv.40.51.2: *Lepidus molem ad Tarracinam, ingratum opus, quod praedia habebat ibi privatamque publicae rei impensam inseruerat.*

84. Canneto: A. Hesnard, *MEFR* 89 (1977), pp. 157–168. Shatzman, *SWRP*, p. 242 (no. 3), duly cites the evidence for Lepidus' estates, but sees no connection between his "very considerable" private resources and the possibility that he shipped his wine from Terracina.

while amphoras of his wine were being placed on board? Would Scipio Aemilianus, who had fifty talents on deposit with a banker in 162,[85] have inquired scrupulously into the ways in which the man invested this sum? The importance of such questions for the dynamics of the relationship between attitudes and conduct is large, whatever the answers to them may be.

We can strongly suspect, moreover, that the answers to all of these questions were negative. For when in 70 Cicero brought up against Verres the latter's ownership of a huge and handsome cargo ship,[86] he did not base his objections on the provisions of the *plebiscitum Claudianum*. Indeed, if Verres could show that he had built the ship at his own expense, Cicero admitted that he would be satisfied and find nothing actionable in the conduct.[87] He knew better than to rest his case on the illegality of a senator building or owning a ship, for the counsel for the defense had disposed of that argument easily enough: "The statutes forbidding that are ancient things, what you yourself, Hortensius, often call dead letters."[88] A *nobilis* such as Q. Hortensius Hortalus clearly recognized that the *plebiscitum Claudianum* had long since lost its binding force, and however much Cicero, the *novus homo*, might appear to yearn for earlier days when strictness prevailed in the state and severity in the courts, he too was realistic enough to see the futility of parading the contents of such legislation before members of a jury who belonged to the post-Sullan senate.[89] After a passing reference to the continued existence of the law, he hurried on to other arguments, making it clear that if Verres could have been supposed to need a merchant vessel to export produce from some *maritimum fundum* in Italy, one could hardly think the worse of him.[90]

If the *plebiscitum Claudianum*, and perhaps other and similar statutes, could be described in 70 as *antiquae et mortuae* while remaining formally binding, it is most improbable that the formal revival of such

85. Polyb. 31.27, the passage which must have been intended by Harris, *WIRR*, p. 80.

86. Cic. II *Verr.* 5.44: *navem vero cybeam maximam, triremis instar, pulcherrimam atque ornatissimam.*

87. II *Verr.* 5.47.

88. II *Verr.* 5.45: *Antiquae sunt istae leges et mortuae.*

89. II *Verr.* 5.45, on which see J. R. Hawthorn, *G&R* 9 (1962), pp. 57–58; cf. also Broughton (above, note 30), p. 152.

90. II *Verr.* 5.46. Rougé, *OCM*, p. 259, attributes to Cicero's words a censorious implication which seems to me unnecessary.

legislation in Caesar's *lex de repetundis* of 59[91] succeeded where earlier provisions had failed. On the contrary, repeated attempts at such restrictive legislation are often better interpreted as evidence for the strength of the social tendencies which were working to counteract them. In Ming-Ch'ing China, a statute prohibited the higher nobility from allowing their family members or servants to engage in trading or commercial activities; so flagrant, however, were the violations that the censor general was compelled to complain to the throne in 1407 that nobles and others engaged in the salt trade had "become a real menace to the interest of the government and the people"; and subsequent attempts to enforce the law met with no better success.[92]

The analogy with Ciceronian Rome is no more than approximate, since in Ming Ch'ing China social positions were rigidly predetermined. Even so, respective conditions were not wholly dissimilar. We now know that in this period a senator's financial needs were greater than they had ever been before, since "the prizes of political life were now much bigger . . . , the competition for the prizes was now much fiercer, [and] the means of achieving the prizes were now much less easily controllable"; in consequence, Roman aristocrats were finding it increasingly necessary to seek wealth in ways that a Roman traditionalist would not have condoned.[93] The tension between traditional agricultural values on the one hand and, on the other, the developing availability of maritime profits and the need to exploit them, may be partly reflected in the contorted logic of Cicero's discussion of maritime cities in *De Re Publica*, introduced earlier.[94] After rehearsing the philosophers' conventional objections to cities like Carthage and Corinth, where *cupiditas mercandi et navigandi* destroy social stability and so corrupt the state, he concludes *in his vitiis inest illa magna commoditas*: "All the products of the world can be brought by water to the city in which you live, and your people, in turn, can convey or send whatever their own fields produce to any country they like"; Rome, on a great river, near but not on the sea, enjoys the advantages

91. *Dig.* 50.5.3, cited above in Chapter 1, section I and note 17.
92. Ping-Ti Ho, *The Ladder of Success in Imperial China* (New York 1962), pp. 81ff.
93. T. P. Wiseman, "Senators, Commerce, and Empire," *Liverpool Classical Monthly* 1 (1976), pp. 21–22. See further H. Schneider (above, note 8), pp. 241 ff., stressing the link between increasing criticism of greed and the growth of acquisitive practices.
94. Cic. *De Re Pub.* 2.7–10. Cf. above, chapter 1, note 18.

of a maritime city, untainted by its corrupting vices.[95] The substance of the passage derives from the Old Oligarch, who had described Athens as a magnet for world-wide commerce; but, as has now been acutely noticed,[96] the tone of the Old Oligarch was unremittingly hostile. Actual Roman conditions, together with the desire to glorify Rome at the expense of Greece, combined here to lead Cicero to a conclusion contradictory to his premise.

In short, we may be confident that at least some of the unspecified *negotia* of late Republican senators, the evidence for which has only recently begun to be systemmatically collected and discussed by modern scholars,[97] will have included financial investments in shipping and commercial enterprises—clear evasion of the *plebiscitum Claudianum* and similar legislation. It remains, however, to inquire more closely into the social mechanisms of this evasion, since they are important for our understanding both of Roman economic history, and of the relationship between attitudes and conduct, the dynamics of which it is the chief aim of this chapter to illuminate.

III

Plutarch's description of the Elder Cato's financial interest in shipping is not only our earliest evidence, but also our most detailed account of the organization of business arrangements: "His method was as follows: he required his borrowers to form a large company (ἐπὶ κοινωνίᾳ), and when there were fifty partners, and as many ships for security, he took one share in the company himself and was represented by Quintio, a freedman of his, who accompanied his clients in all of their ventures. In this way his entire security was not imperilled, but only a small part of it, and his profits were large."[98]

In the organization of the commercial partnership described here, three principal features may be distinguished: first, a multiplicity of levels of financial commitment on the part of Cato, who both lent capital to an unspecified number of borrowers, and took out one share in the partnership himself; second, an indirect participation on the

95. *De Re Pub.* 2.9.

96. Ps.-Xen. *Ath.Pol.* 2.7–8, on which see now Gabba, "Riflessioni" (above, note 64), p. 97. See further A. D. Momigliano, *CR* 58 (1944), p. 2.

97. Wiseman, *NMRS*, pp. 197–202; Shatzman, *SWRP*, pp. 241–439.

98. Plut. *Cat. Mai.* 21.5–6.

part of Cato, who empowered his freedman Quintio to represent his interests; third, the considerable size of the company and its apparent profitability.[99]

We should like to be able to compare these arrangements with those of other private commercial partnerships (*societates privatae*)[100] in the late Republic, so as the better to test how typical they were; the meager evidence, unfortunately, is inadequate for such a test. But it is important to emphasize that the little we do know is not in conflict with the overall impression conveyed by Plutarch. *Societas* between C. Quinctius and Sex. Naevius involved at least these two freeborn partners and possibly others; P. Quinctius inherited his brother's share; their profitable business involved a well-cultivated grazing farm in Gaul.[101] The *mercatores* of Puteoli, whom we have met before in the *Verrines*, complained of Verres' ill-treatment, in Sicily, "of their partners, of their freedmen, and of their fellow freedmen."[102] Here is a *societas* of traders also active in the provinces, in which free partners are participants, but freedmen again play a prominent role. When the Puteolan *mercator* P. Granius charged that Verres murdered his freedmen in Sicily and confiscated his ship and its cargo, Granius' position in the commercial enterprise becomes clear: he owned the ships and was financing trade, with his freedmen, like Cato's Quintio, acting as his representatives.[103] Could *liberti* enter into private partnerships with *ingenui*? Freedmen could certainly act in independent fashion, organizing partnerships of their own: that appears to be the implication of a passage in the *Satyricon*, in which the freedmen *socii* of an undertaker, also a *libertus*, are said to have enriched themselves at their former master's expense.[104] And the social pattern is confirmed by a late Republican inscription, in which a *libertus* appears as *socius* with his patron in a business which

99. On the characteristics of the partnership, cf. Broughton (above, note 30), pp. 151–152; Rougé, *OCM*, pp. 355, 357–358, 426–428.

100. *Dig.* 17.2.59; cf. Gaius 3.148–149, with the notes of F. de Zulueta, *The Institutes of Gaius* (Oxford 1946) ad loc; W. A. J. Watson, *The Law of Obligation in the Later Roman Republic* (Oxford 1965), pp. 125ff; J. A. Crook, *Law and Life of Rome* (London 1967), pp. 229ff. For recent legal debate on the nature of *societas*, see M. Kaser, "Neue Literatur zur 'Societas,' " *Studia et Documenta Historiae et Juris* 41 (1975), pp. 278–338.

101. Cic. *Quinct.* 11–13.

102. Cic. II *Verr.* 5.154.

103. Ibid., 5.154.

104. Petr. *Sat.* 38.13.

is not named; the patron was also a freedman.[105] That the social composition of the private *societas* was normally heterogeneous, and that slaves, freedmen, and other dependents as well as freeborn partners, were normally all involved in their severally appointed functions, might have been guessed from the sophisticated organization of the public companies (*societates publicanorum*), which are much better documented;[106] and it must be inferred from Cicero's revealing description of such private arrangements: "partnerships, with their slaves, their freedmen, and with their clients."[107]

Brunt has correctly observed that "the Roman law of *societas* never permitted the formation of trading companies with limited liability of more or less permanent duration in which many could hold shares" and grow powerful through "the accumulation and concentration of capital"; he concludes that "the *negotiatores* were unorganized individuals."[108] But Cato's company included fifty partners, and his profits were large; the profitable *societas* of Quinctius and Naevius in Gaul endured for many years;[109] *socii* could marshal clients, freedmen, and slaves, and deploy them in trade with the provinces. The partners themselves could be men of standing, owning ships and financing trade without ever going on board themselves as *naukleroi* or *magistri*—as Plutarch implies, and as the presence of the *actio exercitoria* in the Praetor's Edict confirms.[110]

Moreover, such relationships as these must have been deeply embedded into the late Republican institutional fabric. Otherwise, it is difficult to understand how Cicero could include actions stemming from *societas* with those of *fiducia* and *tutela* as those most deeply affecting a man's reputation, and argue that, while it was reprehensible to break faith or deceive one's ward, it was equally reprehensible for a man "to deceive a partner who had joined with him in business."[111]

---

105. *CIL* I², 1596 = *ILLRP* 938; on which see Treggiari, *RFLR*, p. 105.

106. See Badian, *Publicans and Sinners* (above, note 75), pp. 67–81, a full response to the question (p. 67) "how, without managerial training and schools of business administration, could the Romans organize companies that could handle contracts of a size dwarfing most private fortunes?"

107. Cic. *Parad. Stoic.* 46: *qui cum servis, cum libertis, cum clientibus, societates.*

108. Brunt, *Equites*, pp. 125–126.

109. Cato: above, note 98; Gaul: Cic. *Quinct.* 14.

110. Rougé, *OCM*, pp. 233–234, 389–390; observed also by M. W. Frederiksen, *JRS* 65 (1975), p. 166.

111. Cic. *Rosc. Com.* 16: *socium fallere, qui se in negotio coniunxit.*

We have no way of knowing what proportion of the men who carried on *negotia* were formally involved in partnerships, but even those for whom no *socii* are explicitly attested needed to rely upon a network of dependents, associates, and contacts, carefully and systematically developed over time, in order to conduct their affairs successfully. L. Aelius Lamia, for example, who supported the *publicani* of Syria, and who may have had *negotia* in Bithynia, furthered his *negotia* in Africa through *procuratores*, *liberti*, *familia*, and was helped as well by his friendships, in this case by Cicero's direct intervention on his behalf with the governor of Africa Vetus.[112]

Roman company law may have remained at a rudimentary level of development; all the same, large-scale business enterprises such as those directed by Lamia apparently managed well enough. While to characterize such men or such enterprises as "unorganized" is technically correct in an age familiar with sophisticated shipping cartels, conglomerates, and large corporations, it nonetheless tends to divert the historian from recognizing such organizational characteristics as these enterprises did possess, and from considering the implications of these for the larger Roman social framework, in which the upper-class attitudes towards commerce and trade play their part. These characteristic forms of organization may be summarized as follows.

First, the organization of *societates* and also that of less formal trading relationships, could cut across the boundaries of rank and status, and involve men of very different social levels: freedmen play prominent roles, but so also do *ingenui*, who might be *viri municipales* but also might be men of equestrian or senatorial rank. Here is the fundamental Roman social unit, the *familia*, enlarged and extended to perform functions far more complex than fulfillment of domestic needs. One such interconnecting web of relationships, among men of varied levels of rank and status, of varying degrees of closeness, and involving various types of expectations and obligations, the Romans knew as *clientela*. When Cicero explicitly includes *clientes* in a description of *societates privatae*, he establishes the relevance of the concept of *clientela* to a proper understanding of Roman economic, as well as of Roman political relationships.[113]

---

112. Cic. *Ad Fam.* 13.62, 12.29.2; cf. Nicolet, *Ord. éq.* 2, p. 764; Wiseman, *NMRS*, p. 197n2; and see further below, Chapter 3, section III.

113. Cic. *Parad. Stoic.* 46 (quoted above, note 107); see also Frederiksen (above, note 110), pp. 166–167.

Second, since no Roman would freely choose to be known as *cliens*—
Cicero declared that "it is bitter as death to have accepted a patron or
to be called clients"[114]—other language might be used instead to
conceal real differences in rank, standing, and function. A slave, when
manumitted, could be called a "friend" by a former master,[115] but new
vocabulary did not automatically abolish conditions of dependence or
domination. In general terms, this means that conventional Roman
semantics can hinder our understanding of actual social relationships
and their various functions. Specifically, there could be "friendship"
both between equals and unequals, and services performed by both
types of "friends" might be of many kinds, including activities which
had lucrative dimensions. This is clear both from passages in Cicero's
works, and from the fact that although a loan to a friend was called
"*mutuum*, to distinguish it from *faenus*, of which the sole aim was
profit," the difference in terminology did not prevent loans to friends
from being interest-bearing in the late Republic.[116]

114. Cic. *De Off.* 2.69; *Patrocinio vero se usos aut clientes appellari mortis instar
putant.*

115. Cic. *Ad Fam.* 16.16. 1 (Quintus to Cicero): *De Tirone, mi Marce, ita te
meumque Ciceronem et meam Tulliolam tuumque filium videam ut mihi gratissimum
fecisti cum eum indignum illa fortuna ac nobis amicum quam servum esse maluisti.* On
Tiro's manumission, see S. Treggiari, *Liverpool Classical Monthly* 2 (1977), pp. 67–72.

116. Cicero's distinction between *prodigi* and *liberales* (*de Off.* 2.56) is highly instructive: *Liberales autem, qui suis facultatibus aut captos a praedonibus redimunt aut
aes alienum suscipiunt amicorum aut in filiarum collocatione adiuvant aut opitulantur
in re vel quaerenda vel augenda.* cf. *Ad Att.* 1.13.6 (Messalla had purchased the house
of Autronius for HS 13,400,000): "You wonder what concern it is of yours. Only that
after this transaction I am considered to have made a good bargain, and persons have
begun to realize that it's legitimate to make a respectable show in the world with
purchases financed by one's friends," (*homines intellegere coeperunt licere amicorum
facultatibus in emendo ad dignitatem aliquam pervenire*); cf. also *Ad Fam.* 14.1.5:
"Just this will I say: if my friends are loyal, money will not be lacking; if not, you cannot
achieve results with *your* money" (*tantum scribo: si erunt in officio amici, pecunia non
deerit; si non erunt, tu efficere tua pecunia non poteris*). *Mutuum* and *faenus*: J. A. Crook
(above, note 100), pp. 210–211, and p. 240: "When we look at the supposedly gratuitous contracts we find the need to make many qualifications and exceptions . . .
Mutuum, for example, was strictly loan without consideration; but in practice money
was not lent for nothing, and little understanding of the financial pattern of Roman
society would be achieved by anyone who confined himself to the gratuitous concept
of *mutuum*"; Shatzman, *SWRP*, p. 82, with refs. in nn. 40, 41. For late Republican
aristocrats as financiers, see now J. Andreau, "financiers de l'aristocratie à la fin de
la République," in *Le dernier siècle de la république romaine et l'époque augustéenne*
(Strasbourg 1978), pp. 47–62. From the lender's viewpoint, the important distinction
was between "friendly" loans and loans for profit. But the attitude of the borrower needs

Third, in the patterns of participation described above, a man's actual visibility in commercial and trading relationships might be—and in the case of Cato, L. Aemilius Lepidus, Scipio Aemilianus, or of P. Granius and of L. Aelius Lamia certainly was—inversely proportionate to his share of the profits.

Once we are prepared for the possibility that men of different social ranks and positions could be involved in the same trading enterprises, and for situations in which a man's profits and his visibility might be in inverse proportion, certain features of our evidence appear in changed perspective, and important consequences follow. For one thing, the large numbers of freedmen concentrated in the foreign or Italian trading centers—Delos, for example, where of the "Romaioi" whose status is known, forty-eight were slaves, ninety-five were freedmen, and eighty-eight were *ingenui*;[117] or in centers of manufacture and distribution like Capua, Puteoli, Aquileia, Ostia—ought not to be interpreted in isolation, without reference to the extended *familia* or larger units of organization of which they were often a part; and without reference, especially, to the Roman and Italian patrons of *liberti* themselves, who will have provided much of the capital for their enterprises, and who will have realized, often, disproportionate shares of the profits. The economic advantages of manumission of slaves are pertinent here: a *libertus* could perform services for a former master which could not be performed by slaves, and ex-slaves owed continuing obligations to their former masters—obligations often sanctioned by law, but still more often a matter simply of actual practice.[118] In other words, small and humble men, moving in their apparently restricted orbits and small units of production, can typically imply the involvement of larger and more distinguished men, and of systems of production and distribution of some specialization, efficiency, and complexity.

Moreover, the very nature of our Roman evidence can perhaps help to illuminate realities of the Roman social system. The historian who seeks to identify these larger and more distinguished men and to document their involvement with commerce and trade, finds the path encumbered: in the inscriptional material from the trading centers it

also to be considered in order to determine whether, in any instance, the loan was undertaken for purposes of consumption or for those of capital investment.

117. Hatzfeld, *Trafiquants* (above, note 22), pp. 247–248; accepted by P. A. Brunt, *Italian Manpower 225 B.C.–A.D. 14* (Oxford 1971), pp. 212–213.

118. For references, see below, Chapter 5, note 30.

is typically the small men who are in the foreground; whereas in the upper-class literature from Rome, the larger men are rarely named, and when they are the language in which economic activities are described (*negotium exercere* and cognates) is, as we have suggested, normally imprecise and unspecific. Indeed, the greater a man's *dignitas*, the more likely that his involvement was indirect and discreet, camouflaged behind that of an undistinguished freedman, client, partner, "front man," or "friend."[119] A similar pattern of participation can be seen in operation at other times and places; for example in seventeenth century England, where Sir Percival Willoughby could possess ships to transport his coal down the river Trent to Lincolnshire, but found it disreputable to buy grain there as freight for the return voyage and for resale in Nottingham. Yet Sir Percival found a way to achieve his desired ends without compromising his standing as a gentleman: it was pointed out to him that "your worships need nott be seene in the premises, but onely your servantes."[120] If for "servante" we read "freedman," or "procurator," or "freeborn, nonsenatorial partner," or even "friend," the analogy with Rome is striking.

IV

It is precisely here, around this concept of indirect involvement, that it becomes possible to clarify the relationship between senatorial attitudes towards commercial activities, and actual upper-class practice in the late Republic. Values and conduct were not sharply at variance—nor could they be, if social institutions could continue to function effectively for so long. As we have seen, legislation prohibiting senators from active engagement in seaborne commerce was repeatedly enacted; expressions of disdain toward petty huckstering, toward *mercatores* and *navicularii*, were frequent; senators remained landowners by definition, kept their hands off the public contracts, and did not overtly and directly engage in buying and selling on the internal market, or overseas. But on the other hand, neither can repeated acts of legislation, or the frequent expressions of disdain, or the upper-class emphasis upon the pursuits deemed appropriate for men of rank (*dignitas*), be combined to imply the existence of a dominating "ideology,"

---

119. See, e.g., Broughton (above, note 30), pp. 125–126; Gabba, "Riflessioni" (above, note 64), pp. 94–95; Wiseman, *NMRS*, p. 78; H. Pavis d'Escurac, "Aristocratie senatoriale et profits commerciaux," *Ktema* 2 (1977), pp. 344–345.

120. L. Stone, *The Crisis of the Aristocracy, 1558–1641* (Oxford 1965), p. 336.

which directed the members of the elite solely toward their landed estates and luxury villas, and away from an interest in the various other means of acquiring wealth, including those of commerce, trade, and manufacture. For we have seen also that the laws prohibiting senators from owning ships could be evaded and could be described, even by a member of the Roman nobility, as "dead-letters"; that pejorative references to *mercatura* are counterbalanced by notices of the high levels of mercantile wealth, and of the respectability of the men who attained them; that a senator's *negotia* might well include the part-possession of ships, shares in shipping partnerships, and investments in seaborne commerce; and that terms such as *negotia* and *amicitia* can have economic dimensions.

The truth is, rather, that traditional values and actual conduct remained interdependent, integrated, and at least formally compatible; and that this equilibrium—sometimes precarious—was achieved through flexible adjustments of existing institutions, rather than by abandoning *patria instituta ac mores* in favor of a new set of what we might call "economic" values. Indeed, given the innately conservative tendencies of the Romans it could hardly have been otherwise. Laws prohibiting senators from owning ships, and aristocratic contempt for banausic activities, did not prevent senators from realizing commercial profits; nevertheless, the laws and the ethos affected conduct profoundly, by encouraging forms of enterprise which increased the importance of subsenatorial roles and minimized senators' visibility and direct involvement.[121] The social organization of Roman trade, in which the institutions of the *familia* and *clientela*, and the claims of *amicitia*, were extended and expanded so as to permit a man of *dignitas* to exploit fresh opportunities for gain without essential compromise of his reputability, simultaneously reveals the continuing potency of "noneconomic" values in the Roman social system, and the readiness of the institutions within the system to adapt to changed conditions.

These, like all generalizations, are subject to the charge of oversimplification; they must be tested against concrete evidence and in spe-

---

121. Cf. R. de Roover's observation on the Scholastics, usury, and banking: "The church's ban against usury did not arrest the development of banking; nevertheless, it affected this development very profoundly, because the bankers managed to evade the ban—in a licit way—by operating on the exchange instead of lending outright." See J. Kirshner, ed., *Raymond de Roover: Business, Banking and Economic Thought* (above, Chapter 1, note 60), p. 345.

cific historical situations; this will be attempted in the next chapter. Nor do I intend, in what has been written above, to suggest that Roman attitudes and Roman conduct were consistently in perfect equilibrium, that their interrelationship was static and never subject to stress. "Aristocratic codes of behavior have generally proved feeble defenses against the temptations of really big money."[122] One is inclined to agree; on the other hand, upper-class Roman invocations of the *mos maiorum* should not be viewed too cynically, or simply dismissed as irrelevant. To characterize the "conventional" Roman attitude towards money-making, defended by Cato, as "quite unreal," "grotesquely in-apposite in the conditions of the late Republic,"[123] or as a reflection of an "antiquated value-system,"[124] does not quite do justice to the complexity of the relationship between attitudes and practices, which in fact, through the social mechanisms described above, could function in a manner which was mutually reinforcing. The dictum that "every form of profit seeking was unsuitable for senators," when considered in the light of the social organization of Roman trade, was something more than a fiction, and something less than a norm.

122. Stone, *Crisis of the Aristocracy* (above, note 120), p. 335.
123. Wiseman, *NMRS*, pp. 77–82.
124. P. Garnsey, in Finley, *Property*, p. 127.

3

Senators and Commerce

Upper-class attitudes and practice must be seen as interdependent; the social organization of Roman trade permitted members of the privileged classes to exploit economic opportunities—including those offered by overseas trade—while essentially preserving a system of values which in modern parlance we should describe as "noneconomic." This chapter first offers two concrete illustrations, with detailed exposition, of such exploitation, and then explores two of the implications to which they give rise. Others have collected and categorized the information pertaining to late Republican senators and equestrians, their careers and their sources of wealth. Here the combination of literary with archaeological evidence in the two case studies, the subsequent analysis of conventional literary descriptions of such activities, and the discussion of how typical they were, may serve as useful prolegomena to a comprehensive historical treatment of the place of commerce, trade, and manufacture in Roman society—one in which proper account is taken both of the types, quantities, and distribution of pertinent archaeological materials, and of the curiously oblique character of many of the pertinent passages in the Romans' literature.

I

C. Sempronius Rufus was certainly in the senate in 43 B.C., and apparently *praetorius* already in the preceding year;[1] if so, and if nor-

---

1. Senator: Cic. *Ad Fam.* 12.29.2, although, as D. R. Shackleton Bailey has reminded me in correspondence, it is just possible that *Sempronianum decretum* could mean "a degree involving Sempronius." A shade of doubt attaches also to the precise meaning of *praetorius* in Hor. *Sat.* 2.2.50, but it at any rate establishes that Sempronius Rufus was a senator, if the scholiasts are to be trusted: see Porphyrio, Acro, and Comm. Cruq. *ad loc.* For these and other details of his career, including his introduction of the chicks of storks as elements in haute cuisine, cf. F. Münzer, *RE* 2A

mal patterns apply, he must have held the quaestorship in the middle
to late fifties and must have been a senator by May of 51, when in a
letter to Atticus Cicero refers to him contemptuously as Rufio, and
interprets his failure to call in at the Cumanum as a failure in *gratia*:[2]
just possibly Cicero had been helpful in smoothing Rufus' way into the
senate. But as the letter makes clear, it was not Cicero whom Rufus
was anxious to avoid but rather a local inhabitant of Puteoli, C. Vestorius. What was the social and economic position of this *vir municipalis*, who does not fit the Roman stereotypes in terms of either status
or wealth? In a private letter to a civilized and urbane contemporary,
and on other occasions, Cicero could joke that Vestorius was a mere
business hog, ignorant of higher things.[3] But it was at Vestorius' table
that Cicero was dining as he wrote, a fact which establishes Vestorius
as sufficiently respectable to play host to a Roman consular, at least
outside of Rome; and Vestorius was *familiaris* of both Cicero and Atticus.[4] At the other end of the social spectrum, Vestorius had efficient
local contacts whom Cicero does not name and doubtless did not know:
exploiting them, Vestorius resolved details of a local inheritance to
Cicero's full satisfaction in 44, and was responsible for a plan whereby
two damaged shops or apartment blocks, a part of the inheritance,
were put into habitable condition, tenants found, and profit realized:
HS 80,000 and perhaps as much as HS 100,000 per year. Vestorius
was later remembered for other enterprises: he introduced to Italy a
form of manufacture previously associated with Egypt, thus earning
the admiration of Vitruvius, who found the method of production ingenious; still later, one of the *vici* of Puteoli bore the family name, a
reflection of the family's wealth and longstanding local influence.[5]

(1923), 1436–37; Broughton, *MRR* 2, p. 465. He is not discussed in the most recent
investigations of economic interests of senators in the late Republic, Wiseman's *NMRS*
and Shatzman's *SWRP*.

2. Cicero held the quaestorship in 75, the praetorship in 66; if the career of
C. Sempronius Rufus was not anomalous, and there is no indication that it was, he
will have been within the senate when first mentioned by Cicero, *Ad Att.* 5.2.2 (May,
51). Rufus was again characterized as Rufio Vestorianus in 44 B.C.: *Ad Att.* 14.14.2.

3. *Ad Att.* 14.12.3: *in arithmeticis satis exercitatum;* for other jokes about Vestorius'
lack of culture, see *Ad Att.* 4.19.1; 6.2.3.

4. For references, see Gundel in *RE* 8A (1958), 1789–90; D'Arms, *RBN*, pp.
52–53.

5. *Ad Att.* 14.9.1, 14.10.3, 14.11.2, and elsewhere: on the inheritance, see further
S. L. Mohler, *TAPA* 63 (1932), pp. 82–86; *RBN*, pp. 53, 200. That *tabernae*, normally

Here is an independent business man, operating simultaneously on a number of fronts, not a "middleman" in the conventional sense of the term, for he did not act as an agent for others. Instead, he has something in common both with the *argentarius* of Cicero's description ("in a position to command favors of men of every rank") and with the property speculators, C. Sergius Orata (like Vestorius, active on the Campanian coast) and Damasippus: all were men who dealt directly with their clients, were involved simultaneously in a number of lucrative pursuits, and occupied positions on the fringe of aristocratic society.[6]

What were the grounds for Vestorius' grievance against C. Sempronius Rufus? There is no direct evidence elsewhere in this letter, although Cicero does make it clear that Rufus was himself no stranger to Puteoli, for he had a villa there; indeed, one found it impossible to walk through the city's business district without catching sight of Rufus, engaged in some transaction or other.[7] But in October of the same year, Vestorius' grievance was publicly aired in the course of a trial in Rome. When a certain M. Tuccius sought to bring C. Sempronius Rufus to trial on an unspecified charge, Rufus attempted by a legal maneuver to turn the tables on his accuser and to prosecute him.[8] But the strategy backfired; M. Caelius Rufus hurried to the assistance of the defense and subsequently gave Cicero the following account of his testimony: "I made a thorough job of Sempronius, even including Ves-

---

interpreted as shops, may mean "apartments" is suggested by the reference to *inquilini*: on this, and on the actual role of Vestorius in the affair—it was probably he who found Cicero's lessee—see now B. W. Frier, "Cicero's Management of His Urban Properties," *CJ* 74 (1978–79), p. 2. Vestorius' manufacture: Vitr. 7.11.1; Plin. *NH* 33.162; on which cf. below, note 19. *Regio vici Vestoriani et Calpurniani: CIL* X, 1631, on which see G. Camodeca, *Puteoli—Studi di Storia Antica* 1 (1977), pp. 73–74. The text is dated to A.D. 93/4, and new evidence now reveals a C. Vestorius Felix active in Puteoli in A.D. 53 (F. Sbordone, *RAAN* n.s. 51 [1976], p. 156): the family thus may have remained locally prominent (*pace* D'Arms, *JRS* 64 [1974], p. 113n80), and their absence from the inscriptional records may be entirely a matter of chance.

6. Cicero on *argentarii: De Off.* 3.58 *argentarius apud . . . omnes ordines gratiosus;* cf. *Caec.* 10 *Romae argentariam non ignobilem fecit.* Orata and Damasippus: E. Rawson, in Finley, *Property,* pp. 100–102.

7. *Ad Att.* 5.2.2: '*Non vidisti igitur hominem* [*sc. Rufus*]?' *inquies* [*sc. Atticus*]. *Qui potui non videre cum per emporium Puteolanorum iter facerem? In quo illum agentem aliquid credo salutavi.*

8. Under the *lex Plotia de vi: Ad Fam.* 8.8.1.

torius and the story of how . . ."⁹ The text of the remainder of this
sentence is corrupt, but whatever the substance of the "story" (*fabula*),
it was severely damaging to the case of Sempronius Rufus, for he was
convicted for malicious prosecution. There is one final allusion to the
altercation, in the spring of the following year. Cicero, who was by now
en route to Cilicia, responded to a report from Atticus on the matter
by expressing amazement at the naiveté (εὐήθεια) of Sempronius Rufus, and envy of the *potentia* of Vestorius;¹⁰ the latter had clearly
proved himself a formidable adversary.

It has been suggested recently that Rufus owed Vestorius money.¹¹
In the light of our knowledge both of Vestorius' shrewd pursuits of his
various economic interests and of the importance of the port of Puteoli
(figures 17, 19) as a commercial center in the late Republic, the suggestion is plausible enough as far as it goes, but greater specificity
would be particularly welcome, since it might help to clarify the types
of relationships that could exist between Roman senators and *viri municipales* such as these—relationships which are largely taken for
granted by the Romans, and about which our literary authorities, for
the most part senators themselves, are almost uniformly mute or
unrevealing.

As a beginning, we may note that Vestorius of Puteoli and the M.
Tuccius who brought charges are united by one bond of common interest: opposition to the senator C. Sempronius Rufus. To discover
additional connective links between Vestorius and Tuccius might provide a way forward. Here the first step was taken in 1939, when it was
observed that Cicero once mentions his acceptance of an inheritance
from a certain Galeo, who died in 47.¹² The cognomen is extremely
rare, and even though M. Tuccii are rather better attested in the Republic, they are not numerous; it was suggested that the M. Tuccius
mentioned by Caelius in 51 and the Galeo mentioned by Cicero in 47
might be the same person, and precisely M. Tuccius L. f. *Tro*[*mentina
tribu*] Galeo, whose existence had long been known from stamps on

9. Ibid. 8.8.1: *Totum Sempronium usque eo perago ut Vestorium quoque interponam,
et illam fabulam narrem.*
10. *Ad Att.* 6.2.10.
11. For Shackleton Bailey's suggestion, see *Att.* 3, p. 192 *ad loc.*
12. *Ad Att.* 11.12.4, on which see F. Münzer, in *RE* 7A (1939), 767 (no. 6).

amphorae of late Republican date.[13] Until very recently it has been impossible to bring fresh and independent evidence to bear on this hypothesis, which consequently has tended to be ignored by Ciceronian scholars and in historical works.[14] But now a preliminary analysis has been published of the cargo of a Republican Roman commercial vessel bound from Italy to Gallia Narbonensis and wrecked off the island of Planier, southwest of Marseilles.[15] The new material (figure 7) greatly increases the attractiveness of the earlier prosopographical reconstruction, and also brings the nature of the relationship between M. Tuccius Galeo and Vestorius of Puteoli into sharp and sudden focus.

The cargo included, together with two other types of amphorae and quantities of *terra sigillata*, a number of amphorae bearing the stamp of M. Tuccius L. f. *Tro*[*mentina tribu*] Galeo, and scholars have been able to localize the Italian center of their manufacture. They were produced in a workshop near Apani, in the region of Brundisium in Apulia.[16] The chronology of the pottery of the wreck is fully consistent with a very late Republican date, and the identification of Cicero's Galeo with the producer of the amphorae, plausible in itself, is strengthened by the fact that it was precisely during Cicero's stay at Brundisium that he reported to Atticus his acceptance of the inheritance from Galeo. The mention of the matter at the close of a letter otherwise wholly devoted to politics acquires added point and topicality if Galeo was a local man.[17]

13. For M. Tuccius, praetor in 190, see F. Münzer, in *RE* 7A (1939), 766–767 (no. 5); Broughton, *MRR* 1, p. 356; and, for the distribution of the *gens*, W. Schulze, *Zur Geschichte lateinisher Eigennamen* (Berlin 1904), p. 375. M. Tuccius L. f. Tro. Galeo: *CIL* I², 2654, with Münzer's comments (above, note 12) *ad loc.*; the possible pertinence of Cicero's Galeo had earlier been observed by O. Bohn, *Germania* 7 (1923), p. 15.

14. The identity of Cicero's Galeo is not discussed by SB, *Att.* 5 *ad loc.* (p. 281); Münzer's suggestion is not mentioned in the brief discussion of M. Tuccius' trial in E. S. Gruen, *The Last Generation of the Roman Republic* (Berkeley and Los Angeles 1974) p. 351.

15. A. Tchernia, "Premiers résultats des fouilles de juin 1968 sur l'épave 3 de Planier," *Études Classiques* (Aix-en-Provence) 3 (1968–1970), pp. 51–82; cf. also Tchernia's account in *CRAI* (1969), pp. 292–309.

16. Tchernia, "Premiers résultats," pp. 61–64; see E. L. Will, *Journal of Field Archaeology* 4 (1977), pp. 295–296, who cautions against assuming all "Tuccius" amphorae were produced in or near Brindisi.

17. Cic. *Ad Att.* 11.12: *scr. Brundisi viii Id. Mart.* It must be acknowledged that the tribe Tromentina is not yet otherwise attested in the region of Brundisium, which was apparently assigned to Maecia (L. R. Taylor, *Voting Districts of the Roman Republic*,

Moreover, a series of coloring dyes were recovered from the wreck and constituted a part of the cargo: realgar (*sandaraca*), litharge (*molybditis*), and *caeruleum*, each of which, as has been well shown, was produced in and distributed from Puteoli;[18] in addition, we have Vitruvius' statement that it was C. Vestorius who inaugurated the Puteolan production of *caeruleum*, which had long been manufactured in Alexandria.[19] There can be little doubt that C. Vestorius and Cicero's Puteolan friend are the same man. We can accept the conclusion which Tchernia draws: the products of C. Vestorius of Puteoli and of M. Tuccius Galeo were found on board the same ship; this fact, which squares precisely with a situation discussed in the *Digest*, is sufficient to create presumption as to the closeness of their business relationship.[20] Aspects of the enterprise remain unclear: we do not know whether the vessel initiated her voyage at Brundisium, putting into Puteoli to take on Vestorius' products, or whether Galeo's amphorae reached Puteoli on a different ship and the entire cargo of the wreck was placed on board in the coastal Campanian port, a major entrepôt; we do not know whether Galeo was the seller of the oil (or, just possibly, wine) which the jars contained as well as the manufacturer of the amphorae, although at least one amphora specialist inclines to this belief.

Finally, we do not know how far the financial commitments of Vestorius to the venture extended beyond the products of his own manufacture. We are entitled, of course, to our suspicions, based on general knowledge of the wealth and influence of the man; and suspicion is

---

MAAR 20 [1960], p. 273). Tchernia suggests (p. 64) that the diffusion of the M. Tuccii in this region may derive from the presence of the *praetor* M. Tuccius in Apulia and Bruttium during the years 190–186 (Livy 36.45.9; 37.2.1; 37.2.6; 37.50.13; 38.36.1; 39.23.3–4). If so, it will have been because M. Tuccius had property and freedmen in the region, since at this period the magistrate could not grant citizenship, which required a vote of the people.

18. Tchernia, "Premiers résultats," pp. 64–67. There is ancient evidence for the presence of the latter two substances in the region of Puteoli; the presence of realgar in ancient times is inferred by Tchernia on the basis of a report from the French Bureau of Geological and Mineral Research, attesting its presence in the sulfurous zone of modern Pozzuoli.

19. Vitr. 7.11.1, on which see above, Chapter 3, section I.

20. Tchernia, "Premiers résultats," p. 73; he does not notice the passage on *iactus* (jettison) in the *Digest* (14.2.2.2.), which begins "A number of merchants had on board the same ship a variety of cargoes" (*cum in eadem nave varia mercium genera complures mercatores coegissent*). (These merchants, however, were plainly not *socii*.)

increased by a passage of a letter of Cicero which reveals that Vestorius was actually in Apulia on one occasion late in 54: it is tempting to suppose that he was transacting business at Brundisium with M. Tuccius Galeo already at this date.[21]

In any case, from the size of the vessel, the variety and bulk of its cargo, and the location of the wreck, it is clear that this venture represents commercial shipping on a considerable and well-organized scale. While it may be unnecessary to suppose the existence of a partnership as elaborate as that entered into by the Elder Cato, where capital (and risk) were distributed among fifty partners,[22] neither is it likely that the organization was as simple and primitive as that of the two partners involved in a *sagaria negotiatio*, and whose respective legal rights and obligations were set forth by the jurist Julianus and are quoted by Ulpian in a passage of the *Digest*.[23] The involvement of other participants in the commercial venture seems clearly indicated, and the senator C. Sempronius Rufus is one perfect candidate. This is a man who could be found trafficking in the *emporium Puteolanorum* (a fact not adduced by Tchernia) and against whom both M. Tuccius Galeo and Vestorius had justified claims—claims which the former was prepared to carry to the courts for settlement, and which the latter's *potentia* helped to bring to advantageous resolution.

Here are signs of a Roman senator's significant financial interest in a commercial shipping venture. Would that the lines of its organization were clearer. Conceivably C. Sempronius Rufus merely functioned as a *faenerator*,[24] a supplier of capital at interest, in the operation, but in that case the fact that M. Tuccius Galeo and C. Vestorius pressed

21. Oil or wine: Tchernia, "Premiers résultats," p. 80; seller and manufacturer: A. Hesnard has communicated this opinion to me in conversation. Vestorius and Apulia: Cic. *Ad Att.* 4.19.1: *Credo enim te putasse tuas mulieres in Apulia esse, quod cum secus erit quid te Apulia moretur? An Vestorio dandi sunt dies? An* and *num* have been conjectured in place of *nam*, the consensus of the best MSS; Shackleton Bailey, accepting *an*, notes that "Vestorius lived neither in Rome nor in Apulia but in Puteoli" (SB *Att.* 2 *ad loc.*, p. 224). But *an*, and Shackleton Bailey's own translation, make better sense if Vestorius were actually in Apulia, rather than in Campania: "What is to keep you in Apulia? Or do you have to spare some days for Vestorius (there)?" *Num*, while it would of course change the expected response to the question, would not affect the issue of Vestorius' actual location.

22. Plut. *Cat. Mai.* 21.6, on which see above, Chapter 2, section III.

23. *Digest* 17.2.52.4, on which see Rougé, *OCM*, p. 425.

24. For senatorial involvement in the lending of money in the late Republic, see Wiseman, *NMRS*, pp. 78–81, with the list of names in Appendix IV, pp. 199–201; Shatzman, *SWRP*, pp. 76ff; see also above, Chapter 2, note 116.

their claims against him so confidently and persistently becomes more difficult to explain. The balance of probability is rather in favor of a more formal set of arrangements, in which these men (and possibly others) had entered into an agreement to combine their capital, merchandise, maritime expertise, and knowledge of foreign markets, in order to pursue profits over a long term. Within this formal private partnership (*societas*),[25] C. Sempronius Rufus could have been owner or part-owner of one or more ships.

If the date of the wreck could be established with precision, if we knew more about the mutual obligations of the associates, and about the duration of the partnership, it might be possible to sustain what in the present circumstances can only be tentatively suggested, that M. Tuccius Galeo and C. Vestorius were harassing C. Sempronius Rufus for his failure to pay his proper share of damages attendant upon the loss of this (or another) ship and its cargo through *naufragium*:[26] in all but the most primitive societies the loss of goods from shipwreck or comparable natural disasters, and the subsequent need to determine liability for damages, has tended to generate legal proceedings.

At all events, this commercial grouping of C. Vestorius, M. Tuccius Galeo, and C. Sempronius Rufus illustrates precisely and concretely one feature of organization which was emphasized in the preceding chapter, the principle of social heterogeneity in trading operations.[27] For in this partnership the boundaries of status are blurred, with men of different social levels involved: a municipal notable, a freeborn member of the tribe Tromentina, and a Roman senator. The names, numbers, and functions of the freedmen engaged in aspects of the operations are unknown; we can be certain, nevertheless, that they will have played their part.

II

Writing from Formiae in July of 44, Cicero expresses his satisfaction that Atticus has "had a word with him of Cosa."[28] The man is P. Sestius,

25. For some legal texts, modern bibliography, and a good discussion, see Rougé, *OCM*, "La société en matière commerciale," pp. 423–430, and above, Chapter 2, note 100.

26. See, e.g., *Dig.* 17.2.52.4: *Proinde et si naufragio quid periit, cum non alias merces quam navi solerent advehi, damnum ambo [sc. socii] sentient: nam sicuti lucrum, ita damnum quoque commune esse oportet, quod non culpa socii contingit.*

27. See above, Chapter 2, section III.

28. Cic. *Ad Att.* 15.29.1: *quod cum Cosano egisti, optime.*

quaestor in 63, tribune of the plebs in 57, praetor in 54 or 50, promagistrate (proconsul?) in Cilicia from 49 to 48, *cum imperio* 48–47, and defended by Cicero early in 56: this is clear from a letter written three days before, in which Cicero comments on P. Sestius' failure to return from Cosa in time to meet him in Rome before his departure to the south.[29]

That P. Sestius possessed property in the *ager Cosanus* is a safe inference. There are no direct indications in the literature which help to determine its extent, its architectural typology, or its economic function. Theoretically, the holdings of Sestius might be classed among *voluptariae possessiones*.[30] But the coastline near Cosa differed in a number of ways from the littoral of Latium and Campania, to which this phrase is actually applied, and from the brief account which has been published of the best-known villa on Cosa's coast near the harbor, it is clear that this large estate functioned as a center of production rather than, merely, of consumption.[31] In fact, there is good reason to believe that the holdings of P. Sestius at Cosa were also productive properties, and of a particular type.

Amphorae again point the way. In 1952 the contents of a Roman freighter were recovered from the waters off Marseilles. The Grand Congloué wreck contained nearly 1700 amphorae, most of them stamped on the rim or neck with the letters SES.[32] This was and still remains the largest cache of any single amphora stamp, but the type itself had long been known as #1 in Dressel's classification, and was widely distributed: the jars marked SES, SEST, accompanied often by symbols such as anchor, five point star, palm leaf, trident, double axe (*bipennis*), and crown, are attested at twenty-three different sites in Italy, France, Switzerland, and Spain, and invariably occur in archae-

29. *Ad Att.* 15.27.1; for his career, see Broughton, *MRR* 2, p. 620; F. Münzer, *RE* 2A (1923), 1886–90 (no. 6).

30. *Ad Att.* 12.25.1.

31. *NdSc.* 1927, pp. 208–209, on which see below, Chapter 4, note 31.

32. E. L. Will, "Les amphores de Sestius", *Revue Archéologique de l'Est et du Centre-Est* 7 (1956), pp. 224ff; the first descriptions of these amphorae were those of F. Benoit, "L'archeologie sous-marine en Provence," *Rivista di Studi Liguri* 18 (1952), pp. 249–255; "Amphores et céramique de l'épave de Marseille," *Gallia* 12 (1954), pp. 34–54; and cf., for the final development of his views, *Fouilles sous-marine: l'épave du Grand Congloué à Marseille* (= *Gallia*, suppl. 14) (Paris 1961), esp. pp. 56–70.

ological contexts dateable to the late second or early first century B.C.; two further examples have also turned up in Athens and Delos.[33] The amphorae of the Grand Congloué, on the basis of parallels with these other finds, and finds in the Athenian agora, thus cannot be earlier than the late second century, nor later than the first quarter of the first.

SEST is usually taken to be, and must be, Sestius, and it now appears possible, thanks chiefly to the efforts of E. L. Will, to fix the principal center of the jars' production. For whereas in all other locations the Sestian stamps occur in groups of no more than six, more than eighty examples have appeared at Cosa, where they are concentrated in an area adjacent to the ancient harbor (figure 8); they constitute more than 10 percent of the amphora types which have been locally recovered (figure 9), whether intact or, more often, in fragments. These numbers are a telling sample. This is the largest single concentration of one Roman amphora stamp found anywhere on land—and the figures have recently increased, since six new examples turned up in casual exploration in the summer of 1976, thirteen more in September of the same year. Nineteen new specimens, part of a deposit "noticed in the winter of 1976," have been recently discussed in an article by D. Manacorda, who has emphasized that Cosa is not only the most southerly site on which the stamps have been found, but also the only site at which all but one of the symbols which accompany the SES stamps are attested.[34] Equally significant, the condition of most of the fragments proves that these amphorae had never been filled or shipped: their inner surfaces bear no trace of the pitch with which the containers were coated before being filled with wine, and their outer surfaces no traces of having rubbed against other amphorae during a voyage in the

33. For the distribution of Sestius stamps, see the map in E. L. Will (preceding note), p. 226, fig. 77; cf. that supplied by D. Manacorda (following note), p. 127, fig. 3; Will, "New Light on the Sestius Question," paper delivered at the seventy-seventh General Meeting of the Archaeological Institute of America, Washington, D.C. 29 December 1975, p. 5.

34. E. L. Will, "The Sestius Amphoras from Cosa," paper delivered at the seventy-sixth General Meeting of the Archaeological Institute of America, Chicago, Ill., 30 December 1974, p. 3; at that date, approximately sixty Sestius stamps had been discovered at Cosa; the figure in my text is Professor Will's estimate as of 1 July 1977. See also D. Manacorda, "The *Ager Cosanus* and the Production of the Amphorae of Sestius: New Evidence and a Reassessment," *JRS* 68 (1978), pp. 122–123; E. L. Will, "The Sestius Amphoras: A Reappraisal," *Journal of Field Archaeology* 6 (1979), pp. 339–350. For the port, see A. M. McCann, *JFA* 6 (1979), pp. 391–411.

hold of a ship.[35] Thus, the unused condition of the mass of Sestius amphora fragments found at Cosa signifies that Cosa was the place of the containers' manufacture.

Since we continue to be ignorant of many organizational aspects of the wine trade—what was the relationship between the maker of the amphorae, the producer of the goods, and the merchant who purchased both the goods and the containers?—interpretation of any inscription carried on rims or necks of amphorae is never a simple matter.[36] Nevertheless, the Cosan properties of Sestius produced wine jars, and in quantity; that is the most reasonable explanation of the family's attachments, attested on amphorae and in literature, to the town. Moreover, although we have no definitive proof that the *gens Sestia* was concerned with the contents of the amphorae or involved in their shipping, as well as in their production, various considerations combine to point in that direction. Pertinent here, in a general way, is our earlier finding that a man's *negotia* might be multiple, and that he might further them through *clientela*, his own *familia*, or through private partnerships.[37] More suggestive, because they are a part of the history of this particular family, are the two known visits by P. Sestius to Massilia and Gaul, the widespread diffusion of Sestius amphorae, especially in Gaul, and the location of the Grand Congloué wreck itself: the conclusion of the scholar who has conducted a special study of these amphorae is that "the Sestius firm apparently constituted a virtual monopoly in the Western Mediterranean of its day, but mostly in Gaul."[38]

"Virtual monopoly" is an anachronistic phrase, but it is almost certain that the *gens Sestia* produced containers for shipment of wine grown on their own estates, and possibly also on estates of other vintners in the *ager Cosanus*. Current excavation of the villa Settefinestre (figure 10) and other villas near Cosa, when completed, may help to clarify the relationship between the Sestii and other wine growers in

35. F. E. Brown, *Cosa: The Making of a Roman Town*, Jerome Lectures, 13th ser. (Ann Arbor 1980), p. 71.

36. D. Manacorda (above, note 34), p. 126.

37. See above, Chapter 2, section III.

38. Gaul: Cic. *Sest.* 7: *Clara in hoc P. Sesti pietas exstitit et omnibus grata, quod et Massiliam statim profectus est.* E. L. Will, "New Light on the Sestius Question," (above, note 33), p. 5; her publication of the Cosa amphorae is in an advanced state of preparation.

the vicinity.[39] Furthermore, that the family had financial interest in some of the ships by which the jars of wine were transported is both intrinsically probable and seems actually corroborated by another passage in Cicero, which shows that the son of P. Sestius possessed ships which were in use in 44.[40] And this son, apparently, drew upon experience with one branch of the family's lucrative activities to shift into a different but related field: L. Sestius Albanianus Quirinalis, the son of Publius and suffect consul in 23, was among the first in a long succession of members of the Roman governing class to own property— whether in Rome or outside remains uncertain—on which tiles were fired and then distributed.[41]

When did the *gens Sestia* begin their association with Cosa, and with the production, shipment, and distribution of Sestius amphorae to the West? Since P. Sestius held the quaestorship in 63 he can hardly have been born before the mid-nineties, by which time, according to the present estimates, already cited, the Sestius jars were being produced and distributed. It is time to focus upon a more likely candidate as instigator of the family business: L. Sestius, the father of Cicero's friend.

The little which is known of L. Sestius is confined to a series of conventional Ciceronian compliments which served to introduce the jurors to the character of P. Sestius in the trial of 56. The man was *sapiens*, *sanctus*, *severus*, and he was returned first in the list of elections for plebeian tribune *inter homines nobilissimos temporibus optimis*, that is, between the uprising of Saturninus in 100 and the outbreak of the Social War in 90.[42] That is all, except for one further

39. The current excavations of A. Carandini and others at Settefinestre (Ansedonia), bear on the question: the first phase of the villa is dated by the excavator to the early years of the first century B.C.: see D. Manacorda, (above, note 34), p. 122n2; and cf. now A. Carandini and S. Settis, *Schiavi e padroni nell'Etruria romana* (Rome 1979), p. 89.

40. *Ad Att.* 16.4.4.: *navigia praeterea luculenta (L.) Sesti, Buciliani*. E. L. Will first drew my attention to this passage. On this Sestius see SB, *Att. 6 ad loc.* (nos. 411, 395).

41. L. Sestius Albanianus Quirinalis: *PIR* S, 436; F. Münzer, *RE 2A (1923), 1885 (no. 3); for the tiles, see CIL* XV, 1445; *NdSc.* 1891, p. 31; P. Setàla, *Private Domini in Roman Brick Stamps of the Empire* (= Ann. Acad. Sc. Fenn. 10) (Helsinki 1977), p. 41; for the orthography of Albanianus, see SB *Fam.* 2, p. 461 (no. 321).

42. Cic. *Sest.* 6. For reasons not stated and which remain unclear to me, Will

Ciceronian compliment which has not, perhaps, received the attention it deserves. After the tribunate, L. Sestius, in Cicero's words, "did not so much wish to hold other offices as to appear worthy to hold them."[43] The rhetoric is admittedly difficult to penetrate. It may be an attempt to disguise the fact that L. Sestius canvassed for higher political office and failed to get elected; and even if it means what it seems to say there could of course be a number of reasons why L. Sestius chose not to pursue a political career. Nevertheless, the language is remarkably similar to passages in which Cicero, or other senatorial authors, take elaborate rhetorical pains to create the impression that *honestum otium* is as socially acceptable as the *dignitas* which high office confers and which leave the reader with the uneasy feeling that they are being disingenuous. When T. Pomponius Atticus wrote to Cicero saying that there were "many advantageous opportunities which he had preferred to let slip"—he was referring to lucrative *negotia* both in Rome and in the provinces—Cicero responded with strained and self-conscious politeness that his own ambition had led him to pursue honors but that "another and entirely justifiable way of thinking had led Atticus to an honorable independence" (*honestum otium*).[44]

A man like Atticus—wealthy, cultivated well-connected, entirely respectable—might be scarcely distinguishable, in social terms, from a senator. But one difference which did exist between wealthy senators and wealthy equestrians was that the latter could engage, openly and without embarrassment, in kinds and types of lucrative activities (*negotia*) from which senators were both legally and conventionally excluded. Of course, the concept of *honestum otium* can certainly involve more than the single-minded pursuit of profits; literary activities, for example, are often implied.[45] But at the same time, when Cicero urges

---

apparently thinks that the phrase *sapiens, sanctus, severus,* indicates Sestius' suitability for business activities: *Journal of Field Archaeology* 6 (1979), p. 348.

43. Ibid., *Sest.* 6: *Reliquis honoribus non tam uti voluit quam dignus videri.*

44. Cic. *Ad Att.* 1.17.5: *Neque ego inter me atque te quicquam interesse umquam duxi praeter voluntatem institutae vitae, quod me ambitio quaedam ad honorum studium, te autem alia minime reprehendenda ratio ad honestum otium duxit.* On *minime reprehendenda ratio,* see SB, *Att.* 1, p. 5n3, who takes it as representing "the ordinary Roman view"; but cf. Wiseman, *NMRS,* p. 82n2: ("Cicero's self-conscious politeness about Atticus' *negotia*") and H. Hill, *The Roman Middle Class in the Republican Period* (Oxford 1952), p. 48. Atticus had sacrificed his *otium* during Cicero's consulship and at other times (*Ad Att.* 1.17.4 *et aliis temporibus et me ipso consule*) by returning to Rome to be of service: SB, *Att.* 1, p. 12.

45. See below, Chapter 5, section III and note 73.

Ser. Sulpicius Rufus to help a *negotiator* "as far as is consonant with your respectability and *dignitas*," the tone of senatorial superiority is unmistakable, and Atticus' profitable *negotia* were notorious.[46] When he or other *equites Romani locupletes honestique* are characterized by senators as easily able to win the prizes of high offices, "if they had wished to direct their efforts to acquiring political distinction,"[47] we should ask ourselves what were the directions to which they were devoting their efforts instead, and may suspect that the answer may often, if not invariably or exclusively, be: acquisitive activities, involving commerce, finance, and manufacture. Cicero's own words in *De Officiis*, quoted in the previous chapter, considerably strengthen these suspicions; when he includes persons who concentrated exclusively on the managing of their own financial interests within the category of men who lived a *vita otiosa*, he surely had men like Atticus in mind.[48]

In other words, social as well as chronological conditions are better satisfied by our supposing L. Sestius, rather than P. Sestius, to be the manufacturer of the Cosan jars. Cicero's description of L. Sestius as a man "who wished to seem worthy of senatorial offices rather than to hold them" may imply that L. Sestius consciously chose to devote himself to lucrative pursuits after becoming *tribunicius*, or else, just possibly, that his overt engagement in these "nonsenatorial" activities weighed against him, enabling his political opponents to denounce him before the voters of the tribal assembly, and so to prevent his further political advancement.[49]

But this last suggestion is speculative, and should not divert us from our chief purpose, which is to attempt to extrapolate a pattern of participation from the details concerning the *gens Sestia* and its involvement in trade. In contrast to the partnership of Sempronius Rufus,

46. Cicero to Ser. Sulpicius Rufus: *Ad Fam.* 13.22.2; Atticus' *negotia: Ad Att.* 4.4a.2, 4.8.2; S. Treggiari, *RFLR*, pp. 108, 148, citing Nep. *Att.* 13.3, on the efficiency of Atticus' *familia*.

47. Cic. *Clu.* 153: *si sua studia ad honores petendos conferre voluissent.*

48. Cic. *De Off.* 1.92 (quoted above in Chapter 2, note 7); the pertinence of the passage to Atticus has been noticed also by E. Gabba, "Riflessioni antiche e moderne sulle attività commerciali a Roma," in *Seaborne Commerce*, p. 96. The lucrative aspects of equestrian *otium* are not developed in the otherwise excellent discussion of C. Nicolet, *L'ordre équestre à l'époque républicaine*, vol. 1 (Paris 1966), pp. 699ff.

49. It was not until nearly a generation later that the laws disbarring senators from participation in commerce are actually described, as we have seen, as *antiquae et mortuae*: see above, Chapter 2, note 88.

which illustrates the principle of social heterogeneity in a trading enterprise, that of the Sestii illustrates continuity and concentration of economic activities, which endured, even if in somewhat altered form, from before the Social War into the Augustan Age—that is, over three generations and within a single family. This has interesting implications for the ways in which technical knowledge and practical experience might be cumulative over time, presumably leading to more efficient deployment of resources, of men and materials, in production and distribution. And the durability of the enterprises through the last half century of Republican revolution is not without interest, suggesting that forces were at work which might survive the upheavals of civil war. In this connection, the activities of the Avianii and Cossutii, already discussed, are pertinent.[50] Representatives of nonsenatorial families and engaged in the manufacture and distribution of different articles of trade, they are nonetheless similar to the *gens Sestia* in the ways in which they managed to focus and organize their commercial enterprises, and to maintain them over time, despite revolution and the civil wars.

III

What wider significance have these two specialized case studies? Two rather different lines of argument can be usefully pursued.

The first derives from a feature common to these cases. In both, without the evidence provided by archaeological discoveries, it would have been impossible to clarify the character and scope of economic interests. This is not merely a methodological point about the importance to the Roman social and economic historian of archaeological materials: it deserves emphasis, rather, in order to place the character of our literary evidence in clearer perspective.

Negotium gerere and cognate terms are normally imprecise and elusive.[51] When Cicero writes to Atticus about transactions connected with his profitable purchase, through the agency of Philotimus, of a part of Milo's confiscated property, names are disguised and details communicated *en langue voilée*, in Greek.[52] A similar obliquity char-

50. See above, Chapter 2, section I and note 48.
51. See above, Chapter 2, section I.
52. μυστικώτερον: *ad Att.* 6.4.3.; cf. 6.5.1–2; 6.7.1; 6.9.2, recently discussed by D. Lange, "Two Financial Maneuvers of Cicero," *CW* 65 (1972), pp. 154–155.

acterizes the forms of expression relating to all of the trading activities reviewed here. C. Sempronius Rufus was described as *aliquid agens* in the emporium; while it may be purely a matter of chance that the *fabula* involving Vestorius is a textual muddle, Rufio Vestorianus is singled out, elsewhere, for his εὐήθεια, his adversary for his *potentia*.[53] When Vestorius found a way to make commercial property at Puteoli *quaestuosum*, Cicero provides no descriptive details, only laudatory epithets: than Vestorius no man could be *diligentior*, *officiosior*, *nec nostri studiosior*.[54] L. Sestius withdrew from a political career to concentrate upon the manufacture and shipping of his wine in amphorae—but Cicero says nothing of this, creating instead a fine phrase about *dignitas*, actual and potential.[55] The lucrative activities of Atticus in Rome and overseas become, in Cicero's letter, *facultates aut provincialium aut urbanorum commodorum*;[56] in fact, the involvement of all respectable, but nonsenatorial, men in gainful pursuits is regularly defined obliquely, in terms of a choice not to pursue honors, to live a life of *otium honestum*.

The circumlocution and obscurity of this language are not atypical; a rapid glance at the vocabulary used by Cicero in his *commendationes*, requests to provincial governors to promote the *negotia* of his acquaintances, will show this at once. The letters abound with references to the ethical qualities of the man commended, with Ciceronian professions of friendship, with expressions of gratitude to the governors for kindnesses rendered or about to be performed. But the activities of the persons whose characters are thus endorsed are always those of men in search of profits in overseas markets, as is revealed by such occasional but telltale phrases as *"habet . . . negotia quae procurant liberti,"* *"commendo tibi omnia negotia, libertos, procuratores, familiam."*[57] *Homo pudens et officiosus et dignus qui a te diligatur*: the fellow so described may have actually possessed the virtuous and affectionate qualities which Cicero assigns to him; he was also the freedman pro-

53. See above, notes 7, 9.
54. *Ad Att.* 13.45.3.
55. See above, section II and note 43.
56. *Ad Att.* 1.17.5.
57. *Ad Fam.* 13.33; 1.3.2.; cf. 13.31.2; 13.38; 13.43; 13.44, and others, cf. also the *negotia, procuratores, libertos, familiam* of L. Aelius Lamia discussed above in Chapter 2, section II. For the conventions of decorum observed by writers of such letters of recommendation, see H. M. Cotton, *JRS* 69 (1979), pp. 40–41; she correctly notes the need for a special study (p. 41n23).

curator of a man with *negotia*.[58] L. Lucceius benefitted from a proconsul's *benignitas* and *liberalitas* in 59; Cicero expressed his satisfaction
that his own *auctoritas* and *gratia* had counted for something.[59] Behind
this language lie the extensive and longstanding commercial interests
of the family, one of whose members, a Roman *legatus*, was at Samothrace in 92 and was patron of a contemporary freedman active on Delos;
another, Q. Lucceius L. f., owned a great bank at Rhegium in 72; he
was, perhaps, the father of Cicero's friend L. Lucceius, who had property in Puteoli. At Rome the family gave its name to the *vici Lucceii*
near the Tiber, and in the imperial period to the *cella Lucceiana*; humble
members of the *gens* were active in the trade in wine and oil.[60] We
should hardly form an impression of the collective enterprises of this
family from any single passage of Cicero, but in fact the Lucceii are
found paving two Roman streets by the Porta Flumentana, operating on
Delos and in Cilicia, banking in Rhegium, owning property in Puteoli,
keeping storehouses in the *Forum Boarium*, and supplying freedmen
for other wine magazines.

What is the meaning, the social significance, of this obliquity, that
is to say, this tendency to describe lucrative activities as though they
are something else? Self-consciousness hardly makes for clarity of exposition; it promotes, rather, obscurity and periphrasis. There is a sense
in which this language functions as camouflage, an aristocratic literary
convention, related to the negative senatorial attitudes towards commerce and trade. This camouflage is analogous to the indirect ways in
which senators carried out these activities. That is, just as the traditional social institutions of *familia* and *clientela* were not abandoned,
but were proved to be flexible, able to expand to meet fresh needs, so
the traditional vocabulary of morality, friendship and affection continued viable, and came to be applied in a range of situations and contexts

58. *Ad Fam.* 13.21.2.
59. *Ad Fam.* 13.41, 42.
60. Samothrace in July, 92: *ILLRP* 210; Lucceii on Delos: *Inscr. Delos* 1763; banker
of Rhegium: Cic. II *Verr.* 5.165: *quid Q. Lucceius qui argentariam Regi maximam
fecit*; Puteolan connections: the villa of L. Lucceius, *Ad Fam.* 5.15.2; cf. for a local
Cn. Lucceius *Ad Att.* 16.5.3; *Ad Att.* 15.1a.1 (where I accept Shackleton Bailey's
emendation of the puzzling "Lucullus" of the MSS); see further D'Arms, *RBN*,
187–188. *Vici Lucceii* in Rome, near the Porta Flumentana, the *cella Lucceiana*: see
R. E. A. Palmer, "The *Vici Lucceii* in the *Forum Boarium* and Some Lucceii in Rome,"
Bull. Comm. Arch. Com. Roma 85 (1976–1977), pp. 135–161.

very different from those in which it had originated and developed.[61] This Roman maintenance of traditional institutional forms, and of traditional forms of expression, unquestionably impede efforts to reconstruct the character and scope of upper-class participation in commerce and trade. But archaeological materials can assist; the purposes which motivated the preservation of traditional forms can occasionally be glimpsed, and the interrelationship between attitudes and conduct, therefore, better understood.

Second and finally, the activities of C. Sempronius Rufus and of the *gens Sestia* raise the question of typicality: just how common was such senatorial behavior? We may not know how to quantify the results obtained, or how to construct a statistical table. But these two examples of senators in trade are not exceptional; they take their place in a long parade of persons of rank, already identified, who had a multiplicity of acquisitive interests, including commerce, banking, and manufacture, even if their freedmen will normally be found in the forefront of such enterprises. Not surprisingly, many such senators were *novi homines* of equestrian ancestry, the evidence for whose *negotia* has recently been collected: men like C. Vibienus and T. Rufrenus, whose potteries at Arretium were begun and managed by members of senatorial families.[62] To this large late Republican group M. Aquinus must now be added—his family had interests in lead mining in Spain[63]—and also Bucilianus, a somewhat shadowy but ship-owning senator, whom Cicero twice mentions in connection with L. Sestius: the two may have collaborated in commercial enterprises.[64] It is now clear that the foundations of wealth of a number of late Republican senators from Tibur and Praeneste derived from the lucrative possibilities provided by the rich and vast sanctuaries of Hercules Victor and Fortuna Primigenia there (figure 4), and from the commercial links, cultivated by the fore-

61. See above, Chapter 2, section III.

62. See in general Wiseman, *NMRS*, "Appendix IV: Business Interests of Senatorial Families," pp. 197–202; see also Shatzman, *SWRP*, pp. 100–104. For C. Vibienus and T. Rufrenus see Wiseman's fuller discussion in *Mn.*, 4th ser., 16 (1963), pp. 275–283. Cf. also H. Pavis d'Escurac, "Aristocratie senatoriale et profits commerciaux," *Ktema* 2 (1977), pp. 347ff.

63. T. R. S. Broughton, in J. A. S. Evans, ed., *Polis and Imperium, Studies in Honor of E. T. Salmon* (Toronto 1974), pp. 15–16, cited also by Wiseman, "Senators, Commerce and Empire," *Liverpool Classical Monthly* 1 (1976), p. 21.

64. Ad Att. 16.4.4.; cf. 15.17.2.

bears of those senators, between these sanctuaries and cities in the Greek East.[65]

More is now known of the family, and the dying establishment, of the Barronii, who produced a curule aedile at the end of the Republic, and purple garments in quantity at the family vats at Aquinum.[66] More is known also of the *gens Cestia*, of Praenestine origin, with freedmen, other dependents, and *negotia* in the East: C. Cestius Epulo was proscribed for his great wealth, but was spared; he ultimately reached the praetorship, and his earthly remains reached the mammoth and costly pyramidal tomb in Rome by 13 B.C.[67] L. Plotius Plancus (*pr.* 43), it seems, had interests in the production of cosmetics, and the family works were furthered by representatives on Delos, as well as at Capua and Puteoli.[68] Granaries and warehouses owned by senators create, quite legitimately, the presumption that the owners of the buildings had an interest, also, in the products which they housed and in their shipping and their marketing. Cicero writes as though L. Manlius Torquatus might well have owned granaries at Puteoli.[69] The Lucceii are also instructive and the *horrea Lolliana* in Rome, the presence of a second century M. Lollius Q. f. on Delos, and roughly fifty instances of these two praenomina among small members of the *gens* in Rome, are suggestive—especially in the light of a recent attempt to assign the construction of these *horrea* to M. Lollius Palicanus (*tr. pl.* 71 B.C.).[70] Now that the thousands of Roman amphorae on Delos are at last being studied and prepared for publication, it may soon be possible to es-

65. G. Bodei Giglioni, "Pecunia fanatica," *Riv. Stor. Ital.* 89 (1977), pp. 72–73.

66. For P. Barronius Barba of Aquinum, see Wiseman, *NMRS*, p. 217 (no. 65); for the dye works, see L. V. Bugno, *Rend. Acc. Linc.* 26 (1971), pp. 685–695.

67. See in general Wiseman, *NMRS*, p. 224 (no. 118), with a stemma; new evidence is soon to be published by F. Coarelli.

68. See Wiseman, *NMRS*, p. 252 (no. 328), and below, Chapter 4, sections I and II.

69. Cic. *De Fin.* 2.84–85, on which see G. Rickman, *Roman Granaries and Store Buildings* (Cambridge 1971), pp. 171–172.

70. Delos: *ILLRP* 747; cf. F. Münzer, *RE* 13 (1927), 1375, s.v. "Lollius"; M. Lollius Palicanus: F. Coarelli, in P. Zanker, ed., *Hellenismus in Italien* (Göttingen 1976), p. 23; cf. Wiseman, *NMRS*, pp. 237–238 (no. 231). E. Groag believed that the consul of 21 B.C., or his son, were the builders: *PIR*² L, 311, 312; he has been followed by G. Rickman (see preceding note), p. 164. H. Pavis d'Escurac (above, note 62, pp. 348–349) infers commercial interests of C. Trebonius (*cos. suff.* 45), on the basis of *CIL* VI, 9933, which lists freedmen *thurarii* of the *gens* in Rome; the *gentilicium*, however, is too common to inspire confidence.

tablish direct connections between the names on stamps in Delos and the owners of warehouses in Rome and elsewhere.

The Roman notables in the foregoing group, including C. Sempronius Rufus and P. Sestius, are normally senatorial *novi*, the first representatives of their respective families to attain rank. This suggests the need for careful distinctions within the Roman governing class, and very particularly between *nobiles* and the rest: if we are in general ill-informed about the nature and extent of senatorial *negotia* involving commerce and manufacture, we hear less of the *negotia* of members of noble families. But how is this *e silentio* evidence best evaluated? *Nobiles* are indeed more likely than others to have abstained from the grosser, less respectable forms of making profits (*augere patrimonium*). Yet poverty must have compelled some aristocrats to compromise; the patrician M. Aemilius Scaurus was reportedly a dealer in charcoal *ob paupertatem*, and even his son, the consul of 115 B.C., apparently hesitated before embarking upon his political career: he might, but for his eloquence, have ended up as an *argentarius*. [71]

Derogatory smears such as these are of course part of the rhetorical convention in Roman politics, and when—as in the case just mentioned—the sources are not contemporary with the situations which they describe, they are still more suspect. [72] But at the same time, was it not the members of the nobility whose style of life most required consistent spending, and who simultaneously had most to gain by attempting to preserve optical illusion, that is, to take pains to ensure that such lucrative pursuits as they may have had were well disguised, least detectable? A newly published inscription from Karystos in Euboea commemorates Appius Claudius Pulcher. *cos.* 54, for his εὔνοια and, perhaps, εὐεργεσία. [73] This is additional evidence, certainly, for the *amplissimae clientelae* of the patrician Claudii, which were longstanding in southern Latium, Campania, and the Greek East. [74] But why, exactly, Karystos? May the consul have had an interest, also, in Karystian marble, which began to be quarried and transported for use

71. *De Vir. Ill.* 72.1–2; cf. also Pliny *NH* 36.116.

72. Wiseman (*NMRS*, pp. 84–85) is exemplary on the need for careful appraisal of the sources.

73. H. J. Mason and M. B. Wallace, "Appius Claudius Pulcher and the Hollows of Euboia," *Hesperia* 41 (1972), pp. 128ff.

74. Cic. *Ad Fam.* 13.64; see Elizabeth Rawson, "The Eastern Clientelae of Clodius and the Claudii," *Historia* 22 (1973), pp. 219ff; see also her additions and second thoughts in *Historia* 26 (1977), p. 355.

in Rome precisely in this period?[75] An homonymous Pulcher of the succeeding generation exported amphorae far afield, and since the base of the concern was near Mutina, it is very probable that it was primarily the production of the jars and only secondarily their contents which interested this *nobilis*.[76] Who is the roughly contemporary Q. Claudius Pulcher whose name is stamped on tiles at Italian Locri, and what do the tiles suggest about the extent of his lucrative interests?[77] Ships belonging to a certain Lentulus ("no obscure *navicularius* but . . . a patrician Cornelius") were available for transporting Cicero's works of art from the Piraeus to Italy in 67.[78] What were they doing in Greece, what was the bulk of the return cargo, and what percentage of the profits found its way (and by what means) into the patrician's hands?

The degree to which such examples should be viewed as "timebound phenomena," made possible by exceptional historical conditions such as revolution and civil war, is an important subject, requiring greater attention than it can be given here. After Philippi Octavian, in desperate need of ready money, might draw upon the ex-votos of precious metals and cash at the great sanctuaries at Tibur and else-

75. Tentatively suggested by Mason and Wallace (above, note 73), p. 136; Rawson is sceptical, on the grounds that senators were prohibited from owning land in the provinces (*Historia* 26, 1977, p. 355). But even if she is right—and the evidence for such legal prohibitions is far from conclusive—Pulcher could have profited indirectly, through freedmen *procuratores* or other intermediaries.

76. On all this, see Wiseman, *NMRS*, p. 79, p. 80n1, with references.

77. *NdSc.* 1911, suppl., pp. 49ff; cf. E. Rawson, *Historia* 26 (1977), p. 349. The typology of tile would help to establish chronological controls, but Prof. M. Barra Bagnasco informs me that the tiles disappeared during relocation of Locrian archaeological material after 1945.

78. Cic. *Att.* 1.8.2: *si Lentuli navis non erit*; 1.9.2: *Lentulus navis suas pollicetur*; for discussion, see SB *Att.* 1 *ad loc.* (p. 284). Shackleton Bailey tentatively suggests that the man was P. Cornelius Lentulus Spinther (*cos.* 57), adding that Lentulus may have been returning to Italy from an assignment in the East. Rather, the ships were probably on a commercial voyage: as F. Coarelli has observed in an as yet unpublished paper, no Lentulus is attested in an eastern province in the months immediately prior to the date of Cicero's letter. Moreover, the contents of the two letters make clear that Cicero was currently in closer touch with Lentulus than was Atticus: it appears as though Lentulus was in or near Rome. On the basis of a stamp L. Lentu(lus) P. f. on (wine) amphorae of type Dressel I B, examples of which have turned up at Laurion and in the Athenian Agora, Coarelli is inclined to identify Cicero's Lentulus with L. Cornelius P. f. Crus (*cos.* 49). For the sources of wealth of the two Lentuli, cf. the economic prosopography of Shatzman, *SWRP*, pp. 333–334 (no. 127), pp. 334–335 (no. 129)—no mention of ships, however, in either entry.

where, and later might proscribe the wealthy men who derived their riches from the sanctuaries and from the trade which they generated. But the Rubellii Blandi of Tibur apparently came to no harm, neither the late Republican *negotiator* nor his direct linear descendants, the Augustan senator and his consular son.[79] Indeed, our earlier discussions of continuity, of both assets and activities, from late Republic into the Augustan Age, should be borne in mind, and just occasionally it is possible to trace the accumulation of wealth and rank over as many as five generations, from the Ciceronian Age through the Flavian dynasty.

We may consider the Volusii Saturnini. Tacitus asserted that L. Volusius Q. f. Saturninus, the consul of 12, was the founder of the vast wealth of the family as well as of their *nobilitas*.[80] In the first particular, Tacitean conciseness obscures the fact that the consul's father was in all likelihood the Q. Volusius involved in "financial transactions none too perspicuously described" in Cilicia early in 49.[81] He was clearly a man of wealth and rank, one for whom Cicero had high regard.[82] Moreover he, rather than the homonymous consul of A.D. 56, may be the Q. Volusius Saturninus whose name appears on a lead pipe at the enormous family villa (figures 13, 14) which has been excavated beside the Roma nord entrance of the Autostrada del Sole, near Lucus Feroniae, since the first phase of that villa was unquestionably constructed around the middle of the first century B.C.[83] And if he built the villa, it is likely also that he was builder and first owner of the *horrea*

79. Time-bound phenomena: cf. Finley, *Property*, pp. 4–5. Octavian and the sanctuaries: see G. Bodei Giglioni (above, note 65), pp. 33ff, 72–76; on the Rubellii Blandi cf. Cic. *Ad Fam.* 12.26.1 (the *negotiator*), Wiseman, *NMRS*, p. 256 (no. 360) (senator), Tac. *Ann.* 6.27.1, 14.22.2 (consul).

80. Tac. *Ann.* 3.30.1.

81. *Ad Fam.* 5.20.3, on which see Shackleton Bailey, *Philologus* 105 (1961), pp. 76ff; cf. also *Ad Att.* 5.11 (where the MSS record a Cn. Volusius), *Ad Att.* 5.21.6 with SB's comments *ad loc* (3, pp. 234–235), *Ad Fam.* 5.10.2; on his identity see H. Gundel, *RE* 9A (1961), 903ff (no. 5); and esp. M. Torelli, "Feronia e Lucus Feroniae in due iscrizioni latine," *Archeologia Classica* 25–26 (1973–74), p. 748.

82. For his rank (*praefectus?*), see Broughton, *MRR* 2, pp. 246, 254; R. Syme, *Historia* 13 (1964), pp. 156–166; Wiseman, *NMRS*, pp. 277–278 (no. 514).

83. *RE*, suppl. 9, 1857, no. 15 (citing *CIL* XV, 7389); cf. R. Bartoccini, *Autostrade* 5 (1963), pp. 11–13. For the date (60–50) of the original nucleus of the villa—which awaits proper publication—see M. Moretti and A. M. Sgubini Moretti, *La villa dei Volusii a Lucus Feroniae* (Rome 1977), pp. 6, 16, 20; this supersedes the earlier report in *Autostrade* 10.8 (August 1968), p. 4 (with plan, p. 7); Torelli (see note 81 above), pp. 747–749.

Volusiana in Rome: one of the four known wine amphorae bearing the family name is precisely dated to A.D. 3, and among the inscriptions in the Augustan tomb of the Volusii on the Via Appia a *horrearius* of Q. Volusius Saturninus is recorded.[84] This Q. Volusius has traditionally been identified with the consul of A.D. 56, who has also, in consequence, been assumed to be the founder of the *horrea Volusiana*.[85]

However, now that the late Republican villa is known, and it is clear that Cicero's contemporary, also very probably a Q. Volusius (Saturninus), was almost certainly its builder, there is excellent reason to assign the founding of the *horrea* to Q. Volusius (Saturninus) of the late Republic. There is reason also to suppose that the financial transactions in Cilicia, the first phase of the immense agricultural villa, clearly attested business dealings in both Rome and in Ostia, valuable urban property located near the Tiber island in the heart of Rome's commercial district, as well as the Roman *horrea*, were distinct but related family enterprises.[86] Inscriptions from the *lararium* of the villa prove that the Volusii were still in residence and in possession in A.D. 92, and that the villa itself remained in use until the close of the Antonine Age:[87] here are two centuries of economic continuity, their foundations solidly established by Q. Volusius (Saturninus) of the late Republic. A family history such as this one suggests the advantages in attempting to view lucrative phenomema diachronically, even if our evidence does

84. Amphorae: *CIL* XV, 4571 (A.D. 3), 4646, 4771, 4784; cf. H. Loane, *Industry and Commerce in the City of Rome* (Baltimore 1938), p. 115n6. *Horrearius: CIL* VI, 7289, on which see P. Romanelli, *Diz. Epigr.*, s.v. *horrea*.

85. Cf. G. Rickman (above, note 69), who proposes an Augustan date for the foundation of the *horrea* on the basis of Tac. *Ann.* 3.30; the discoveries at Lucus Feroniae, however, are not discussed, nor does Rickman mention Cicero's contemporary, Q. Volusius.

86. Neither the Ciceronian Q. Volusius nor the *horrea Volusiana* are noticed by the authors of the report in *Austostrade* (above, note 83); cf. Torelli (above, note 81), p. 748, where the Republican nucleus of the villa is assigned to Cicero's contemporary; the *horrea* and their founder, however, are not discussed. For a freedman *negotiator* of L. Volusius Saturninus, see *CIL* VI, 9653; for Ostia, See *CIL* XIV, 178 (L. Volusius Celer, *ex domo Volusi Saturnini consularis*). Property in Rome's commercial district: a travertine *cippus*, dateable to 27 and still in place in A.D. 48, records an *insula Volusiana*; the inscription, which is being published by S. Panciera, came to light during the construction of the offices of the fifth Ripartizione del Comune di Roma.

87. *Autostrade* (above, note 83), p. 9; for the inscriptions, see J. M. Reynolds, *JRS* 61 (1971), pp. 142ff; W. Eck, *Hermes* 100 (1972), pp. 461ff. T. P. Wiseman's forthcoming study of the Valerii Catulli of Sirmio demonstrates similar family and economic continuity.

not equip us for historiography based upon the principle of *la longue duree*, and to focus on multiple forms of a family's wealth, rather than the moment of their acquisition.

In these efforts to explore the implications of two case studies, we have ranged far from C. Sempronius Rufus, the *gens Sestia*, and the late Republic. The names of other members of the ruling class might have been added, and other forms of their lucrative activities—investment in urban property, for example[88]—might have been discussed. But generalizations must be based upon concrete and specific examples. The aim here has been to use two of these to indicate, in outline, the importance for the historian of empirical analysis of the relationship between articles of trade and attitudes towards trade—between what the Romans made and did, and what upper-class Romans thought and said. To advance this inquiry, it will be helpful now to turn to a recent collection of material, more or less complete, and to scrutinize it afresh for its social and economic implications. The evidence for the villa society on the Bay of Naples lends itself admirably to this purpose; not only is the heterogenous source material conveniently assembled, geographically restricted, and distributed over a considerable period of time, but the area itself was a resort, its society notorious among Roman authors for conspicuous consumption, *luxuria*. Here, if anywhere in the late Republic and early Empire, it ought to be possible to witness the Roman governing class speaking with disregard for revenue, writing as though they built and spent for ostentation and not for gain—and possible, too, to test these pronouncements against the surviving documentary and archaeological evidence. While the results of such an inquiry cannot be expected to lead to a radically different view of the villa society in question, they may help us to see the evidence in broader context, and hence to achieve better perspective.

---

88. See now Peter Garnsey, "Urban Property Investment," in Finley, *Property*, pp. 123–136; B. W. Frier, "Cicero's Management of His Urban Properties," *CJ* 74 (1978–79), pp. 1–6, suggesting that the management of such properties through middlemen was "extremely common among Roman property owners" (p. 6): the mechanism removes investors from direct involvement in real-estate deals, while at the same time insuring a steady return on their property.

Luxury, Productivity, and Decline:
Villa Society on the Bay of Naples

I

He who sets out to collect the ancient evidence for the owners of estates on the Bay of Naples (map 2)—*crater ille delicatus*, in Cicero's famous phrase[1]—will quickly encounter the peculiar conditions which the investigation imposes: our literary sources offer a plentiful supply of names of the owners of coastal properties, but from the villas themselves—and the archaeological remains are also abundant—information of this kind is rarely, if ever, available. Of the forty-four notable Roman proprietors of the Ciceronian Age whom I was able to identify in a book published in 1970,[2] only two are known from sources outside literature, and may be said to be the exceptions which prove the rule. Were it not for the carbonized rolls of papyri, the writings of Philodemus of Gadara, and for passages in Cicero which connect Philodemus with L. Calpurnius Piso Caesoninus, surely neither Comparetti nor subsequent scholars would have considered Piso the owner of the vast estate at Herculaneum, a replica of which the late J. Paul Getty had constructed on a sumptuous scale in Malibu, California.[3] At Pompeii, the evidence for a *villa maritima* belonging to Sex. Pompeius Magnus is distressingly indirect; the villa itself has not been found, only a small shrine with a votive inscription erected by a freedman, Sex. Pompeius

1. *Ad Att.* 2.8.2.
2. D'Arms, *RBN*, pp. 171–201 (Catalogue I).
3. Philodemus and Piso: Cic. *In Pis.* 68; the question of ownership: H. Bloch, *AJA* 44 (1940), pp. 490–493, and cf. *RBN*, pp. 173–174; the villa: D. Mustilli, *RAAN* n.s. 31 (1956), pp. 77–97. The villa at Malibu: N. Neuerburg, *Herculaneum to Malibu: A Companion to the Visit of the J. Paul Getty Museum Building* (Malibu, California, 1975).

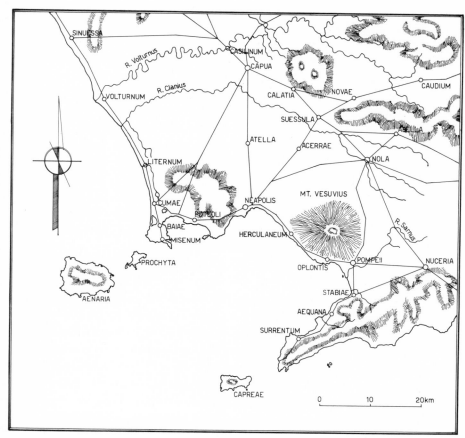

2. Campania and the Bay of Naples in Roman times.

Sex. l. Ruma.[4] And since the Pompeian Pompeii were many, and the praenomen Sextus is not found among them until a considerably later date,[5] to identify Ruma as freedman of the famous Pompeius was perhaps to succumb to the alluring, but dangerous, temptation to as-

4. *CIL* X 8157; on which see A. Sogliano, "Pompei e la gens Pompeia," *Atti della R. Accad. Arch. Lett. di Napoli* n.s. 8 (1924), pp. 17–42; M. Della Corte, *Case ed abitanti di Pompei*, third edition, ed. P. Soprano (Naples 1965), pp. 444–445.

5. P. Castrén, *Ordo Populusque Pompeianus, Polity and Society in Roman Pompeii*, Acta Instituti Romani Finlandiae (Rome 1975), pp. 205–206: the Sex. Pompeii are dated to the period of Nero.

sociate purely local discoveries with the major personalities of Roman history.

One might object that, since archaeological remains generally are relatively meager in the Republican period, their infrequency also in Campania provides no true test. What, then, of the Empire? From the Augustan Age to A.D. 400, the evidence for the names of the forty-seven known owners is somewhat more diverse, as we might have expected: ten proprietors are identifiable from names preserved on *fistulae acquariae*, three purely from inscriptions, and three from a combination of literary and epigraphical materials. But literature remains by far the most important source of information, yielding the names of thirty-one owners.[6] In only one case can literary testimony be combined with the inscriptional evidence which issues from a villa which has actually been excavated, that of M. Vipsanius Agrippa; and despite the ingenious efforts of Rostovtzeff, some scholars may still feel that the evidence for ownership on which he based his arguments is not strong.[7]

This same unsatisfactory compartmentalization of the literary and archaeological material, it is fair to say, holds true of the most recent discoveries, those of the past six years. The late R. N. Paget identified what he considered to be the remains of a number of coastal villas along the Bacoli peninsula; the new fascicule of *Forma Italiae*, which treats the territory between Baiae and Misenum, documents this material with unprecedented fullness; and we now have preliminary observations on the magnificent villa of Torre Annunziata (figure 6).[8] One scholar believes that evidence from the villa indicates that Oplontis may have belonged to Poppaea Sabina;[9] that would be of particular interest, given her other known associations with the region,[10] and we

6. *RBN*, pp. 202–232 (Catalogue II).

7. Rostovtzeff, *SEHRE*[2], pp. 552–553, n.31; see further *RBN*, pp. 231–232 (no. 46).

8. See M. Borriello and A. D'Ambrosio, *Baiae-Misenum*, Forma Italiae, reg. 1, vol. 14 (Florence 1979), index, s.v. "Villa." The new villa: A. De Franciscis, "La villa romana di Oplontis", *PdP* 28 (1973), pp. 453–466.

9. A. De Franciscis, in B. Andreae and H. Kyrieleis, eds., *Neue Forschungen in Pompeji* (Recklinghausen 1975), pp. 15–16.

10. A freedman of Poppaea is mentioned on a *fistula aquaria* found near the Lucrine Lake: *CIL* X, 1906; there were *figlinae Arrianae Poppaeae Augustae* in the *ager Pompeianus* by A.D. 63: V. Arangio-Ruiz and G. Pugliese Carratelli, "*Tabulae Her-*

await the full presentation of these views. Meanwhile, it has to be said that not one of these newly discovered villas has yielded the name of any proprietor, for any period of its history.

For owners' names we must continue to look to ancient literature, or the documentary sources. Continued rereading of the authors has advanced our knowledge, even if it has not always resulted in any increase in absolute numbers of owners of villas. Arguing largely from the evidence of the Bobiensian scholiast, I had assigned a second villa to C. Marius *in agro Baiano*, in addition to the better attested estate at Misenum—but recent work has cast doubt on the reliability of that source, and Marius' second villa may, in consequence, have to be withdrawn from him.[11] C. Sempronius Rufus, as we have seen, had a villa at Puteoli.[12] L. Plotius Plancus, brother of Munatius, was found hiding in a retreat at Salernum when proscribed by the triumvirs in 43 B.C. Both the Elder Pliny and Valerius Maximus have versions of this tale, and Plotius may well have had a villa there.[13] Now comes the attractive suggestion that the Scaurus mentioned in the *Cena Trimalchionis*, who preferred to stay with Trimalchio in his town house even though *habet ad mare paternum hospitium*, was one of the consular M. Aemilii Scauri; whether this was an actual, rather than purely fictional Scaurus may certainly be questioned, but a consular is a better candidate for ownership than the Pompeian magistrate with whom Scaurus is normally identified.[14] Epigraphical and other documentary evidence, too, can be invoked: Appius Claudius Pulcher (*cos.* 38 B.C.), who built the theater at Herculaneum, surely had some local connection, very possibly a villa, and less distinguished names are known from stamped lead pipes.[15] More interestingly, one of the recently published tablets found in Pompeian territory is dated A.D.

---

culanenses IV," *PdP* 9 (1954), pp. 56–57. For the hypothesis that Poppaea came originally from Pompeii, see A. W. Van Buren, in *Studies Presented to D. M. Robinson* 2 (St. Louis 1953), pp. 970–974.

11. *RBN*, pp. 26–28; but see now E. Badian, *JRS* 63 (1973), pp. 121–132.

12. See above, Chapter 3, section I; Cic. *Ad Att.* 5.2.2 (*e sua villa*).

13. Plin. *NH* 13.25, Val. Max. 6.8.5; cited also by Shatzman, *SWRP*, p. 389 (no. 184).

14. R. Duncan-Jones, "Scaurus at the House of Trimalchio," *Latomus* 32 (1973), pp. 364ff; cf. Pet. *Sat.* 77.5.

15. Appius Claudius Pulcher: *CIL* X, 1423, 1424; Shatzman, *SWRP*, pp. 323–324 (no. 116); lead pipes: see *RBN*, pp. 202–203, 206, 209, 212, 214, 216, 218, 223.

40 and refers to *praedia* near Puteoli owned by a Domitia with a second name which has been restored as L[iv]ia.[16] Reexamination of the tablet reveals that the name was rather Domitia Lepida, the aunt of Nero, whose *piscinae* at her villa at Baiae are mentioned by Tacitus, and whose estates there, according to Cassius Dio, inspired the emperor to hasten her death by poison.[17]

But enough has been said to illustrate the observation with which we began: rarely, if ever, can literary and documentary evidence for notable proprietors be combined and associated with a particular group of existing remains, at least in such a way as to constitute what an impartial observer might accept as satisfactory proof of villa ownership. Furthermore, when documentary evidence of ownership is actually discovered in an impressive villa, the "owner," in addition to being associated always with the very last phase of the villa's history, relates closely to the local social and economic milieu, rather than to that of the great political families of Rome: witness L. Istacidius Zosimus, if he was indeed the last owner of the Villa of the Mysteries at Pompeii.[18] These limitations of our evidence will seem less constricting when they are considered in broader perspective, in relationship to what is known about ownership of villas elsewhere in the Roman West. Thus, more than six hundred villa sites have been identified in Roman Britain; the numbers are probably even greater for Gaul; for Belgium, a survey of sites completed more than a generation ago listed roughly three hundred and fifty villas; and when one adds the plentiful villa remains from the Rhineland and the provinces of the Upper Danube, together with those of Spain, Africa, and other parts of Italy, the total number of villa sites actually excavated or partially studied will be well in ex-

---

16. C. Giordano, *RAAN* n.s. 46 (1971), p. 195, no. 19, lines 6–7.

17. Tac. *Ann.* 13.21.6 (referring to the year A.D. 55); Cass. Dio 61.17.2; cf. Suet. *Nero* 34.5, and *RBN*, pp. 211–212. The reading Domitia Lepida is now certain (F. Sbordone, *RAAN* n.s. 51 [1976], pp. 146, 167), confirmed, as T. Renner has pointed out to me, by the fact that Lepida's holdings are described as *praedia Barbatiana* (note 24, below): the name must derive from the cognomen of Lepida's first husband, M. Valerius Messalla Barbatus (*PIR* V, 88).

18. A. Maiuri, *La Villa dei Misteri* (Rome 1931), pp. 28–29; 33: the identification of the owner rests upon the presence of the name L. Istacidius Zosimus on a *sigillum* found in a room (no. 55) "nel rustico ambiente." On the local origin of the *gens Istacidia* see G. O. Onorato, *Iscrizioni Pompeiane* (Florence 1957), p. 120, no. 20; P. Castrén (above, note 5), p. 178: nineteen examples of the name are recorded at Pompeii, all of which bear one of two praenomina, Lucius or Numerius.

1. Museo Torlonia harbor relief, Ostia.

2. Tomb of Flavius Zeuxis, Hierapolis, Phrygia.

3. Sarcophagus of Annius Octavius Valerianus.

4. Model, reconstruction of temple of Fortuna Primigenia, Praeneste.

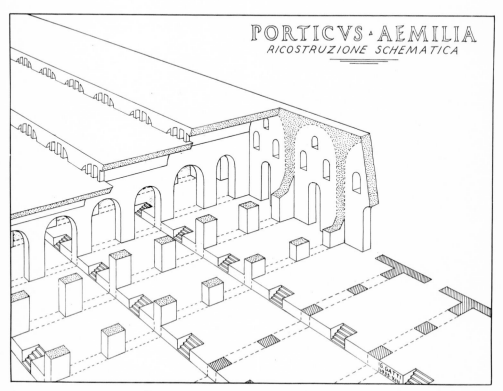

PORTICVS · AEMILIA
RICOSTRUZIONE SCHEMATICA

5. Reconstruction of Porticus Aemilia, Rome.

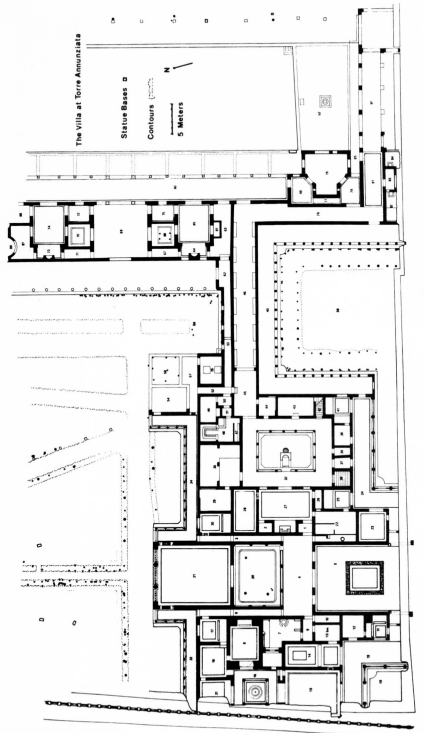

The Villa at Torre Annunziata

Statue Bases ☐

Contours (⸱⸱⸱⸱)

5 Meters

N

6. Plan of Villa Oplontis, Torre Annunziata.

7. General view of the Planier wreck.

8. Sestius trademarks from Cosa and the Portus Cosanus. All stamps occur on rims of amphorae of Type 4A (Dressel 1A). Accompanying devices are, respectively, (a) anchor, (b) trident, (c) five-pointed star, (d) eight-pointed star, (e) sigma (or TIUS in ligature?), (f) caduceus, (g) palm branch, (h) double axe, (i) lighted altar(?).

9. Amphorae from Cosa, antiquarium of the American Academy in Rome, Ansedonia.

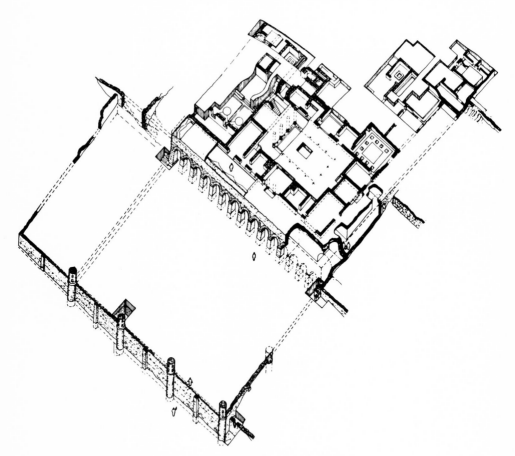

10. Plan of Villa Settefinestre, Ansedonia.

11. Remains of *villa maritima*, Capo di Sorrento.

12. Fish-breeding tanks, villa at Sperlonga.

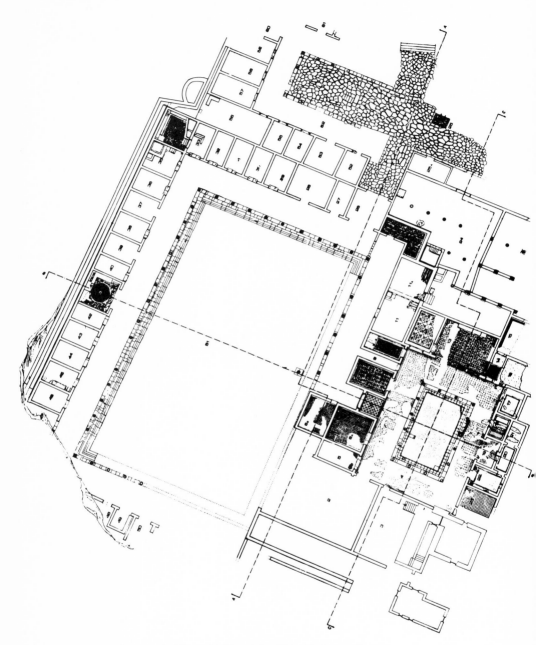

13. Plan of Villa of the Volusii, Lucus Feroniae.

14. Air view of Villa of the Volusii, Lucus Feroniae.

15. Mosaic inscription *salve lucru*[*m*], casa di Sirico, Pompeii.

16. Air view of Ostia.

17. Air view of Pozzuoli.

18. Model, reconstruction of Hadrian's Villa, Tivoli.

0   100   200   500 m.

19. Plan of ancient Puteoli.

20. Epitaph of M. Claudius Trypho, Puteoli.

21. Tomb of Ti. Claudius Eutychus, Ostia (Isola Sacra, tomb 78).

22. Terracotta plaque, tomb of Eutychus, Ostia (Isola Sacra, tomb 78).

23. Building of the Seviri Augustales, Ostia.

24. Portrait of T. Flavius Damianus of Ephesus, Archaeological Museum, Izmir.

25. Epitaph of the L. Faenii, Museo Nazionale delle Terme, Rome.

cess of three thousand.[19] In contrast, the number of cases in which an owner's name can be attached with assurance to a given site is infinitesimally small. Thus, in comparative terms, we are unusually well informed about the owners of estates in the Bay of Naples, where the villa society was historically atypical also in other respects; indeed, relative to other areas, it is the abundance rather than the limitations of our information which makes the dominant impression. Nevertheless, the clear recognition of the fact that our evidence for ownership, even here, is compartmentalized and restricted can be instructive: above all, it ought to guard us against assuming that the famous Roman villa owners known to us from Roman upper-class writers can be actually associated with extant archaeological remains, however opulent and extensive. *Narcissus Aug[usti] libertus* is named in tiles found in the villa S. Marco at Stabiae, and from a passage in Cassius Dio it is a fair presumption that the notorious freedman, *ab epistulis* to the emperor Claudius, had property on the Bay of Naples.[20] It is a plausible hypothesis that the two Narcissi are in fact the same man, but the idea that the tiles prove Narcissus to have been the owner of the villa, which we find proposed in a book on Roman houses, villas, and palaces published as recently as 1975,[21] is far less plausible; they reveal no more than that the brickyards of this imperial freedman supplied tiles for the villa. The careful study, recent begun, of Campanian tiles, brickstamps, amphorae, *fistulae*, *sigilla*, and *vascula*,[22] will bring greater

19. Britain: A. L. F. Rivet, *The Roman Villa in Britain* (London 1969), p. 209; the index of the periodical *Gallia*, for the period 1943–1962, lists more than one hundred villas which were either discovered or studied anew during this period alone; Belgium: R. de Maeyer, *De overblijfselen der romeinsche villas in Belgie* (1940); the Rhineland: see, e.g., E. M. Wightman, *Roman Trier and the Treveri* (London 1970), pp. 139–150 ("the villas"), with pp. 158–159, distribution map of the villas; cf. C. M. Ternes, "Les villas romaines du Grand Duché de Luxembourg," *Helinium* 7 (1967), pp. 121–143; Pannonia: E. B. Thomas, *Römische Villen in Pannonien* (Budapest 1964); O. Paret, *Die Römer in Württemberg*, vol. 3 (1932), p. 27, estimates that there were approximately eight hundred villa sites at that date in Württemberg. See further J. Percival, *The Roman Villa: An Historical Introduction* (London 1976), pp. 16ff; *Enciclopedia dell'arte antica*, suppl. (1970), s.v. "Villa," pp. 911ff.

20. Villa San Marco: L. D'Orsi, *Gli scavi archeologici di Stabia*[2] (Milan 1965); Cass. Dio 61.34.4, on which see *RBN*, p. 141.

21. A. G. McKay, *Houses, Villas and Palaces in the Roman World* (Ithaca, N. Y., 1975), p. 118. The man's ownership of property is more likely when his name appears on a lead pipe, as it does in Rome: *ILS* 1666 = *CIL* XV, 7500.

22. See A. Carandini et al., *Instrumentum domesticum di Ercolano e Pompei* (Rome 1977); cf. P. Castrén (above, note 5), p. 22n6.

clarity and precision to the entire problem of the applicability of such
material to the study of the ownership of property in the Bay of Naples.

II

The Roman senators C. Sempronius Rufus and L. Lucceius were owners of villas near Puteoli in the late Republic. But mention of the villa
of the former is incidental to the account of his trafficking in the
emporium of the city where, as we have seen, Rufus was very probably
engaged in commercial shipping; and the Puteolan property of L. Lucceius is but one segment of a more intricate family mosaic, which
includes commercial *negotia* in Cilicia, a freedman on Delos, buildings
and depositories near the Tiber in Rome, and banking in Rhegium.[23]
The *praedia* of Domitia Lepida, as we now know from the financial
transactions recorded in the new Pompeian documents, included *horrea* near Puteoli as well as fish ponds at Baiae;[24] Poppaea Sabina
owned *figlinae* near Pompeii;[25] the tiles of Narcissus are not confined
to the villa at Stabiae, for ten examples of the same stamp were reported
long ago at Herculaneum.[26] The Campanian brickyards of the empress
Livia must have been highly productive, with wide distribution, in the
early years of the reign of Tiberius, for tiles from her *officinae* have
turned up at Puteoli, Neapolis, Stabiae, Capreae, Pontiae, and, most
recently, at Cumae.[27]
The great value of such evidence is this, that it reveals that Roman
dignitaries, and members of the Imperial family as well, had varied
lucrative interests around the Bay of Naples—an impression which
emerges only very rarely and then indirectly from our literary author-

23. C. Sempronius Rufus: above, Chapter 3, section I; L. Lucceius: above, Chapter
3, section III.
24. F. Sbordone, *RAAN* n.s. 51 (1976), pp. 146, 167: *horreum vi[ce]simum sex-
[tu]m quod est in praedis Domitiae L[ep]idae Barbatianis superioribus.*
25. V. Arangio-Ruiz and G. Pugliese Carratelli (above, note 10), pp. 56–57: *figlinae
Arrianae Poppaeae Augustae*; it may also be presumed that the freedman of Poppaea
whose name appears upon a lead pipe in the territory of Puteoli (*CIL* X, 1906) was the
operator of an *officina* belonging to the empress.
26. *CIL* X, 8042, 82.
27. Puteoli: *NdSc.* 1902, 630; Neapolis, Stabiae, Capreae: *CIL* X, 8042, 60; *RAAN*
19 (1938), pp. 83ff; Pontiae: *NdSc.* 1926, p. 222: for the date, see J. B. Ward-Perkins,
PBSR n.s. 14 (1959), p. 154n4; Cumae: M. E. Bertoldi, *Bollettino d'Arte* 58 (1973),
p. 40. Cf. also *PIR*[2] L, 301, p. 78; *RBN*, p. 84.

ities, who tended rather to view the area as a setting for conspicuous consumption, and the *villae maritimae* themselves as symbols of luxury, comfort, and civilized leisure—*otium*. It might be added, parenthetically, that a number of the early archaeological reports of such villas reinforce the point of view of Roman writers, in their concentration on the luxurious residential quarters as illustrative of the activities of the "owner," and in their comparative neglect of service quarters and the other more practical and efficient aspects of the sites.[28]

Now, it is certainly true that our ancient authorities tended to regard the luxury villas as belonging to a special class; it is enough to recall the terminology they used to describe them: *voluptas* (rather than *fructus*), *luxuria*, *voluptariae possessiones*, *amoenitas*, *otium* are recurring words and phrases.[29] But actual situations could be more complicated: to one man in the market for a villa in a seaside city, productivity, not scenery, was the principal concern—and this despite his own insistence that he was there *otiandi, non negotiandi causa*.[30] In fact, like other attempts to classify and categorize, these too are partially a matter of convenience and at least to some extent arbitrary, and an historian's excessive reliance on such terminology may divert him from the important question: how far was this villa society economically parasitic and how far symbiotic, linked in more than a superficial way to the urban centers, to the waters, and to the countryside near which these villas were situated? Or, put another way, what was the relationship between the *villae maritimae* (figure 11) and the economy of the region?[31]

28. Even though certain of A. Maiuri's publications set a new standard of quality in description of "service," as against "residential" quarters (cf. *La Villa dei Misteri*[2] [Rome 1947], passim; *La Casa del Menandro e il suo tesoro di argenteria* [Rome 1933], pp. 191ff), it is only recently that such phrases as "ambiente rustico" and "stanze del quartiere servile" have begun to receive detailed analysis: see K. D. White, *Roman Farming* (Ithaca, N. Y. 1970), chap. 13, (pp 415–441), "Farm Buildings and Their Relationship to Various Types of Organization."

29. See, e.g., Varro, *De Re Rust.* 1.13.6–7; Vell. Pat. 2.33.4; Cic. *Ad Att.* 12.25.1; and, in general, *RBN*, pp. 40–42.

30. Cic. *De Off.* 3.58–59.

31. Finley, *Economy*, p. 201n46, observes that "the word 'villa' has lost all specificity as used by archaeologists and historians." But so far as I know, neither Finley nor other scholars have directed attention to the question of the degree to which estates predominantly or outwardly luxurious might have had productive features. A careful analysis of the evidence might prove useful, and help to clarify what at the present

To begin with, the trading and manufacturing centers of Puteoli and Capua offered attractive financial possibilities. Cicero read, wrote, and feasted on shell fish during periods of leisure at his Cumanum, and Hortensius, *piscinarius*, raised fish for pleasure in his ponds at Bauli, but the former was on close terms with a number of rich Puteolani, and both of these consulars owned income-producing property at Puteoli.[32] L. Plotius Plancus, in his retreat at Salernum in 43, was betrayed by the strong odor of perfume emanating from his person. We should like to know what his connections may have been with the Plotius *unguentarius* whom Cicero mentions at Puteoli in the previous year, or the freedman L. Plotius L. l. Philippus, who had interests in the East but came from Capua, a major center for the production of cosmetics.[33] L. Manlius Torquatus had a villa near Cicero's Cumanum, and philosophical interests—but might well have had interests, also, in *horrea* at Puteoli, where the ships of C. Rabirius Postumus, a senator's nephew, put in from Egypt, laden with a cargo of papyrus, linen,

---

appear to be ambiguous reports. The villa of Orbetello near the port of Cosa was described long ago and constitutes a case in point: it has been said to contain large storage areas for grain, with walls as much as seven feet in thickness, yet the author of the report concludes that "tutto denota un gran lusso ed un grande sfarzo, e la preoccupazione di predisporre ogni conforto" (*NdSc.* 1927, pp. 208–209). In all likelihood, the combination of productive and luxurious features was frequent, and assumed diverse forms (despite Shatzman, *SWRP*, pp. 24–25, where the economic typology is oversimplified). Interesting suggestions have been advanced by C. Gatti (below, note 59), by G. Mansuelli, *Enciclopedia Dell'arte antica*, vol. 7 (1966), p. 1168, s.v. "Villa," and by J. E. Skydsgaard, *JRS* 61 (1971) p. 277; and see now J. Percival, *The Roman Villa* (above, note 19), pp. 17–18 *et alibi*. A recent book on the English Country House would also have profited from closer attention to the lucrative aspects of aristocratic estates, and to the lucrative interests of their aristocratic owners: see J. H. Plumb, *New York Review of Books* (Oct. 26, 1978), p. 7, reviewing Mark Girouard, *Life in the English Country House: A Social and Architectural History* (New Haven 1978).

32. Cicero and shellfish: *Ad Att.* 4.10.1; Hortensius and the ponds at Bauli: Varro, *De Re Rust.* 3.17.5; Pliny *NH* 9.172; Cicero's Puteolan friends: *RBN*, pp. 52–55 and n82 (p. 54); property at Puteoli: *Ad Att.* 7.3.9 (Hortensius); *Ad Att.* 13.48.1, 46.3, 37.4, 45.2. (Cicero); see further J. H. D'Arms *AJP* 88 (1967), pp. 195–198; *RBN*, pp. 53, 182.

33. *Unguenti odor*: Pliny *NH* 13.25, Val. Max. 6.8.5; Plotius *unguentarius*: Cic. *Ad Att.* 13.46.3; L. Plotius Philippus: *CIL* X, 4291; he appears also on Delos as a *competalistes*: see Hatzfeld, *BCH* 36 (1912), p. 68. See further, on Capua as a center of cosmetics, M. W. Frederiksen, "Republican Capua: A Social and Economic Study", *PBSR* n.s. 14 (1959), pp. 110–111; and below, Chapter 7, section II.

and glass. In 67 B.C., ships of a patrician Cornelius Lentulus were at Piraeus, bound for Italy: they would probably have put in at Puteoli, where P. Cornelius Lentulus Spinther had estates.[34]

Even if an owner of a luxury villa was not actually exploiting the economic possibilities of the nearby urban centers and increasing his wealth, he would still need the towns and cities, and the larger the size of his domestic staff, the longer his periods of residence, and the grander, more tastefully decorated, and less productive his *villa maritima*, the greater would have been his urban needs. One wishes that Cicero in his Cumanum, or the Younger Pliny, whose account of his Laurentine villa is so full of other information, had told us the exact size of the *familia* normally in residence;[35] or that the latter writer had informed us where and from whom Silius Italicus, in Neapolis, had bought the numerous statues which decorated his villas in the area.[36] But Pliny does explicitly say that Ostia was close by to minister to his needs,[37] as Puteoli was to supply those of L. Marcius Philippus, when he gave his famous dinner to Caesar and two thousand other guests;[38] and distribution centers for statuary, marble columns and fittings, are known at Baiae and Puteoli, while *marmorarii* are mentioned in the inscriptions, and Campanian architects had a high reputation.[39]

34. L. Manlius Torquatus: Cic. *De Fin.* 2.84; on which see Dubois, *PA*, p. 112n1, and see above, Chapter 3, note 69. C. Rabirius and C. Rabirius Postumus: Cic. *Rab. Post.* 40, 45; for the Campanian connections of C. Rabirius, see Cic. *Rab. Perd.* 8; for the extent of their financial and commercial interests, see Rougé, *OCM*, pp. 278–279; Wiseman, *NMRS*, pp. 197, 199. P. Cornelius Lentulus Spinther: above, Chapter 3, section III and note 78; his Puteolan holdings: *RBN*, p. 177 (no. 10).

35. Pliny *Ep.* 2.17.9: *Reliqua pars lateris huius servorum libertorumque usibus detinetur plerisque tam mundis, ut accipere hospites possint*; cf. 2.17.24: *praecipue Saturnalibus . . . cum reliqua pars tecti licentia dierum festisque clamoribus personat.* But from these general remarks, the only references in the letter to the domestic staff, no safe inferences as to numbers can be drawn.

36. Pliny *Ep.* 3.7.8: *Plures isdem in locis villas possidebat, adamatisque novis priores neglegebat.*

37. Pliny *Ep.* 2.17.26: *Suggerunt adfatim ligna proximae silvae; ceteras copias Ostiensis colonia ministrat.*

38. Cic. *Ad Att.* 13.52.1; on the wealth of Philippus and his reputation for luxurious living, see *RBN*, pp. 189–190 (no. 28).

39. Capitals and columns of Attic workmanship have been discovered at Puteoli: Dubois, *PA*, pp. 130–131; casts for statues at Baiae: Walter-Herwig Schuchhardt, "Antike Abgüsse antiker Statuen," *Archäologischer Anzeiger* (1974), pp. 631–635; *marmorarii*: *CIL* X, 1648, 1873, 1549 (*redemptor marmorarius*); cf. *NdSc*. 1888, p. 640. Architects: Decimus Cossutius, employed by Antiochus Epiphanes in the

At his villa near Ostia, moreover, Pliny noted with pleasure how many of his requirements could be satisifed on his own property.[40] Recent emphasis upon the Roman upper-class fondness for self-sufficiency on their estates[41] prompts two questions: Could not even the luxurious *villae maritimae* have complements of productive lands or be situated near well-stocked waters? If so, might not a proprietor's desire to be "self-sufficient" lead quite naturally to a desire to realize profit through the sale of surplus?

Archaeological reports are generally more informative, naturally, about residential blocks and artifacts than about outlying buildings and surrounding lands, and it was no doubt generally true that the seaside villas in the Phlegraean Fields, as Varro remarked about their accompanying fishponds, tended to empty, rather than fill, their owner's pocketbooks.[42] Still, installation even of those costly fishponds (figure 12), as has been observed in a recent study of *peschiere*,[43] might transform a modest *fundus maritimus* into luxury property, and so greatly increase its value as real estate: C. Sergius Orata, who engaged in ostreaculture at the Lucrine Lake *nec gulae causa sed avaritiae*,[44] ac-

building of the Olympieion in Athens, is the first known architect associated with Roman rule, and his name is distinctly Campanian: see J. M. C. Toynbee, *Some Notes on Artists in the Roman World*, Collection Latomus, vol. 6 (Brussels 1951), p. 9; later, there is L. Cocceius Auctus, architect of the Augustan temple at Puteoli: *CIL* X, 1614 with Mommsen's note *ad loc.*, and cf. H. W. Benario, *Classical Bulletin* 35 (1959), pp. 40–41. The patron of Cocceius, C. Postumius C. f. Pollio, left his signature on the Augustan temple at Terracina (*CIL* X, 6339). Pompeii: M. Artorius M. l. Primus probably restored, in the Augustan period, the large theater: *CIL* X, 841 (= *ILS* 5638a), cf. 807, and G. O. Onorato (above, note 18), p. 124 (no. 27); the name is indigenous to Campania: M. W. Frederiksen (above, note 33), p. 116. Herculaneum: P. Numisius P. f. Men[enia tribu] *architectus* built the theater, which also dates from the Augustan period: *CIL* X, 1443, 1446; the family is found early at Capua, later at Puteoli: Frederiksen (above, note 33), p. 118.

40. Plin. *Ep.* 2.17.25–27, and especially 28: *Villa vero nostra etiam mediterraneas copias praestat, lac in primis; nam illuc e pascuis pecora conveniunt, si quando aquam umbramve sectantur.*

41. See Finley, *Economy*, pp. 36, 50, 109–110, and elsewhere, on self-sufficiency.

42. Varr. *De Re rust.* 3.17.2: *Potius marsuppium domini exinaniunt quam implent*; *RBN*, p. 41.

43. G. Daniela Conta, "Peschiere marittime nel mondo romano," in G. Schmiedt (and collaborators), *Il livello antico del mar tirreno* (Florence 1972), p. 217.

44. That a *fundus maritimus* could be essentially productive is clear from Cic. II *Verr.* 5, 46. Sergius Orata: above, Chapter 3, section I; Val. Max. 9.1.1; Pliny *NH* 9.168; cf. *RBN*, pp. 18–20. On property speculation in general cf. Wiseman, *NMRS*, p. 81, and see now E. Rawson, "The Ciceronian Aristocracy and Its Properties," in Finley, *Property*, pp. 99–102; and see below, note 60.

quires sharper relief when viewed in this speculative context. And, whereas pisciculture might often have purely snob appeal, one Roman knight was lured into buying a *villa maritima* near Syracuse only when persuaded that the waters near the property attracted vast quantities of fishermen and countless fish of the highest quality.[45] A cultured Roman took a genuine interest in agricultural production,[46] and there are hints in the literature that proprietors around the Bay of Naples were not, in this respect, exceptions: there were *vilici* and *procuratores* on one of Cicero's seaside estates, *iugera* at another;[47] Pollius Felix had vineyards and arable fields at his villa on the Sorrentine peninsula,[48] and one *villa Baiana* described by Martial is explicitly contrasted, in terms of productivity and the efficiency of *vilicus*, *vilica*, and *vernae*, with an estate near Rome where the staff was fed entirely by produce brought from the capital.[49]

Again, even if coastal villas were themselves essentially nonproductive, the hinterland of *Campania felix* offered excellent agricultural possibilities. As was rightly emphasized some years ago, the economic relationship between *fundi* in the *ager Campanus* and expensive villas at Cumae and Puteoli, was elucidated by Cicero as early as 63 B.C.: revenue derived from agricultural production offset the expenses of maintaining luxury property on the Campanian coast.[50] L. Papirius Paetus may be an example of what Cicero had in mind; an Epicurean, he lived comfortably and quietly at Neapolis—which did not prevent him, however, from showing great concern over possible confiscation of his nearby productive lands in 46 B.C.[51] Finally, could not commercial and agricultural wealth be, in practical terms, so interdependent that they were often difficult to distinguish? We may not yet be willing to infer too much from the activities of Trimalchio, a fictional

45. Cic. *De Off.* 3.58–59; cf. A. J. N. Wilson, *Emigration from Italy in the Republican Age of Rome* (Manchester 1966) p. 59.

46. J. E. Skydsgaard, *JRS* 61 (1971), p. 277.

47. Cic. *Ad Att.* 14.15.4; *ad Att.* 14.16.1; cf. *RBN*, p. 50n61, with refs. *ad loc.* (*vilici, procuratores*). Mart. 11.48.1–2 (*iugera Ciceronis*).

48. Stat. *Silv.* 2.2.98–99.

49. Mart. 3.58 (villa of Faustinus).

50. Cic. *De Leg. Agr.* 2.78: *Neque istorum pecuniis quicquam aliud deesse video nisi eius modi fundos quorum subsidio familiarum magnitudines et Cumanorum ac Puteolanorum praediorum sumptus sustentare possint*, on which see Frederiksen (above, note 33), p. 121.

51. Cic. *Ad Fam.* 9.16.7; 17.1, 20.1; cf. *RBN*, pp. 191–192 (no. 30).

figure; nevertheless, he owned ships whose cargoes consisted of wine, beans, and lard, which very probably came from his own estates near the Campanian coast.[52]

We should not underestimate the uncertainties and difficulties which hinder us from placing this fragmentary evidence from the Bay of Naples in clear and precise economic perspective. Whereas the owners of some luxurious *villae maritimae* exploited the possibilities which were locally or regionally at hand, in the cities and the hinterland, for acquiring wealth, others' sources of revenue lay further away: P. Vedius Pollio indulged his expensive habits at the villa Pausilypon, but his productive estates lay elsewhere in Campania, and his amphorae reached Apulia, Africa, and Cisalpine Gaul.[53] We may be impressed by the self-sufficiency of Faustinus' villa at Baiae, where the slaves did the fishing, yet Seneca was confident that at the villa of Servilius Vatia at Cumae, the owner ate the fish from his own well-stocked ponds only when storms made it impossible for the local fishermen to supply him.[54] We should probably concede that when in the *Digest* one group of *urbana praedia* are defined as "estates which serve only the ends of pleasure"[55] the word "pleasure" should be allowed a certain latitude of meaning, so as to include the Roman upper-class attitude which favored self-sufficiency, and profit from surplus, even on luxury estates. Yet there remain the other passages, in which insane and extravagant spending on the construction of luxurious seaside properties is explicitly contrasted with concern for *fructus*, and prodigality is contrasted with the *avaritia* which leads to acquisition of productive estates.[56] It remains to be shown whether any of the coastal villas on the Bay of Naples resembled the isolated maritime estate identified some years ago at Stes Marie de la Mer at the southern edge of the Camargue at the mouth of the Rhone, which probably served as a major center for

52. Petr. *Sat.* 76.6; the "typicality" of Trimalchio is discussed below in Chapter 5. *Seplasium*, also a part of Trimalchio's cargo, is an appropriate Campanian product: see above, note 33. Interdependence of commercial and agricultural wealth: Wiseman, *NMRS*, pp. 78ff; see further below, Chapter 7, section I, with note 42.

53. Pollio and Pausilypon: Cass. Dio 54.23.5; *RBN* pp. 229–230 (no. 44); estates at Beneventum: *CIL* IX, 1556 = *ILS* 109; amphorae at Carthage: *AE* 1971, no. 487; amphorae in Cisalpine Gaul: *AE* 1972, no. 188.

54. Faustinus: Mart. 3.58.27; Servilius Vatia: Sen. *Ep. Mor.* 55.6.

55. *Digest* 50.16.198: *praetoria voluptati tantum deservientia.*

56. E.g., Varro *De Re Rust.* 1.13.6–7; Sen. *Ep. Mor.* 89.20–21; see in general *RBN*, pp. 40–42 (late Republic), pp. 117–119 (Empire).

the salting and marketing of fish; or whether any local proprietor re-modelled his private docking facilities, in a manner comparable to that of one enterprising Ephesian, so as to accommodate commercial maritime traffic.[57]

Functionally, the proper analogues with the majority of the coastal Campanian villas are probably to be sought elsewhere—at Giannutri, Sirmio on Lake Garda, Leptis Magna and Hadrumetum in Africa, the villa near Wittlich on the Lieser in Treveran land, the early phases of the villa of Val Catena on the island of Brione Grande on the Adriatic.[58] They differ from their architectural counterparts of Zliten in Libya, Uthina, and Thabraca in Tunisia, all of which seem to have been the luxurious appendages of highly productive estates in the hinterland.[59] Nevertheless, to accept the bulk of literary tradition essentially at face value, and to place all of the villas on the Bay of Naples in a special category, to regard them entirely and solely as the consumers, and never as the producers, of income, is to adopt rather a one-dimensional approach. In fact, more emphasis upon the economic function of the villa in the Phlegraean Fields is entirely justified and appropriate. A new study of the Ciceronian aristocracy stresses their feverish buying

57. Stes Marie de la Mer: *Gallia* 22 (1964), pp. 588–590; and one may compare the (unpublished) establishment, containing deep vats for the salting of fish and possibly the production of *garum*, which was excavated some years ago at Neapolis (Nabeul), on the coast of Cap Bon, Tunisia. For similar evidence from Spain and Portugal, see T. R. S. Broughton, "Trade and Traders in Roman Spain," in J. A. S. Evans, ed., *Polis and Imperium, Studies in Honour of E. T. Salmon* (Toronto 1974), pp. 16ff, and cf. in general M. Ponsich and M. Tarradell, *Garum et industries antiques de salaison dans la Mediterranée occidentale* (Paris 1965) (= Bibl. hautes études hisp. 36). Damian of Ephesus: see below, Chapter 7, section 2.

58. Giannutri: *NdSc.* 1935, pp. 134ff; Sirmione: A. Boëthius and J. B. Ward-Perkins, *Etruscan and Roman Architecture* (London 1970), pp. 330–332; Leptis Magna: E. Salza Prina Ricotti, "Le ville marittime di Silin," *Enciclopedia dell' arte antica*, suppl. (1970), s.v. "villa," pp. 913–915 (with plans); G. Guidi, "La villa del Nilo," *Africa Italiana* 5 (1933), pp. 1ff; cf. S. Aurigemma, *Africa Italiana* 2 (1929), pp. 246–261; Hadrumetum: P. Romanelli, *Africa Italiana* 3 (1930), p. 56; P. Gauckler, *Inventaire des mosaiques de la Gaule et de l'Afrique* 2 (Paris 1910), no. 126 (villa of Sorothus); villa near Wittlich: E. M. Wightman (above, note 19), pp. 152–153; villa of Val Catena: Ward-Perkins, *Etruscan and Roman Architecture*, pp. 322–323, with references in n15, p. 570.

59. Zliten: S. Aurigemma, *I mosaici di Zliten* (Rome-Milan 1926), pp. 85ff, 265–266 and passim; Uthina ("villa of the Laberii"): P. Gauckler, "Le domaine des Laberii a Uthina," *Monuments et memoires Piot* 3 (1896), pp. 177–229; Thabraca (Tabarka): P. Gauckler (above, note 58), no. 940; P. Romanelli (above, note 58), p. 54. On all this see C. Gatti, "Le ville maritime italiche e africane," *Rend. Ist. Lombardo* (Cl. lett., sci. mor., stor.) 91 (1957), pp. 285–305.

and selling of properties of all kinds, as a form of investment; this practice has now been suggestively analyzed in a Campanian context. Varro, realistic appraiser of Roman attitudes, would certainly approve such efforts: after distinguishing between estates for profits and estates for delectation, he makes it clear that both types of property were highly saleable assets.[60] Profits were never a negligible consideration in Roman eyes.

III

On the slopes of Tusculum, a mere fifteen miles from Rome, the senatorial elite constructed luxury villas and gathered for brief periods of respite (*otium*) in the late Republic: one could scarcely walk the streets without encountering a Roman consul.[61] Cicero in 51 called Cumae a "Rome in miniature," such were the numbers of people then about.[62] Between these senatorial proprietors, even between persons of comparable *dignitas*, there were notable differences both then and in the early Empire. We are inclined to doubt, for example, whether at Cumae in 51 C. Sempronius Rufus had much to do with the eminent Hortensius, and inclined to wonder whether, somewhat later, at Baiae consular *novi homines* like Valerius Asiaticus, from Narbonensis, mingled on the same terms with persons like Hordeonius Flaccus, whose distinctive nomenclature (and other evidence) suggests that he and the sources of his wealth were native to the region.[63] But even at Tusculum the social scene was a complicated, even rather motley conglomerate: the great Lucullus had an *eques* as a neighbor in the lavish villa im-

60. Property deals: E. Rawson, "The Ciceronian Aristocracy and Its Properties", in Finley, *Property*, pp. 85ff; on which see M. W. Frederiksen, "Changes in Agrarian Structures in the Late Republic: Campania," to be published by the Istituto Gramsci in Rome. See now, for the thesis that property could exert strong emotional attachments for owners, S. Treggiari, "Sentiment and Property: Some Roman Attitudes," in A. Parel and T. Flanagan, eds., *Theories of Property* (Calgary 1979), pp. 53–85: a useful corrective to some of the arguments of Rawson, but she fails to persuade me to modify the view of Campanian developments presented here. Varro's remarks: *De Re Rust.* 1.4.2.

61. Cic. *De Leg.* 3.30, on which see Wiseman, *NMRS*, pp. 32, 48.

62. Cic. *Ad Att.* 5.2.2: *Habuimus in Cumano quasi pusillam Romam: tanta erat in iis locis multitudo.*

63. Valerius Asiaticus: Tac. *Ann.* 11.1.3, on which see *RBN*, p. 229 (no. 43); Hordeonius Flaccus: J. H. D'Arms, *Historia* 23 (1974), pp. 497–504.

mediately above his property, and a *libertinus* in that immediately below.[64]

And the signs, some already noticed, in documentary and inscriptional sources suggest a similar pattern for the Bay of Naples and raise the question: how many of the owners of these properties were representatives of the municipal or regional gentry, less illustrious but more integrally related to the social forces of the Campanian area itself? The cases of C. Sergius Orata, C. Vestorius, and Pollius Felix, known from literature, ought to prepare us for the possibility that ownership of luxury villas could be primarily a matter of financial resources, only secondarily a matter of political distinction and social prestige—and Orata, Vestorius and Pollius, and also the sources of their wealth, came from the region of Puteoli.[65]

To be sure, modern comprehensive collections and studies of the municipal notables in the urban centers of the Campanian region—Capua, Puteoli, Neapolis, Pompeii—important for their own sake and indispensable preliminaries as well for deeper social analyses, are relatively recent phenomena,[66] and the idiosyncrasies of such material need to be recognized before useful inferences can be drawn. For example, a recently published list of the seventy known municipal notables from Puteoli, when its contents are set next to the names of the ninety-two Roman dignitaries who owned villas in the Campi Flegrei, exposes very few examples of close onomastic congruity.[67] At first sight the failure of the same names to appear on the different lists

64. Cic. *De Leg.* 3.30.

65. Orata: see above, note 44; Vestorius: see above, Chapter 3, section I; Pollius Felix: Stat. *Silv.* 2.2.133, on which see *JRS* 64 (1974), p. 111.

66. Capua: Frederiksen (above, note 33), pp. 80–130; Puteoli: J. H. D'Arms, "Puteoli in the Second Century of the Roman Empire: A Social and Economic Study," *JRS* 64 (1974), pp. 104–124; for Neapolis there is no full-scale study, but see the two papers by E. Lepore, in *PdP* 7 (1952), pp. 300–332, and in *Storia di Napoli* 1 (Società editrice Storia di Napoli) (Naples 1967), pp. 289–333; Pompeii: E. Lepore, "Orientamenti per la storia sociale di Pompei," in *Pompeiana: Raccolta di studi per il secondo centenario degli scavi di Pompei* (Naples 1950), pp. 144–166; J. Andreau, "Remarques sur la société pompéienne," *DdArch.* 7 (1973), pp. 213–254; and see now the study of P. Castrén (above, note 5).

67. *JRS* 64 (1974), pp. 122–124. By "close onomastic congruity" I mean identity of both *praenomina* and *nomina gentilicia*: recurrence in different lists of *gentilicia* only, especially when the *gentilicia* themselves are common and widely distributed, is not a firm enough foundation upon which to construct Roman family relationships.

might seem to suggest that owners of luxury villas constituted, socially and economically, as well as politically, a class apart, and that the members of the local aristocracies were not the persons who owned such villas. But that inference may not be valid, for the two lists are of very different dates: that of Puteolan *domi nobiles* derives principally from inscriptions of the late second century, whereas our literary evidence for senatorial proprietors is concentrated in a much earlier period, prior to the reign of Trajan.

In fact, the new material, despite its idiosyncrasies, is already proving instructive in a number of ways. In general terms, it provides solid reinforcement for the idea that this local aristocracy was in fact regional, for branches of the same families are found to be active in a number of urban centers, and to have a variety of interests spread throughout Campania (and elsewhere): nearly all of the financial and legal transactions mentioned in the tablets of C. Sulpicius Cinnamus occurred in Puteoli, but the tablets themselves were discovered in a building in the maritime suburbs of Pompeii.[68] More specifically, the Puteolan list raises the possibility of a close linear connection between a local Julio-Claudian magistrate, descendant of a freedman, and C. Cassius, assassin of Caesar, who had property on the Bay of Naples:[69] this will not be the only case in which Roman dignitaries established luxury villas, and freedmen, in the Bay of Naples, nor the only case in which the freedmen went on to establish wealth, and their descendants ultimately rose to political prominence in the nearby towns. At Pompeii, the Istacidii were numerous and politically prominent already in the Augustan Age; this brings L. Istacidius Zosimus, of the last phase of the villa Item, into sharper social focus.[70] By the same token, in the last years of the Republic a number of wealthy inhabitants of the commercial city of Puteoli—a Cluvius, Vestorius, Blossius, Hor-

68. For the tablets, see *JRS* 64 (1974), p. 107, n. 21; for the building, see O. Elia, *RAAN* n.s. 35 (1960), pp. 29ff.

69. J. H. D'Arms, "Tacitus, *Annals* 13.48 and a New Inscription from Puteoli," in *The Ancient Historian and His Materials, Essays in Honour of C. E. Stevens* (Farnborough 1975), pp. 155–165; the text has also been published by G. Guadagno, *Rend. Accad. Naz. Lincei*, 8th ser., Class. sci. mor., stor., fil. (1975), pp. 361ff, where the passage of Tacitus is not discussed.

70. See J. Andreau, *Les affaires de monsieur Jucundus*, Collection de l'école française de Rome 19 (Rome 1974), p. 114n3; P. Castrén (above, note 5), p. 178.

deonius, Cossinius, Cossutius[71]—would certainly have qualified, in financial terms, for ownership of the luxurious *villae maritimae* then in fashion. In the time of Augustus, who brought, as we now know, a colony to Puteoli (figures 17, 19), who may have expanded the city's *territorium*, and who increased and stabilized its prosperity,[72] other local men or colonists and their descendants would qualify.[73] These might be primarily townsmen and only secondarily farmers, with freedmen and financial interests both in Puteoli and elsewhere in Campania; their sources of wealth, indeed, might be various, diversified, no more susceptible to uniform classification than the luxurious and sprawling *villae maritimae* themselves, built on hilltops or out into the Bay, on platforms or staggered terraces, with porticoes and peristyles, offering different panoramas.

We should not, of course, suppose that social and economic conditions in the region remained static, or underestimate the implications of major historical changes—civil war, acts of imperial policy, the eruption of Mt. Vesuvius—for villas and villa owners. And the rate of change could be slow or rapid. From a socio-economic perspective, the differences between Scipio Africanus Maior and Vetulenus Aegialus at Liternum are vast;[74] but, if C. Antistius Vetus, who acquired Cicero's Cumanum, actually came from a Campanian branch of the Antistii, social differences are detectable also in this case.[75] Uncertainties remain, and the tools of analysis must be further sharpened, before we shall be able to say with confidence what proportion of the owners of the luxurious Campanian *villae maritimae* were in fact the illustrious Roman dignitaries whom our upper-class authors permit us to identify, and what proportion were of different social type: municipal magistrates who might themselves be descendants of important local

71. See in general *RBN*, pp. 52–55 and n82 (p. 54); *Historia* 23 (1974), pp. 497–504 (Hordeonius); *AJA* 77 (1973), pp. 152, 161–162 (Blossius); *JRS* 64 (1974), p. 109 (Cossutius).

72. On Augustan developments at Puteoli, see in general M. W. Frederiksen, "Puteoli" in *RE* 23 (1959), 2043; *RBN* pp. 81–82. The Augustan colony: see below, Chapter 5, note 46.

73. E.g., C. Avianius Flaccus, on whom see above, Chapter 2, section I, and *HSCP* 76 (1972), pp. 207ff; for the C. Calpurnii, cf. *JRS* 64 (1974), p. 113n78.

74. Scipio: Sen. *Ep. Mor.* 86.4, with *RBN*, pp. 1–2; Vetulenus Aegialus: Sen. *Ep. Mor.* 86.14–21; Pliny *NH* 14.49.

75. Pliny *NH* 31.6, on which see *RBN*, pp. 70, 172 (no. 2).

families, or the linear descendants of ex-slaves of an emperor or a Roman senator, who could boast the regional economic interests which were noted long ago in a study of owners of villas around Pompeii.[76] Nevertheless, it is possible, even likely, that both of these broad social groups were represented among the owners, not merely the Roman dignitaries whom we know from senatorial literature. That possibility will seem less surprising if we recall that social distinctions, so numerous and so keenly noticed in Rome itself, would tend to be less sharply defined away from the capital, particularly in a region with strong cultural traditions of its own, such as the Campanian coast. In Neapolis, after all, everyone wore not the toga but the chlamys.[77]

IV

Nunc Campaniam petamus.[78] But when and for what reasons did the desire to build or to buy *villae maritimae* cease in this region? At the end of this discussion, it may be appropriate to devote a few words to the end of the Bay of Naples as a fashionable setting for these coastal villas. The problem is a difficult one: much of the archaeological material is either unreported or awaits proper publication; the hints in the literature after the Flavian period are few, scattered, and difficult to interpret; and there is little in the modern scholarship to guide us, for social and economic historians, understandably perhaps, have shown greater interest in the building rather than the abandonment of centers of *villeggiatura*.

Nevertheless, a general impression emerges from the fragmented evidence. The Bay of Naples was most fashionable as a resort center from the Ciceronian through the Flavian periods, but thereafter it failed to sustain its earlier momentum. Such architectural remains of villas as have been recognized and studied between Cumae and Posillipo often have their late Republican, Augustan, and early imperial phases, but disclose very little brickwork or masonry which can be securely dated later than the Domitianic period,[79] and although the evidence

76. R. C. Carrington, "Studies in the Campanian *Villae Rusticae*," *JRS* 21 (1931), pp. 111–115.

77. Cic. *Rab. Post.* 26.

78. Sen. *Tranq. An.* 2.13.

79. See the references to villas, only partially studied, in *RBN*, pp. 131–132n66; cf. p. 130n59, for remains on three stories at Marechiaro, Posillipo; cf. *Enciclopedia dell'arte antica* (above, note 58), p. 912 (villas at Gragnano, and S. Sebastiano al Vesuvio).

from Baiae is later, much of this territory was the emperor's personal domain, not in the hands of private citizens, and hence was an exception in any case.[80] Literary references which seem rather to suggest continuity are sometimes ambiguous. The references—deprecatory or sympathetic—to senatorial *successus* at Puteoli and Cumae in the *Historia Augusta*, Ammianus Marcellinus, and Symmachus[81] have at times an excessively traditional, rather artificial flavor, as if the great days of luxurious leisure in these parts were past, and were either being rhetorically condemned, or nostalgically reinvoked.

Furthermore, other evidence would seem to suggest that the privileged classes were now finding other places in which to build or to buy their seaside villas. Martial mentions villas at Baiae, but also the coastal estates at Formiae, Altinum in Venetia, and elsewhere.[82] The Younger Pliny employs the phrase *Baiano more* to describe both seaside and elevated villa sites,[83] but the villas in question were at Comum; his other coastal estate was the Laurentine villa, whence he could see "the roof tops of villas—sometimes clustered together, sometimes spaced at intervals."[84] The Antonine consular T. Caesernius Statius Quinctius Macedo Quinctianus had his villa not on the Bay of Naples but in Istria on the Adriatic coast, near his native Aquileia,[85] and we have already mentioned the second century (and later) estates

80. A. De Franciscis, "Underwater Discoveries around the Bay of Naples," *Archaeology* 20 (1967), pp. 212–214. But the extent and exact location of the imperial *palatium* remain *sub iudice*; cf. *RBN*, pp. 109–111.

81. SHA, *Tacitus*, 19.5 (on which see *RBN*, p. 158, and n. 201); Amm. Marc. 28.4.18; Symmachus *Ep*. 8.23.3. Symmachus as well as earlier senatorial contemporaries were locally engaged in building and repairs: *Ep*. 1.1.2 (Bauli); 6.9, 6.11.3 (Baiae); 6.66.3 (Puteoli), and especially 2.60.1–2 (Neapolis). But the six villas on the Bay of Naples represent but a small fraction of Symmachus' holdings (*RBN*, p. 228); furthermore, as a recent writer has observed, it is scarcely surprising that the pursuits of leisure figure so prominently in a period in which "the political heyday of the senate was so far in the past": J. Matthews, *Western Aristocracies and Imperial Court, A.D. 364–425* (Oxford 1975), p. 9. Note also the tendentious quality of the literary description of villas near Trier in the *Mosella* of Ausonius, which has been seen as an attempt to restore confidence among the cultured and wealthy classes who could afford to invest in land: E. M. Wightman (above, note 19), p. 165; cf. Matthews, p. 83, on Ausonius' properties.

82. Mart. 10.30, 4.25.1.

83. Plin. *Ep*. 9.7.3, on which see *RBN*, p. 120n21.

84. Plin. *Ep*. 2.17.27; R. Lanciani discovered traces of twenty-five villas in the territory: *Mon. Accad. Lincei* 16 (1903), p. 245.

85. A. Degrassi, "Aquileia e l'Istria in età romana," in *Studi aquileiesi offerti a G. Brusin* (Aquileia 1953), p. 55; see below, Chapter 7, note 35.

in Britain, Gaul, the Rhineland, and North Africa.[86] The cognomen *Baiae* was attached to one estate near Utica:[87] this may mean that Italian Baiae continued to serve as the standard against which villas elsewhere were measured; alternatively, it may suggest that other sites and locations had come to take the place of the original. This they would the more naturally do, if there is truth in the recent suggestion that under the Republic senators were in fact legally banned from owning land in the provinces; all that had of course changed under the Empire, as early as the time of Seneca.[88]

Undoubtedly, the pattern of distribution of luxurious seaside estates was more complicated, and the outline sketched here does not do it full justice. After all, even when the Bay of Naples was the preferred setting for luxury villas it was not the only fashionable center; similarly, the abandonment of the Phlegraean Fields by the rich was certainly a gradual process, and never total. So long as new building and other signs of wealth were visible in the urban centers of the region—and it has been argued elsewhere that they continue to be detected at Puteoli into the Severan period[89]—villas may be presumed to have existed; furthermore, the familiar imperial trends—third century decline and signs of economic revival under Constantine—are to some degree reflected also in the Campanian region.[90] It is possible, too, that on this coastline as elsewhere, the very paucity of late remains, paradoxically, can be in fact a proof of continuity. That is to say, the ancient site has disappeared because it was transformed in late antiq-

86. Above, notes 58–59.

87. *CIL* VIII, 25425, from Roman baths at Sidi Abdallah, near Bizerte (Tunisia). This well-known mosaic, probably of the fourth century, depicts a maritime scene and a shoreline encircled by buildings; the inscription, set into the lower right-hand corner of the mosaic is an acrostic which names a Sidonius, and begins: *Splendent tecta Bassiani fundi cognomine Baiae*. The *tecta* thus refer to the coastal property, the *fundi Bassiani* of the inscription, and hence Baiae here denotes the name of the estate (see also *Révue Archéologique* 4th ser., 7 [1906], pp. 465–466, no. 183). "Baiae" can also mean, by metonomy, "baths": cf. *TLL* 2, col. 1684, line 55ff, s.v. "Baiae"; *CIL* VIII, 25362 (= *ILS* 8960), and the new inscription in baths of Sullecthum (Salakta) in Tunisia which has been published by A. Beschaouch: *Rend. Accad. Naz. Lincei*, 8th ser., 23 (1968), pp. 59–68 (= *AE* 1968, no. 610), where, however, the author has misinterpreted the sense of "Baiae" in the inscription from Sidi Abdallah, mentioned above.

88. E. Rawson (above, note 60), pp. 90–91.

89. *JRS* 64 (1974), pp. 104–124.

90. On third century crisis and fourth century revival, see *RBN*, p. 121 with the references in n. 27; *PdP* 27 (1972), pp. 255–270.

uity into something else, something more fortified: in this regard, it would be interesting to know the full building history of the site presently occupied by the Castello di Baia.

Still, if there is some substance to this notion of a partial decline of the "Crater" as a villa center and pleasure resort after the Flavians, it is incumbent upon us to seek reasons for the change. They were no doubt various, due to the combination of factors, and no single explanation should be expected to suffice. The destruction of the Vesuvian towns, Herculaneum, Pompeii, Stabiae, in A.D. 79 dealt a heavy blow. Even though Statius could refer to *Stabiae renatae*, other evidence suggests that the eruption was fatal, and that the area never really recovered at any time in antiquity.[91] Furthermore, the increasing concentration of property—everywhere—into the hands of the emperors (Josephus bears witness to vigorous imperial competition in the construction and extension of emperors' palaces at Baiae)[92] may have tended to displace or discourage the builders of private villas. Less significant factors, we may suspect, were Tacitus' insistence that there was a general decline of luxury under the Flavians; the rise of the port of Ostia, and its increasing displacement of Puteoli, as the principal maritime artery of Rome; and important new developments, more inward-looking and self-contained, which came to characterize the layouts and architecture of villas—Hadrian's "Xanadu" at Tivoli (figure 18), or the villas of Sette Bassi and of the Quintilii outside Rome, are spectacular examples.[93] These factors do not usefully advance our analysis, for it is clear, first, that the roots of luxury were far deeper, and more durable, and its effects more widespread, than Tacitus suggested; second, that the vitality of Puteoli was not significantly undermined, at least for a long time, by the rise of Ostia; and third, that the loosely organized seaside villas continued to be built and to remain in fashion simultaneously with the newer developments in sumptuous

91. Stat. *Silv.* 3.5.104; F. De Capua, *RAAN* n.s. 19 (1938), pp. 113–114. A. De Franciscis is more optimistic concerning the revival of the Vesuvian territory in later antiquity: see his comments in *Neue Forschungen in Pompeji* (above, note 9), p. 17; and for presumed reoccupancy of a Vesuvian villa after the eruption see G. Cerulli Irelli, *NdSc.* suppl. 1965, pp. 166–173.

92. Josephus *Ant. Jud.* 18.248–249; the passage ostensibly applies to the reign of Gaius but is valid also for Domitian's period: *RBN*, p. 102.

93. Tacitus and the decline of luxury: *Ann.* 3.55.1–6, on which see *RBN*, pp. 123–124; Ostia and Puteoli: *JRS* 64 (1974), pp. 104ff; the new villa architecture: Ward-Perkins (above, note 58), pp. 328–334.

domestic architecture—it is simply that these *villae maritimae* appear elsewhere than in Campania.

No, better reasons for change are provided by other factors. Partly, we may suspect, the shores of the Bay of Naples had come to be excessively built upon. Already in the Augustan Age, Strabo could say that the luxury buildings, from Misenum to Cape Athenaeum, presented the aspect of one single city; and actual remains, as well as paintings, emphasize the Roman fondness for ample space in which to build, to create the loose and sprawling architectural effects, through *xystoi*, gardens, porticoes, terraces, peristyles, pergolas, which characterized these villas,[94] and thereby leave their owners satisifed that in their domination of the sites, man had indeed subjugated nature.[95] More open and more ample pieces of coastal territory, and hence the possibility of the gratification of desires like these, were by now available primarily in other places.

Yet, in the final analysis, neither the alterations in local or regional conditions, nor what F. Braudel has termed "the fashions and fancies of the rich"[96] are sufficient to explain the change, which should be placed, instead, in a broader context. It is remarkable that, after the Flavian period, no single center replaced the Bay of Naples as a concentration point for the luxury villas of the rich. Instead of the substitution of one fashionable resort area for another—a common enough phenomenon in our own day—we find, rather, isolated examples of such luxury properties, more loosely and widely distributed—in north Italy, in Africa, on the Rhone, the Rhine, the Danube, the Adriatic. Ought we not to connect this development with changes in upper-class imperial society as a whole? The provinces were now providing senators

94. Strabo on the Bay of Naples: Strab. 5.4.8. Architectural characteristics of the *villa maritima*, which combine to create loose, relaxed, informal effects: Ward-Perkins (above, note 58), pp. 321ff; see especially the comment on p. 323, relating Campanian painting to local villa architecture by stressing "the broader layout of these seaside, or lakeside, villas, with their long, low porticoes and deliberately informal grouping, to which it was essentially the setting of trees, rocks, and water that gave unity and meaning. This was architecture in a landscape."

95. The domination of nature is a familiar theme in the literary descriptions of these villas: cf. Stat. *Silv.* 2.2. 45–59 (on the villa of Pollius Felix), with the excellent analysis of H. Drerup, *Gymnasium* 73 (1966), pp. 190–191.

96. F. Braudel, *The Mediterranean and the Mediterranean World in the Age of Philip II*, vol. 1, English edition (New York 1972), p. 338, describing "the social takeover of the countryside by the money of the towns."

in ever increasing numbers; this new elite tended to maintain their ties with their homelands, as the widespread distribution of the villas helps to show. Trajan, and Marcus Aurelius later, found it necessary to prescribe that a certain percentage of the property of all senators be invested in Italian land: the need for compulsion suggests that men from the provinces were indeed treating Italy and the capital "not as their native land, but as a mere inn for use on their visits."[97] Furthermore, this new political elite, so socially and geographically mixed, was different from the much more homogeneous group of Italian senators of Cicero's day or even of the early Empire, who need not—and could not—travel far from Rome or their native estates to congregate on the shores of the "Crater," and constitute a *pusilla Roma*.[98] Roman society was smaller then, and persons knew each other, perhaps a necessary condition for creation of centers of fashionable ease. Then senatorial *peregrinatio* had meant visiting one's various villas, in the countryside and in the Bay of Naples. Now it had come to be applied to occasional visits to Italy from the provinces.

Finally, in contrast to the geographical horizon, that of politics had not widened but contracted. As always, after the Augustan Age, one must reckon with the emperor himself, with his maintenance, on the one hand, of established social forms, and with his power, on the other, to reshape them, to move them in different, distinctively imperial, directions. The author of a large new book on the emperor in the Roman world believes in continuity, asserting that the Republican senatorial pattern of villa life, in both Latium and Campania, persisted on the part of the emperors through the first three centuries; and indeed there are clear signs that imperial villas on Campania's coast, Baiae in particular, were not abandoned.[99] Nevertheless, this emphasis on continuity is misleading, since it is precisely with the Flavian period that the imperial holdings on the Bay of Naples begin to assume secondary importance to the emperor's preferred retreats in Alba, Alsium, Lorium, and other places. The *consilium* of Domitian met at the Alban estate of the *princeps*; that of Trajan can be seen (thanks to the Younger Pliny) at work and at leisure at the villa at Centum Cellae; and although

97. Trajan: Plin. *Ep.* 6.19.4; Marcus Aurelius: SHA *Marc.* 11.8.
98. Cic. *Ad Att.* 5.2.2, quoted above, note 62.
99. F. Millar, *The Emperor in the Roman World* (Ithaca, N.Y. 1977), pp. 16, 24ff.

Hadrian died at Baiae, much of his reign was spent in travel; when not on the move he, his advisors and members of the imperial bureaucracy congregated at the immense new villa at Tibur (figure 18).[100]

A much later age produces a striking case of a monarch's decisive role in the decline of what had once been a flourishing resort center. We may consider the analogy presented by the châteaux of the river Loire and its tributaries. There the most splendid of the *châteaux de plaisance*—Chaumont, Amboise, Blois, Chambord, Chenonceaux, Azay le Rideau—were either constructed or elaborately renovated in the fifteenth and sixteenth centuries, and still later, in the early years of his reign, a youthful Louis XIV in search of fresh air would leave Paris with a nomadic court and pass days in a number of opulent retreats, Chambord among them.[101] But the decision to create the palace at Versailles and to establish the court there were decisive factors in the decline of the Loire châteaux.[102] The parallel with the influence of the Roman emperors on villa life on the Bay of Naples, while not precise, is at least suggestive: where the *princeps* went, at least some of the senatorial aristocracy would be, or feel, constrained to follow, with inevitably damaging consequences for *villeggiatura* on the Campanian coast. Is it surprising that the villa life on the Bay of Naples did not survive in a world so fundamentally changed, a world of wider geographical, and narrower political, horizons?

100. *Albanum* of Domitian and the *consilium Principis*: Juv. 4.37ff, *CIL* IX, 5420 (= Bruns, *FIRA* VII. 5, p. 226); see further J. A. Crook, *Consilium Principis* (Cambridge 1955), pp. 48–51. Trajan and Centum Cellae: Plin. *Ep.* 6.31. The normal size of imperial *consilia* is unknown, although the numbers 11, 20, and 36 are attested: see Crook, p. 59n3. Hadrian: ibid., pp. 56–65, 108.

101. See in general, I. Dunlop, *Châteaux of the Loire* (New York 1969); for the nomadic court of Louis XIV in the years 1661–1672, see P. Goubert, *Louis XIV and Twenty Million Frenchmen*, trans. A. Carter (New York 1970) pp. 79ff.

102. Dunlop (preceding note), p. xxviii; for the king and the court at Versailles after May 1682, cf. Goubert (preceding note), pp. 173–176.

5

The "Typicality" of Trimalchio

I

In the foregoing pages the name of Trimalchio, the most famous freedman in Latin literature, has surfaced more than once, together with those of other characters in the *Satyricon*,[1] as if their behavior and pronouncements had some special claim upon the attention of the Roman social and economic historian. Which behavior, it may be asked, and what pronouncements? The responses need to be developed carefully, for two reasons. First, there exist no general accepted criteria for distinguishing humor from realism in the *Cena*. Even if most would today agree that the characters of Petronius do not float entirely removed from realistic moorings, it remains open to anyone to argue that a given passage is not material from which we can legitimately extract historical information; that, whereas the *Satyricon* as a whole is a composite product of experience and imagination, in individual sections the latter gains the upper hand.

Second and paradoxically, historians, who are especially inclined to take Trimalchio's economic behavior and social attitudes seriously, even going so far as to regard them as "typical," have given very different answers to the question "typical of what?" This disagreement derives from two fundamentally different sets of assumptions about the contours of the Roman social landscape, and about the types of economic behavior appropriate to persons situated in different parts of the terrain. These assumptions themselves are now familiar from the discussion in Chapter 1,[2] and need not be summarized; but the ways in which they have affected interpretations of Petronius' *Satyricon*, and

1. Above, Chapter 1, section II; Chapter 2, section III and note 104; Chapter 4, section I.
2. Above, Chapter 1, section II.

especially of its principal character, do require illustration. What, in fact, were the principal sources of Trimalchio's wealth, and how do his attitudes relate to them?

Rostovtzeff discovered in Trimalchio "a typical representative" of the class of rich businessmen in Italian and provincial cities, the men active in commerce and trade, who comprised his "bourgeoisie"; "characteristically, too, [Trimalchio's] main occupation was first commerce and only in a second stage agriculture and banking."[3] The emphasis upon the commercial basis of Trimalchio's wealth of course coheres neatly with Rostovtzeff's larger view of imperial social and economic developments; and it is symptomatic of that larger view that to Rostovtzeff, the fact that Trimalchio was a freedman is incidental: what matters is that he was "nouveau riche," "parvenu," with wealth derived from trade.[4] We may suspect that it is owing largely to Rostovtzeff's influence that French labels like "nouveau riche" and "parvenu" continue to stick to Trimalchio[5]—as though he might, with minimal adjustments, pass easily for Molière's bourgeois gentilhomme. And this despite the important paper of Paul Veyne, published in 1961.[6] He, like Rostovtzeff, found the Satyricon "profondement réaliste et même typique; c'est un excellent document d'histoire."[7] But to Veyne, it was not Trimalchio's commercial activity, but his desire to abandon it to become a landed proprietor, that is historically significant: and the key to Trimalchio's attitude, his "structure mentale," Veyne derives in turn from his juridical status, that of an ex-slave. What Veyne calls the freedman's "metamorphosis" from an "homme économique" into a landowner and money lender is explained as a pathetic attempt by Trimalchio to achieve respectability—pathetic for the reason that a

3. Rostovtzeff, SEHRE[2], pp. 57–58.

4. Ibid., p. 58: "I am inclined to think that Petronius chose the freedman type to have the opportunity of making the nouveau riche as vulgar as possible"; p. 551n25: "new rich families of parvenus, some of them former slaves like the Trimalchio of Petronius."

5. See, e.g., Duff, Freedmen, p. 230; W. Arrowsmith, Petronius, The Satyricon (Ann Arbor 1959), p. xi; J. Gagé, Les classes sociales dans l'empire romain (Paris 1974), p. 139; J. Schmidt, Vie et mort des esclaves dans la Rome antique (Paris 1973), p. 164.

6. P. Veyne, "Vie de Trimalcion," Annales E.S.C. 16 (1961), pp. 213–247 (hereafter cited as Veyne, "Trimalcion").

7. Veyne, "Trimalcion," p. 213.

libertus cannot improve his juridical status: the word "parvenu" is inappropriately applied to Trimalchio, for he never arrived.[8]

This thesis has now been authoritatively endorsed by Finley, for whom also "Trimalchio remains an authentic spokesman."[9] Finley's emphasis is upon the activities and social circles from which Trimalchio, as freedman, was excluded, but also upon his wealth, "his esoteric luxury and his acceptance of certain 'senatorial' values, the ownership of large estates as a 'non-occupation' and the pride in his economic self-sufficiency."[10] There is no discussion of Trimalchio's commercial activities here, nor is there in MacMullen's book on Roman social relations, where, after characterizing Trimalchio's maritime enterprises as commercial "experiments," the author continues: "This much and no more for the Rostovtzeffian idea of how to get rich. For thereafter Trimalchio entrusted his profits to loans and real estate (some urban, the vast majority agricultural)."[11] Yet for this scholar too, "Trimalchio is typical."[12]

The main evidence for Trimalchio's behavior and attitudes remains where it has always been, in the *Cena*. If social and economic historians can discover such different Trimalchiones in Petronius, and are persuaded that their respective Trimalchiones are typical, it is surely time to return once again to the text of the *Satyricon*, recognizing that it sometimes faithfully reflects, sometimes comically distorts, contemporary Roman institutions and social realities. Interpretation, that is, the attempt to discern Petronius' intent, requires that we recognize both for what they are. What are needed are critical calibrations which are as precise as we can make them, equally attentive to literary tradition, historical and geographical context, and points of language. Trimalchio's own long autobiographical review[13] must serve as the point of departure, for it is precisely this passage which has generated the widely divergent modern interpretations outlined above. If Trimalchio is to continue to be regarded, as seems likely, as "typical of his class,"

8. Veyne, "Trimalcion," pp. 244–245; cited also by Finley, *Economy*, p. 37.
9. Finley, *Economy*, p. 61.
10. Ibid., pp. 50–51; cf. p. 36: "Trimalchio may not be a wholly typical ancient figure, but he is not wholly untypical either."
11. MacMullen, *RSR*, p. 50.
12. Ibid., p. 102.
13. Petr. *Sat.* 75.8–77.7.

"an authentic spokesman," a detailed review of this and other pertinent evidence seems essential.

II

To Rostovtzeff, Trimalchio was a trader "first" and moved into agriculture and banking "only in a second stage"; Veyne characterizes the shift from shipping to land-based activity as "metamorphosis"; others too divide Trimalchio's activities into discrete temporal units.[14] Common to all of these interpretations is a tendency to infer that Trimalchio's various lucrative enterprises occurred sequentially and separately, rather than simultaneously and in combination; and that inference easily gives rise to another, namely that trade and agriculture were mutually exclusive, rather than complementary activities. Petronius' words do not in fact support such inferences. After inheriting the equivalent of a senatorial fortune (*patrimonium laticlavium*) from his former master, Trimalchio says *concupivi negotiari*.[15] He does not tell how he financed the construction of five ships, or from whose estates he acquired the wine with which he loaded them; we therefore have no right to presume that his inherited fortune was entirely in land, or that he sold all of such estates as were part of his *patrimonium* in order to build ships, or that his cargo of wine was produced on estates which belonged to others[16]— yet all of this seems generally to be presumed. When his first ships were wrecked and he lost thirty million HS at one go, Fortunata sold her jewels and Trimalchio built more ships, better and bigger.[17] But again, Trimalchio does not say that the sale of jewelry realized enough to finance the second venture: indeed, that is inherently implausible, and it is more likely that this was the point at which some of the *fundi* which belonged originally to his patron were sacrificed. On his next voyage— the cargo consisted of wine, pork, beans, perfume and slaves—he cleared ten million HS;[18] what proportion of the cargo belonged to Tri-

14. Rostovtzeff, *SEHRE*[2], pp. 57–58; Veyne, "Trimalcion," p. 237; H. W. Pleket, *Talanta* 5 (1973), p. 37; MacMullen, *RSR*, p. 50 Cf. also J. H. Oliver, "Marcus Aurelius: Aspects of Civic and Cultural Policy in the East," *Hesperia*, suppl. 13 (1970), p. 60: he too accepts the firm dichotomy between agricultural and business pursuits, arguing that Trimalchio's move from commerce to land is evidence for Petronius' having "telescoped three generations into one."

15. *Sat*. 76.2–3.
16. *Sat*. 76.3.
17. *Sat*. 76. 4–5, 7.
18. *Sat*. 76.8.

malchio, and which parts were shipped upon consignment by others, is again not specified.

In other words, Trimalchio's account to this point is entirely compatible with his simultaneous participation in both commercial and agricultural activity. At this stage he bought back (*redemi*) his patron's *fundi*, built his house, bought slaves and cattle, and continued to prosper.[19] But these investments imply only an expansion, a still greater diversification, of his gainful pursuits; that is, he must still have considered himself, and be considered, as a *negotiator*. For disengagement from active participation in trade is not mentioned until the next sentence, where the words are important: *Postquam coepi plus habere quam tota patria mea habet, manum de tabula: sustuli me de negotiatione et coepi [per] libertos faenerare.*[20] The sentence proves that Trimalchio remained simultaneously involved in lucrative ventures on both sea and land not just until he had successfully recouped his losses, or until he had amassed a fortune which far exceeded the *patrimonium laticlavium* which he had inherited, or indeed until his personal holdings had grown to approximate those of all of Asia: he continued to combine commercial and agricultural activities, working steadily to increase his wealth, until his fortune had actually begun to surpass that of his native land. The notions of strict compartmentalization of Trimalchio's interest, and of his abrupt and sudden shift from initial trading "experiments" to agricultural investments, are not supported by Trimalchio's autobiographical account.

After the repeated indications in previous chapters that Roman *negotia* could be multiple, diversified, interdependent,[21] this finding will scarcely seem surprising. Trimalchio's heterogeneity of interests is in fact explicitly confirmed by his assertion, earlier in the *Cena*: *Et in mari et in terra multa possideo.*[22] Further controls, moreover, are available: we may test the "typicality" of Trimalchio's practices by comparing them with the acquisitive activities of the two other richest characters in the *Satyricon*. Lichas of Tarentum both captained and owned the merchant vessel upon which Encolpius, Giton, and Eumolpus hastily

19. *Sat.* 76.8: *Statim redemi fundos omnes, qui patroni mei fuerant. Aedifico domum, comparo venalicia, coemo iumenta.*

20. *Sat.* 76.9.

21. See above, Chapter 2, section I; Chapter 3, section I (C. Vestorius); Chapter 3, section III (the Lucceii, Volusii Saturnini).

22. *Sat.* 39.8.

embarked, but he also possessed landed estates and a *familia nego-tians*.[23] So also the imaginary millionaire whom Eumolpus imperson-ated in order to deceive the citizens of Croton. He lost only a fraction of his wealth when twenty million HS went down in shipwreck: thirty million more were invested in Africa, *fundis nominibusque depositum*; his *familia* of slaves, distributed throughout Numidia, was large enough to sack Carthage; and he pretended to be awaiting the arrival of another of his ships from Africa, loaded with slaves and with cash.[24] All three of these are fictional fortunes, but the typology is wholly realistic. This is proved by surviving tombstones erected by traders from the port cities of Ostia and Puteoli. *Liberti*, like Trimalchio, and also like him *seviri Augustales* in their respective cities, they engaged in highly diversified economic activities: carpentering, wine, ships, and money-lending in the case of the Ostian, whereas the Puteolan (figure 20) was a *negotiator*, *vascularius*, and *argentarius*.[25]

Next, what exactly were Trimalchio's activities after he withdrew from active participation in "business" (*negotiatio*)? "Agriculture and bank-ing" is the usual response, the former consisting of "the ownership of large estates as a non-occupation," the latter of loans, these too pre-dominantly agricultural in character, not commercial.[26] In this way, scholars have tried to square Trimalchio's practices with the approved Ciceronian procedure for "gentlemanly" disposition of commercial prof-its—Cicero recommended, it will be recalled, investment in land.[27] They have also elevated the fabulous descriptions, elsewhere in the *Cena*, of the extent and self-sufficiency of Trimalchio's estates, to the same high level of reliability, as evidence, as Trimalchio's own words

23. *Sat.* 101: *Lichas Tarentinus, homo verecundissmus et non tantum huius navigii dominus, quod regit, sed fundorum etiam aliquot et familiae negotiantis, onus defer-endum ad mercatum conducit.*

24. *Sat.* 117, 141.

25. Ostia: A. Licordari, *Rend. Acc. Linc.* 29 (1974), pp. 313ff; the Puteolan in-scription, the epitaph of M. Claudius Tryphon, is unpublished. See the discussion below, Chapter 6, section II.

26. Rostovtzeff, *SEHRE²*, p. 58; Veyne, "Trimalcion," p. 237: "Ce qui est char-actéristique, c'est que Trimalcion ait abandonné le commerce pour la propriété foncière et l'usure; parce que seule la terre anoblissait"; Finley, *Economy*, p. 50; MacMullen, *RSR*, p. 50.

27. Cic. *De Off.* 1. 151 (discussed above, Chapter 1, section I and Chapter 2, section I). For modern attempts to associate Cicero's words with Trimalchio's practice, see e.g., Duff, *Freedmen*, p. 125; Veyne, "Trimalcion," p. 239; Rougé, *OCM*, pp. 12–13; H. W. Pleket, *Tijdschrift voor Geschiedenis* 84 (1971), p. 245.

in his autobiographical review. And they have, finally, arrived at an overall interpretation of Trimalchio as a freedman who, albeit in vain, adopted "senatorial" attitudes.

We must ask again: what does Trimalchio actually say? To begin with, it should be noted that the standard translation and interpretation of the text, "I began to finance freedmen," is based upon a doubtful reading. Buecheler recognized long ago that *libertos faenerare*, the reading of the MSS, seemed impossible Latin, even for Trimalchio, and he reasonably adopted *per*, an old conjecture of Heinsius:[28] Petronius probably wrote *coepi per libertos faenerare*. The implications of the emendation are important. Socially, the force of *per* is exquisitely, and appropriately, pretentious, removing Trimalchio from the hurly-burly of trafficking which Romans of the senatorial and equestrian orders held to be demeaning, and raising him instead to a new plateau, from which he could maintain an interest in profits while remaining aloof from the arenas of actual transaction.[29] On the other hand, in economic terms, lending money at interest through freedman intermediaries suggests far more ambitious and extensive enterprises than simply lending at interest to freedmen. As is well known, legal provisions obliged an ex-slave to provide a specified number of days of work and, more generally, *officia*, to their former masters, and in practice the freedman's continued services must have often exceeded the explicit requirements of the law, to the profit, primarily, of the *patronus*.[30] The *libertus* of a Tiberian con-

---

28. F. Buecheler, *Petronii Arbitri Satirarum Reliquiae* (Berlin 1862) *ad loc.*; although Buecheler abandoned the reading in subsequent editions, it was revived by L. Friedländer (*Petronii Cena Trimalchionis*, Leipzig 1891 [2nd ed., 1906]) *ad loc.*, and has been incorporated in K. Müller's editions (2nd ed., Munich 1965). A parallel for *faenerare* used transitively as in the MSS with the sense of "lend money to," and hence a shade of uncertainty as to the correctness of Buecheler's emendation, are presented by Mart. 1.76.6: *haec [sc. Minerva] sapit, haec omnes faenerat una deos.*

29. See in general above, Chapter 2, sections III–IV; and ct., for a close verbal parallel (adduced also by Friedländer), SHA *Pert.* 3.4.: *mercatus est per suos servos.*

30. See above, Chapter 2, section III, and, for further discussion see A. Arthur Schiller, "The Business Relations of Patron and Freedman in Classical Roman Law," first published 1935 and reprinted in A. A. Schiller, *An American Experience in Roman Law* (Gottingen 1971), pp. 24–31; L. Juglar, *Quomodo per Servos Libertosque Negotiarentur Romani* (Paris 1902), pp. 60–69 (especially useful for the legal sources); J. Gaudemet, *Institutions de l'antiquité* (Paris 1967), pp. 554ff, esp. 561–562 (*obsequium, operae, bona*); Treggiari, *RFLR*, pp. 68–81; for criminal penalties for freedmen who failed in "dutifulness" to patrons, see *Digest* 37.14.1 (cited by J. A. Crook, *Law and Life of Rome* [London 1967], p. 53). Duff, *Freedmen*, "Legal Relations between Patron and Freedman," pp. 36–49, has been largely superseded by later

sular boasts on his tombstone that when his patron entrusted all of his wealth to his management, he, the freedman, increased it;[31] another *libertus*, a famous goldsmith, sold his products at good profits, with the patron receiving the major share: "He did nothing," his gravestone declares, "which did not meet with his patron's approval."[32] Some of the numerous freedmen of the A. Egrilii, C. Nasennii, and A. Livii, notable Ostian families, probably protected and advanced through their commercial activities the fortunes of their former masters; and freedmen of the D. Iunii are found managing Ostian shops and turning back the main profits to the owner of the *insula* where they were located.[33]

Indeed, manumission, and the greater independence which it permitted, worked often to the distinct economic advantage of the *patronus*, as the jurist Gaius explicitly confirms.[34] Such independence could further the formation of profitable partnerships, the *societates* already discussed, which we have seen included *ingenui*, as well as *liberti* and *colliberti*, and which must have flourished in the major trading centers: they diversified ownership, distributed financial risk, and involved the use of representatives.[35] We should like to know with how many freedman intermediaries Trimalchio's liquid assets were out at loan, and something of the sizes of the sums involved. Petronius does not tell us; we have only Trimalchio's vast wealth, and his highly developed acquisitive instincts, to guide us. Taken together, they suggest that the return on Trimalchio's loans was handsome.

What is the evidence for the opinion of Veyne and others that *faenerare* ("to lend money at interest") applies only, or even predomi-

---

works. See M. Kaser, *Das römische Privatrecht*[2], vol. 1 (1971), pp. 299–301, with full bibliography, and cf. below Chapter 6, section IV.

31. *ILS* 1949. P. A. Brunt, *Latomus* 34 (1975), p. 633 implies that landed estates were the source of the wealth of Zosimus' patron M. Aurelius Cotta: there is, however, no explicit evidence.

32. *ILS* 7695, M. Canuleius Zosimus.

33. For freedmen of the Ostian Egrilii, Nasennii, and Livii, see the full discussion below, chapter 6, section III; freedmen of the D. Iunii: Meiggs, *RO*[2], p. 224 (*horti et aedificia et tabernae*); cf. the *praediolum cum taberna* bequeathed by a patron to fifteen freedmen (*Dig.* 32.38.5): no doubt they too had been managing the properties during their patron's lifetime.

34. Gaius, *Inst.* I.19: *Iusta autem causa manumissionis est si quis . . . servum procuratoris habendi gratia aut ancillam matrimonii causa apud consilium manumittat.* But see below, Chapter 6, section IV, with notes 106ff.

35. See above, Chapter 2, section III; for a *societas* composed of Trimalchio's *colliberti*, see *Sat.* 38.13.

nantly, to agricultural investments?[36] There are certainly numerous instances in the literary and legal texts in which landowning and money-lending are treated as complementary activities; a famous passage in one of Pliny's letters is a frequently cited example.[37] But in other literary passages and in inscriptions, profit from *merces* is juxtaposed with interest on loans,[38] proof that money-lending need not invariably imply landed investments; the Roman jurists have full discussions of bottomry loans (*nauticum faenus*),[39] and the procedure through which a banking intermediary arranged to handle maritime loans is spelled out in detail in a papyrus.[40] Since Trimalchio mentions only the lending of money in this present passage, and we know that for much of his life he was directly involved in shipping and trade, it is surely essential to inquire, in the present context, what types of economic activities his loans might actually have financed.

The geographical setting of the *Cena* is pertinent here. The numerous topographical pointers in the text—to a *Graeca urbs* with a harbor on the coast of Campania, close to Baiae and Cumae, near the *crypta Neapolitana*, in easy reach of Pompeii, with a road past a necropolis which connects with Capua—can be combined with other references

36. Veyne, "Trimalcion," p. 239: "Quant à l'usure, elle ètait considérée simplement comme une activité annexe de l'agriculture."

37. *Sum quidem prope totus in praediis, aliquid tamen faenero*: Plin. *Ep*. 3.19.8, cited by Veyne, "Trimalcion," p. 239 (and cf. above, Chapter 1, section I); cf. Hor. *Sat*. 1.2.12 (describing Fufidius): *dives agris, dives positis in faenore nummis*; Sen. *Ep. Mor*. 41.7: *Multum serit, multum faenerat*; Tac. *Ann*. 14.53.6: *tantis agrorum spatiis, tam lato faenore*; see further Veyne, "Trimalcion," p. 239n2; Wiseman, *NMRS*, pp. 78ff; MacMullen, *RSR*, p. 51 and refs. in n74 (p. 165).

38. E.g., Sen. *Ep. Mor*. 17.10; 119.1,5: *Opus erit tamen tibi creditore; ut negotiari possis, aes alienum facias oportet . . . circumspiciebam, in quod me mare negotiaturus inmitterem*; Firm. *Math*. 3.7.4. At Ephesus as early as 85 B.C. a law listing different forms of debt begins with a casual reference to "lenders of money by way of maritime loans." *SIG*[3] 742, lines 50–51.

39. *Dig*. 22.2.6 and 7; *Pauli Sententiae* 2.14.3 with *Dig*. 22.2.4 pr; *Dig*. 45.1.122; see Rougé, *OCM*, pp. 351ff; for a recent discussion of *pecunia traiecticia* see W. Litewski, "Römisches Seedarlehen," *Iura: rivista internazionale di diritto romano e antico* 24 (1973), pp. 112–183, and Litewski's review of A. Biscardi, *Actio Pecuniae Traiecticiae*, in *Zeitschrift der Savigny Stiftung* 93 (1976), pp. 418–422; see further G. E. M. de Ste. Croix, "Ancient Greek and Roman Maritime Loans," in H. Edey and B. S. Yamey, eds., *Debits, Credits, Finance and Profits, Essays in Honor of W. T. Baxter* (London 1974), pp. 41–59.

40. *P. Gr. Vindob*. 19792, on which see L. Casson, "New Light on Maritime Loans," *Eos* 48.2 (1956), pp. 89–93 (note that it is the ship itself, rather than the owners' land, which is here pledged as security); Rougé, *OCM*, pp. 348ff.

to the city's architectural, cultural, and administrative character;[41] the case for identifying Trimalchio's city with the port of Puteoli (figures 17, 19) is strong, and today is nearly universally accepted.[42] Alternatives are no longer seriously considered, and a sceptic must justify his reservations on the wholly different grounds that, while there are recognizable realistic urban features in Petronius' account, much is imaginary; the city is therefore a "composite creation" and cannot be named.[43] But elsewhere Petronius includes some elements of fantasy in his account of the town of Croton[44]—proof (if it were needed) that imaginative detail in Petronian cities is compatible with an actual place. All conditions remain satisfied by Puteoli, and there are other arguments in its favor.[45]

The types of activity financed by Trimalchio through his freedman intermediaries, then, can be inferred from the type of society in which the *Cena* was placed: not merely an international port and commercial emporium but, after Rome, the most important economic artery in Julio-Claudian Italy.[46] We are required to think of commercial loans

41. *Graeca urbs*: Sat. 81.3; coastal Campania: 81.1; Baiae, Cumae, Pompeii: 53; *crypta Neapolitana*: frag. 16; Capua: 62.1. Architectural features: *capitolium* on a hill (*ad clivum*), 44.18; amphitheater, 45.4; circus, 70.13; basilica, 57.9. Oriental contacts: 38.3. Administrative character: seviral college, 30.2, 65.5, 57.6; a *colonia*, 44.12, 57.9; aediles, 44.3; *vigiles*, 78.7.

42. The subject has been endlessly discussed; for a summary of other views, and arguments for Puteoli, cf. K. F. C. Rose, "Time and Place in the Satyricon," *TAPA* 93 (1962), pp. 402ff; and, more recently, J. P. Sullivan, *The Satyricon of Petronius* (Bloomington, Ind., 1968), pp. 46–47.

43. P. G. Walsh, *The Roman Novel* (Cambridge 1970), p. 76.

44. *Sat.* 116ff, as has been rightly observed by M. S. Smith, *Cena Trimalchionis* (Oxford 1975), p. xix. But Smith's own discussion of the location of the *Cena* (pp. xviii-xix) is agnostic, though he recognizes that "a stronger case" has been made for Puteoli.

45. The name Petronius is attested in a monumental inscription of the Augustales in Augustan Puteoli (*CIL* X, 1873; cf. 1888, 8178, *centuria Petronia*). This establishes the importance of the *gens Petronia* in that city and may have implications also for the identity of the author of the *Satyricon*. If that man was indeed T. Petronius Niger, *cos. suff.* A.D. 62, then the Petronius who lent his name, and more material benefits, to the Puteolan Augustales may have been an ancestor; a local parallel can be cited to show that ascendancy over three generations from municipal *nobilitas* to a suffect consulship is well within the bounds of possibility: on the municipal origins of Hordeonius Flaccus, *cos. suff.* before A.D. 68, see J. H. D'Arms, *Historia* 23 (1974), pp. 497ff.

46. On the importance of Puteoli in the Augustan and later period, see M. W. Frederiksen, "Puteoli," *RE* 23 (1959), 2043; *RBN*, pp. 81–82; cf. the discussion below, Chapter 6, section I. Colonization by Augustus is now securely established:

to shipbuilders and owners of large transport vessels and of the myriad small craft which provided ferry service and other functions in the harbor; of loans to *negotiatores*, traders active both locally and overseas, who were in search of funds to enable them to buy cargoes to ship and sell abroad, or who sought temporary or long-term storage space for their cargoes in warehouses; of loans also to local manufacturers— of glass and purple dye—who relied on materials imported from overseas; and of loans to distributors, seeking local, regional, even more distant markets for their wares. To be sure, until very recently the local documentation of such activities has been meager and largely indirect. Although the proportion of freedmen in the surviving inscriptions of Puteoli is high, these *liberti* offer little explicit indication on their tombstones as to the nature of their livelihood; and although useful inferences can be drawn from the much fuller epigraphical record of Ostia, where *coactores argentarii* appear among the *liberti* with some frequency, this comparative material dates to a somewhat later period.[47] But now, for Puteoli in the period of Claudius and Nero, new evidence provides striking illustration of freedmen engaged in financial dealings of this kind: a series of *mutua* (loans) and *vadimonia* (records of security paid to continue legal action which was generated by failure to repay) are the records of a freedman active in Puteoli but apparently a resident of Pompeii; the individual sums are mostly small, but behind the freedman stands a larger *patronus* in control of the operations— and there stand also larger sums.[48]

Locality, then, matters. Money lent through freedmen will finance different enterprises in places of different economic and social character. Pliny's activities, and his agents, were at work in and around

Puteoli is referred to as *colonia Iulia Augusta* in a document which is dated to A.D. 36 or 39: C. Giordano, *RAAN* n.s. 45 (1970), p. 219 (no. 6, lines 24–25).

47. The proportion of freedmen to freeborn in Puteolan inscriptions is approximately 10:1; see *JRS* 64 (1974), p. 112n71. Ostians: H. Bloch, *NdSc.* 1953, p. 291 (no. 53); *CIL* XIV, 4644. There are at least two unpublished examples from Ostia: Ostian inventory 8226 (A. Egrilius Polytimus), and 8485 (M. Lucceius Hermes); see below, Chapter 6, section II. *Stipulator argentarius: ILS* 7512.

48. These texts were first edited by C. Giordano: see *RAAN* n.s. 41 (1966), pp. 107–121; 45 (1970), pp. 211–231; 46 (1971), pp. 183–197; 47 (1972), pp. 311–318. The freedman is C. Sulpicius Cinnamus, his patron—whose status is unknown— C. Sulpicius Faustus. For the Murecine "villa," see O. Elia, *RAAN* n.s. 35 (1960), pp. 29ff. For money lent by Faustus on the security of 13,000 *modii* (more than eighty tons) of Egyptian grain, see *RAAN* 51 (1976), pp. 145–147.

his estates in agricultural Umbria, whereas the freedmen financed by Trimalchio were active in a major trading center. Since Puteoli was of course within easy reach of the fertile parts of Campania—where, indeed, we know that some of Trimalchio's own most productive estates were situated—the chances are good that some of his liquid assets helped to finance agricultural enterprises. In fact, the combination and diversification of economic enterprises which Trimalchio's own words explicitly attest, are historically appropriate to Puteoli, and not only to Puteoli, where landowners and traders tended inevitably to merge their interests, and ultimately tended to be the same people.[49]

We have seen, then, that Trimalchio's loans yielded more substantial profits, and had a more commercial base, than has recently been supposed. When he concludes his autobiographical review with a report of his own personal disengagement from trading activities (*sustuli me de negotiatione*) he does not say—nor does it follow—that he became thenceforth indifferent to profits from that source. Indeed, money-lending at interest through freedman intermediaries supports the opposite conclusion, one which Trimalchio reinforces at the end of his review: "If you've only got a penny, you're only worth a penny; if you've got something, you'll be thought something" (77.6). And he makes the same point with equal emphasis in another place in the *Cena*, where his words are also intended to be taken with a high degree of seriousness. It is time to turn to his epitaph.

III

An epitaph, *titulus sepulchralis*, is a personal as well as a public document; it is a highly select and formulaic arrangement of biographical details, designed to be seen by persons who pass the monument on the roadway. Trimalchio's attention to the composition of his own is characteristically intense. Just after the slaves have pushed onto the couches and have all but jostled the other diners from their places, the atmosphere of confused commotion in the *Cena* abruptly changes. Trimalchio turns suddenly serious (*oblitus nugarum*) and reasserts control; he calls for his will and reads it aloud as his dependents lament (*ingemescente familia*); he instructs Habinnas, first, to see to the erection of his funeral monument according to exact, and ostentatious, specifications, and next to consider carefully (*diligenter*) whether the

49. *JRS* 64 (1974), pp. 121–122.

epitaph which he has composed for himself seems sufficiently appropriate (*satis idonea*).[50] Habinnas would be sure to understand such matters: he is not only a *lapidarius* by profession but also like Trimalchio a member of the *seviri Augustales* (65.5), and the most notable guest at the banquet, for whom the place of honor (*praetorius locus*) was reserved (65.7).

> C. Pompeius Trimalchio Maecenatianus hic requiescit. Huic seviratus absenti decretus est. Cum posset in omnibus decuriis Romae esse, tamen noluit. Pius, fortis, fidelis, ex parvo crevit; sestertium reliquit trecenties, nec umquam philosophum audivit. Vale: et tu.   (71.12)

Many of the elements in this remarkable epitaph have been noticed by the commentators and by other Petronian scholars. Here, as so often elsewhere, Mommsen showed the way: his special contribution was to recognize Trimalchio's epitaph as an unusual member of a familiar species, and to divide the inscription into its component parts, exploiting for each the parallels provided by surviving tombstones of the early Empire.[51] Mommsen pointed out examples of other freedmen pretentiously assuming an agnomen, or second cognomen, and this throws some light on "Maecenatianus." The force of *absenti*, in the second sentence, has also been discussed. Inscriptions confirm that appointment to the sevirate was the highest municipal honor which could be conferred upon freedmen; and there are epigraphical examples from both Rome and the municipalities of magistrates of particular distinction being elected *in absentia*.[52] But there is no parallel in any of the thousands of inscriptions pertaining to the sevirate for a freedman being named to the college while away from his city of residence. Trimalchio inflates the significance of his priesthood by including an element which is in fact appropriate only to a person of distinctly

50. *Sat.* 70.11–71.12. *Diligenter* is an important word: it appears earlier in the description of Trimalchio's frescoes, where also his concern for his public image is paramount (29.4: *Omnia diligenter curiosus pictor cum inscriptione reddiderat*).

51. Th. Mommsen, "Trimalchios Heimath und Grabschrift," *Hermes* 13 (1878), pp. 107ff.

52. For C. Marius, *tertium consul apsens creatus*, see *Inscriptiones Italiae* 13.3: *Elogia* 17, pp. 22–24, and 18, p. 65; Augustus, *Res Gestae* 1.31 (*dictaturam et absenti et praesenti mihi delatam*; cf. Vell. Pat. 2.3.1); C. Cartilius Poplicola of Ostia *octiens duomvir . . . apsens praesensque factus est*: see H. Bloch, *Scavi di Ostia* 3 (Rome 1958), pp. 214ff; cf. also Tac. *Agr.* 41.1.

superior status.[53] This can be seen at once if we look not to inscriptions but to literature, and very particularly to the Ciceronian passage—it has been neglected—in which the townsmen of M. Caelius Rufus, son of an *eques* and not yet embarked upon his own senatorial career, are found electing him to their local senate "during his absence . . . and they bestowed upon him, without his seeking them, those honors which they refused to many who *did* seek them."[54]

In the third sentence the *decuriae* must be, as Mommsen long ago observed,[55] the panels of subordinates of Roman magistrates (*apparitores*); it is again clear from imperial inscriptions, our principal source, that freedmen were indeed eligible to buy membership on at least some of the panels, all of which were located at Rome.[56] But the *decuriae* of quaestorian and aedilician clerks (*scribae quaestorii, scribae aedilicii*) were apparently restricted to *ingenui*, men of freeborn status— they might expect elevation to equestrian rank upon the completion of their duties, and often returned to hold the chief magistracies in their municipalities, including Puteoli:[57] is Trimalchio exaggerating once again when he claims that membership on all the decuries was open to him? In the fourth sentence we now know, thanks to an excellent recent study of the use of prices in the Latin novel,[58] that no very special significance ought to be attached to the figure thirty million HS: Petronius used that same sum on five different occasions, each time to indicate nothing more specific than great personal wealth. There is now a new commentary on the *Cena*, and with it an old interpretation of Trimalchio's never listening to a philosopher: "This may simply make fun of the ignorant glorying in his ignorance, but possibly it is more subtle, a parody of the distrust shown by the upper classes . . . towards philosophers."[59]

53. Cf. Mommsen (above, note 51), pp. 118–119.
54. Cic. *Cael.* 5: *Absentem . . . et ea non petenti detulerunt quae multis petentibus denegarunt.*
55. Mommsen (above, note 51), p. 119.
56. Treggiari, *RFLR*, pp. 153–156; Wiseman, *NMRS*, pp. 72–74; and especially A. H. M. Jones, "The Roman Civil Service: Clerical and Subclerical Grades," *Studies in Roman Government and Law* (New York 1960), pp. 153ff.
57. Jones (preceding note), p. 158, with examples cited in nn. 41–43; Kornemann, *RE* 2A (1921), 852–853. Puteolan examples: *CIL* X, 1725; *CIL* VI, 1944 (= *ILS* 1934).
58. Duncan-Jones, *ERE*, pp. 238–248, esp. 241.
59. M. S. Smith *Cena Trimalchionis* (Oxford 1975), p. 199; for the view that phi-

What one misses in these and other individual pieces of exegesis is any emphasis on the literary coherence of the entire epitaph, and appreciation of the ways in which Petronius intended it—for he certainly did so intend it, as Trimalchio's attentive instructions to Habinnas clearly show—to contribute to our sense of Trimalchio as a personality and to illustrate his attitudes. In both these respects, the third sentence deserves a closer scrutiny than it has previously received. Certainly the sentence as a whole is extraordinary and, in epitaphs, quite without parallel. In the inscriptions of freedmen it is common to find such phrases as "endowed with every mark of distinction to which freedmen can aspire,"[60] or "the local senate conferred upon him all honors appropriate to a freedman."[61] But one will not find instances in which a freedman or any Roman, whatever his *dignitas*, combines on his tombstone a reference to honors which were available to him with a statement that he was disinclined to accept them. This is not the language of epitaph; it belongs to an entirely different literary sphere. One might be tempted to think initially of the official phraseology of polite refusal, employed by the emperor in rejecting divine honors, or by others in positions of high authority: they signify "a courteous indication of disinclination from one who could command."[62] But as the concessive clause makes clear, Trimalchio did not refuse something actually offered but was disinclined to exercise a political option, and for this the relevant parallels are not documentary, but literary. Horace, *libertino patre natus* but of equestrian rank, wrote that given the choice, he would be disinclined to change places with persons of noble birth.[63] Similar locutions are confined without exception to persons of still higher status, junior members of the senate and, above all, members of the equestrian order: we shall

---

losophy is being treated with contempt by an ignorant Trimalchio, see, e.g., E. Marmorale, *Cena Trimalchionis* (Florence 1948) *ad loc.* (p. 157).

60. *CIL* II, 1944.

61. *CIL* II, 2023.

62. The Greek is παραιτεῖσθαι, the Latin *nolle* or *deprecari*. See M. P. Charlesworth, "The Refusal of Divine Honours: An Augustan Formula," *PBSR* (1939), pp. 1–10 (quotation from p. 4); cf. J. Béranger, "Le réfus de pouvoir," *MH* 5 (1948), pp. 178–196. Philosophers and παραιτεῖσθαι: C. P. Jones, *Plutarch and Rome* (Oxford 1971), p. 146n47; *Anth. Pal.* 9, 445. For *nolo* in this sense, by the emperor Nero in an official text, see O. Monteverdi, *Aegyptus* 50 (1970), p. 6.

63. Hor. *Sat.* 1.6.93–94, but the entire poem is instructive; cf. L. R. Taylor, "Horace's Equestrian Career," *AJP* 46 (1925), pp. 161–170.

recall Cicero's description of L. Sestius as a man "who wished to seem worthy of senatorial offices, rather than to attain them."[64] Of one early imperial Roman *eques* it was written: "It was a greater thing to have been able to achieve triumphs, yet not to want them; it was a greater thing for the great to have held back."[65] The language and sentiments are strikingly reminiscent of Trimalchio's own assertion of his disinclination to receive honors. And the similarity in this case cannot be coincidence, for the person so described was the exemplar of the grand but unambitious *eques Romanus*: Maecenas, whose name Trimalchio actually appropriates in his epitaph as the final element of his own nomenclature.

In fact, it is the third sentence which clarifies earlier ambiguities and makes explicit what was earlier only suggested. *Maecenatianus* at the outset of the epitaph is unexpected: Trimalchio did not claim it as part of his name earlier in the *Cena* (30.2). *Absenti* is incongruous in the context of mention of the sevirate and has literary overtones which are curious at first sight.[66] But both words are perfectly suited to the personality whom the third sentence introduces: a man of dignity, like the rich Roman equestrians, conspicuously suited for honors, casually indifferent to those which are bestowed, and disinclined to actively seek those which he could effortlessly obtain. The third sentence, through the parallels provided, respectively, by the couplet from the *Elegiae in Maecenatem*[67] and the passage from the *Pro Caelio*,[68] fully elucidates both *Maecenatianus* and *absenti*: only now does it become patent that Petronius intended to endow Trimalchio's *titulus* with a special literary resonance, evocative of equestrian grandeur. Equestrian, not senatorial grandeur, be it noted, and an equestrian grandeur which is suggested, rather than overtly claimed: the freedman's social pretensions are precisely equivalent with the limits of his social horizon.[69] This is corroborated by the fact that Trimalchio wears on his left hand a ring which is gilded, but not golden, and by the irritated outburst of his fellow freedman when he senses that Ascyltos is pa-

64. Above, Chapter 3, section II, and note 43.
65. *Elegiae in Maecenatem* 1. 31–32: *Maius erat potuisse tamen nec velle triumphos / maior res magnis abstinuisse fuit.*
66. Above, section III, and note 53.
67. Above, note 65.
68. Above, note 54.
69. As has been acutely observed by Veyne, "Trimalcion," pp. 245–246; he does not, however, recognize the pertinence of Trimalchio's epitaph.

tronizing him: *eques Romanus es.*[70] And the humor lies partly in the incongruity of the notion of a freedman's adoption of an attitude appropriate only to persons of greatly superior social status; but especially in his thinking the expression of that attitude appropriate (*idonea*) for his gravestone: to a M. Caelius, a L. Sestius, an Atticus, or a Maecenas, such an act would have seemed not only unsuitable but unthinkable.

Why was Trimalchio disinclined to engage in the pursuit of honors? The way to a response has been prepared above in Chapters 2 and 3.[71] Although our upper-class authors recognized various conditions under which a man's deliberate preference of *otium* to *honores* might be justified and hence his *otium* be designated *honestum*,[72] the activities associated with *honestum otium* are in practice restricted to two types. The first are *otia hospita Musis*, intellectual pursuits, especially those of philosophy and literature.[73] It scarcely needs emphasizing that active engagement in this class of pursuits held no fascination for Trimalchio: that is clear enough from the crudeness of his own verses (55.3), his absurd comparison of the literary merits of Cicero and Publilius (55.5), his garbled generalizations, which prompt the phrase *philosophos de negotio deiciebat* (56.7), and his impossible interpretation of the recitation of the Homeristae (59.3-5). Moreover, his own words in a prominent position in his epitaph are even more emphatic: *nec umquam philosophum audivit.*

Second, we have seen that when *equites Romani locupletes honestique* are described in the literature as worthy to hold high offices of state, should they wish to bend their energies in that direction, these energies were often being devoted instead to acquisitive activities, including commerce, trade, and manufacture. Even though the Romans' system of values did not permit them to express this easily or

70. Ring: *Sat.* 32.3: *Habebat etiam in minimo digito sinistrae manus anulum grandem subauratum*; Ascyltos' neighbor: *Sat.* 57.4.

71. See above, Chapter 2, section I and Chapter 3, sections II and III.

72. *Honestum otium*: Sall. *Hist.* 1.55.9m: *Illa quies et otium cum libertate quae multi probi potius quam laborem cum honoribus capessebant*; see further *RBN*, pp. 70ff (late Republic), pp. 156ff (Empire); W. Kroll, "Die Kultur der Ciceronischen Zeit," *Das Erbe der Alten* 22 (1933), pp. 5–6; J. M. André, *Otium dans la vie morale et intellectuelle romaine* (Paris 1966), pp. 288, 315ff.

73. Sil. Ital. 12.27–36; the association of the phrase with Neapolis, which was regarded as a special haven for the learned and cultivated, is clearly intentional: see Strab. 5.4.7 (the *locus classicus*), with *RBN*, pp. 142ff.

often, we have unimpeachable authority for the view that a life of
honestum otium might be spent in managing and increasing one's private fortune.[74] The nuances of having *negotia* and the cases of L.
Sestius, of T. Pomponius Atticus, and others well illustrate the tendency of upper-class writers to describe the lucrative activities of respectable men obliquely, as though they were something else.[75] The
transition from Republic to Empire brought, with establishment and
regularization of salaried equestrian careers, a fundamental change in
practice: the only explicit example in literature of an *eques Romanus*
avoiding political engagement expressly in order to make money is
early imperial. Tacitus observes that Annaeus Mela, brother of Seneca,
"declined the pursuit of honors, believing that his equestrian rank
offered a shorter road to the amassing of wealth."[76]

Examples of this equestrian preoccupation with their own profits,
under the rubric of *honestum otium*, might be multiplied,[77] and of
course the two types need not be mutually exclusive: witness Atticus,
or the friend of the Younger Pliny, the *eques* Terentius Iunior, who
"having attained honors, preferred leisure" and busied himself on his
country estate, where his intellectual pursuits elicited the approving
comment: "You would think the man lived in Athens, not in a villa."[78]
Moreover, when a notable person retreated from the public gaze it was
easy to impugn, or misunderstand, his motives and to regard his *otium*
as *inhonestum*, linked with *desidia*, *luxuria*, *inertia*, and more exotic

74. Cic. *De Off.* 1.92, discussed above in Chapter 3, section II.

75. Above, Chapter 3, section III.

76. Tac. *Ann.* 16.17.3. Seneca's father and Seneca take a different view, the former
emphasizing Mela's love of philosophy (*Contr.* 2, pref. 3), the latter contrasting Mela's
otium with the *dignitas* of Iunius Gallio (*Cons. Helv.* 18.2): Tacitean malice has been
suspected here. See M. Griffin, *Seneca, A Philosopher in Politics* (Oxford 1976),
p. 84n3.

77. The subject needs further investigation; biographical study of persons with
whom the phrase is associated might prove profitable. See, for the late Republic, SB,
Att. 1, p. 5, citing Papirius Paetus, M. Seius, L. Saufeius, Cn. Sallustius; on
M. Marius of Pompeii, see Cic. *Fam.* 7.1.5 [*Humaniter vivere*], *istam rationem oti tui
et laudo vehementer et probo*; cf. *RBN*, pp. 71ff. For other Republican precedents see
Cic. *Cluent.* 153ff; *Fam.* 11.27.2 (C. Matius); Sen. *Ep. Mor.* 98.13 (Q. Sextius Niger);
Suet. *Aug.* 4 (disparagement of Augustus' own forbears); cf. in general C. Nicolet,
Ord. éq. 1, pp. 702ff. Empire: *RBN*, pp. 156ff; A. Stein, *Der römische Ritterstand*
(Munich 1927), pp. 197–198, and see below, Chapter 7, section I.

78. Plin. *Ep.* 7.25.4: *Paratisque honoribus tranquillissimum otium praetulit . . .
Athenis vivere hominem, non in villa putes.*

vices: Tiberius on Capri is the most notorious example.[79] There were in fact grave and widespread doubts about Maecenas on precisely these counts, to which the *Elegiae in Maecenatem*, Velleius Paterculus, and a letter of Seneca all bear witness.[80]

Maecenas draws us back, at last, to Trimalchio. Those scholars who argue that Petronius drew heavily upon the *Epistulae Morales*, and even scholars who believe that the number of Senecan echoes and borrowings in Petronius has been greatly exaggerated, join together in finding an echo of Seneca's account of Maecenas' loose and effeminate ways in Trimalchio's assumption of the name *Maecenatianus*.[81] But we have shown that it is rather the social attitude expressed in the third sentence of the epitaph which provides the proper explanation for an association between Trimalchio and Maecenas. Nor is it likely that Trimalchio would hint at his own effeminacy in his epitaph, where he has taken such pains to compose something genuinely appropriate and permanently on public view. Trimalchio's *"otium"* is instead to be regarded as *"honestum,"* and we cannot suppose, in order to explain his disinclination to go to Rome, that he preferred to combine intellectual with lucrative pursuits. His rejection of learned activities in his epitaph is as emphatic as is his affirmation of activities of the other type: *Ex parvo crevit, sestertium reliquit trecenties*. Trimalchio was avid of wealth, not honors or learning; like the rich *equites* to whom he pretentiously imagines himself comparable, he declined the more prestigious possibilities of Rome in favor of the more lucrative ones in the

79. See, e.g., Cic. *Sest.* 138; *Brut.* 2.8; Sall. *Cat.* 4.1, with other passages cited in *RBN*, p. 70n175; see further André (above, note 72), index, s.v. *otium desidiosum, Graecum* (which could have distinctly pejorative connotations), *ignobile, luxuriosum, malum* (p. 567). Tiberius: Tac. *Ann.* 4.57.2; Suet. *Tib.* 42.1.

80. *Eleg. in Maec.* 1. 21, 56–57, 105; 2.23: the entire poem is a defense of Maecenas against the charges of weakness and love of ease; Vell. Pat. 2.88.2; Sen. *Ep. Mor.* 114.4–5; cf. Tac. *Ann.* 3.30; Prop. 3.9.23–24; and other references cited by Stein, *RE* 14 (1928), 211.

81. On Seneca and Petronius see Sullivan (above, note 42), pp. 129ff, 193ff; for partial (and guarded) rebuttal, see M. S. Smith (above, note 44), pp. 217–219. But both scholars regard Sen. *Ep. Mor.* 114 as the chief reason for Trimalchio's usurpation of the agnomen Maecenatianus: Sullivan, p. 135; Smith, p. 198 (*ad loc.*). That there were actual Maecenatiani on imperial domestic staffs (B. Baldwin, *Acta Classica* 21 [1978], p. 96) does not explain why Petronius assigned the *agnomen* to Trimalchio. The reasons why Maecenas went into voluntary retirement after 29 B.C. were, and remain, mysterious, despite K. J. Reckford, "Horace and Maecenas," *TAPA* 90 (1959), pp. 198ff.

port of Puteoli, where he could oversee his various financial enterprises and continue to amass wealth.[82]

We are now in a better position to sense the strange, but expressive coherence of this artful literary epitaph. Formally, the opening and closing elements—*hic requiescit*, *vale et tu*—together with the *huic* of line 2, and the paratactic composition and terse quality of the whole, place it in its proper context: that of *titulus sepulchralis*. As regards the social condition of Trimalchio, mention of the sevirate and the *decuriae* are realistic elements, lending verisimilitude, since membership in both institutions was the special prerogative of the ex-slave. But there is also social pretension, suggested by *absenti* and especially *Maecenatianus*, and confirmed and clarified by Trimalchio's appropriation of literary language, oblique and apolitical, which has an unmistakably equestrian ring—directed (as the remainder of the epitaph confirms) towards accumulating profit, rather than upon the abstractions of philosophy. A highly appropriate combination of interests for an inhabitant of a Roman port: we are reminded of Cicero's assessment of the enterprising Puteolanus Vestorius: "a practical mathematician, however ignorant of dialectics."[83]

IV

In the foregoing pages, attention has been focused upon the interpretation of certain of Trimalchio's own words—especially those of his final autobiographical review and of his epitaph—in the belief that they, and the atmosphere of seriousness which Petronius creates for them, constitute the fullest and least ambiguous evidence in the *Cena* for Trimalchio's activities, ambitions, and attitudes.[84] On the interpretation advanced here, the passages present a coherent and mutually reinforcing portrait: Trimalchio's controlling impulses were and remained acquisitive. He focused on multiple and diversified economic pursuits—predominantly commercial and financial, in which he for years participated directly, then through the employment of freedmen intermediaries—which were offered by the major port of Puteoli. There

82. This suggestion was considered first by Mommsen (above, note 51), p. 119, and affirmed more directly by A. Maiuri, *La Cena di Trimalchione* (Naples 1945), p. 212.

83. Cic. *Att.* 14.12.3, on which see above, Chapter 3, section I.

84. This point has been made also by H. C. Schnur, "The Economic Background of the *Satyricon*," *Latomus* 18 (1959), p. 793; he does not, however, discuss the epitaph.

Trimalchio preferred to maintain his residence, despite the more prestigious, but less lucrative rewards in the capital.

But what, then, are we to make of the vast productive estates, described elsewhere in the *Cena*? They certainly require critical attention, but an attention commensurate with that given to them by Petronius and by Trimalchio; and again, this can be determined only by reviewing the passages in which they are described. First, Trimalchio is ignorant of the locations of his immense holdings, inattentive to their management, casual about both their extent and productivity.[85] His attitudes in this respect are inconsistent with those of the astute and acquisitive Trimalchio whom we elsewhere encounter, not simply in those passages already discussed. There is Trimalchio the accountant (*dispensator*, 29.4), and the Trimalchio who is guided and protected by the god of trade (29.5). There are the beaks of his merchant ships depicted at the entrance of his dining room (30.1), and his actual ships at sea (39.8). There are Trimalchio's friends and fellow freedmen, all *homines negotiantes*.[86] There are Trimalchio's revealing *obiter dicta*, and the obsession with buying, selling, and profit which they underscore.[87] And there is, finally, the Trimalchio who is never satisfied, to whom an inherited senatorial fortune is as nothing (76.3)—a Trimalchio not unlike the archtypical Roman whom we meet in a poem later in the *Satyricon*, one who held all the world in his sway but nonetheless loaded his ships and set off in quest of foreign gold: *nec satiatus erat* (119).

Second, transitional phrases often provide useful clues to literary intent. The passage in which Hermeros fixes the limits of Trimalchio's holdings with the expansive phrase *quantum milvi volant*, adding that *omnia domi nascuntur*, is inserted between two explicit references to them, by the narrator Encolpius, as "farfetched tales."[88] That this is

---

85. *Sat.* 37.6: [Trimalchio] *nescit quid habeat, adeo saplutus est*; cf. 37.9: not one out of ten members of his *familia* has ever seen the master; 48.1–2: wine from an estate not yet seen, between Terracina and Tarentum; 53.5: *horti Pompeiani*, existence unknown to Trimalchio.

86. *Sat.* 38.7–10 (C. Pompeius Diogenes); 38.11–16 (C. Iulius Proculus, *libitinarius*); 43.6 (Phileros, *homo negotians*); 45.1 (Echion, *centonarius*); 58.11 (Hermeros); 65.5 (Habinnas, *lapidarius*).

87. E.g., *Sat.* 56.1, remarks on *nummularii*; 70.1: *Ita crescam patrimonio, non corpore*; 75.9: *Bene emo, bene vendo*.

88. *Sat.* 37.1: *Longe accersere fabulas coepi*; 39.1: *Interpellavit tam dulces fabulas Trimalchio*.

how Petronius may have intended them to be taken is partially corroborated by the distinctly artificial flavor of the "self-sufficiency" in question: Trimalchio's lambs are bought and imported from Tarentum, while his bees come from Attica, his mushrooms from India:[89] by what means did they reach Italy, one has only to ask, and at what expense? Hyperbole is scarcely more muted in the speech of the *actuarius* who records the birth of seventy slaves, the storage of five hundred thousand *modii* of grain, and the deposit of ten million HS on one estate in a single day (53), or in that of Trimalchio himself, when he boasts that he need not buy anything, locates one estate on the boundary between Terracina and Tarentum, and pretends to look forward to joining Sicily to his other properties. This boasting leads directly on to ridiculous remarks about his libraries, his literature, and his learning, and the passage of transition begins: *Nondum efflaverat omnia*.[90]

That is to say, attention to the context in which Trimalchio's lands appear, and to the tone of the passages in which they are described, help to determine more exactly their actual function. These are more the luxurious by-products or complements of Trimalchio's financial success, than its principal source; absurd and showy symbols, to which, in the intellectual sphere, his halting Latin verses and inane literary disquisitions are exactly comparable.

To say this is not to deny, of course, that Trimalchio has large social pretensions. His boasting about his lands and his literature are intended to impress his guests; more importantly, we have exposed the equestrian affectations implied by his withdrawal from direct participation in trade, and especially by the phrasing in his epitaph. We do not mean either to imply that the behavior of Trimalchio is uniformly static and predictable; on the contrary, his rapid and erratic shifts of mood, and his total—albeit temporary—absorption in any new matter at hand, are essential ingredients of the man,[91] and no small part, be

89. *Sat.* 38.2–4. Tarentum was famous for sheep (Hor. *Odes* 2.6.10–11; Plin. *NH.* 8.190–191; 29.33), as R. Thomas has reminded me: this supports the view that these items represent a *topos*.

90. *Sat.* 48; cf. 49 *init: Nondum efflaverat omnia*. For a recent attempt—to my mind unpersuasive—to rationalize the extravagances of *Sat.* 53, see B. Baldwin, "Trimalchio's Domestic Staff," *Acta Classica* 21 (1978), p. 95.

91. This aspect of Trimalchio's character has bene rightly stressed by H. D. Rankin, *Petronius the Artist: Essays on the Satyricon and Its Author* (The Hague 1971), p. 28; cf. also Sullivan (above, note 42), p. 153, who cites the remark of Encolpius (52.11): *nihil autem tam inaequale erat; nam modo Fortunatam verebatur, modo ad naturam*

it added, of Petronius' dramatic achievement, since they bring to the dinner party, and hence to the narrative as a whole, a felicitous swiftness of pace.

Finally and especially, this is not to deny the value of Veyne's insistence that Trimalchio's activities and attitudes be seen within a wider social context, or the pertinence of his observation that a Roman freedman's juridical position imposed severe limitations upon what he might realistically expect or aspire to achieve. It is to suggest, rather, that a rigidly hierarchical conception of Roman society, with economic functions sharply compartmentalized by strata, is excessively schematic: Veyne does not allow sufficiently for the fact that actual situations in real lives were more fluid and flexible—as is apparent both from Petronius' writings and from other evidence, less tainted by literary convention. Of the multiplicity of Trimalchio's own economic activity enough already has been said; but Veyne also misleads in treating unembarrassed love of gain as an attitude confined strictly, or even largely, to freedmen. Lichas of Tarentum, described as *homo verecundissimus*, C. Vestorius of Puteoli, and acquisitive municipal magistrates from Aosta to Pompeii, show that the desire to seek and gain riches cuts across social lines, and that respectable city councillors were prepared to express this attitude, unselfconsciously, in various contexts (figure 15).[92]

---

suam revertebatur. See also F. Zeitlin, *TAPA* 102 (1971), p. 660, and *Gnomon* 47 (1975), p. 622: some shrewd observations, although I cannot accept her parallels with modern "maladjustment" and "neurosis."

92. Lichas of Tarentum: above, Chapter 5, section II and note 23; C. Vestorius: above, Chapter 3, section I. *Viri municipales: CIL* V, 6842: *dum vixi quaesi cessavi perdere numquam / Mors intercessit Nunc ab utroque vaco*; cf. V, 6596, a Milanese magistrate's dedication to Mercury, *lucrorum potenti et conservatori*. For Roman worship of *pecunia*, see the literary refs. collected by MacMullen, *RSR*, p. 201n99. The status of the Ostian who begged Hermes (in Greek) to bring him profit, is unknown (Meiggs, *RO*[2], p. 231; on which see now H. Solin, *Arctos* 7 [1972], p. 194); nor is that of the author of the famous Pompeian mosaic inscription, *Salve Lucru[m]* (figure 18): on all this, see P. D. A. Garnsey, *PBSR* n.s. 44 (1976), p. 24. The artistic similarity between Trimalchio's intended funeral monument and that of the Pompeian magistrate C. Vestorius Priscus (on which see J. M. Dentzer, *MEFR* 74 [1962], p. 533) has prompted the acute observation that "la mentalità e il gusto del seviro augustale e dell'edile combaciano alla perfezione. Tale identità di gusto tra famiglie dell'aristocrazia municipale e ceti libertini più abbienti fa comprendere quanto uniforme sia l'ambiente culturale di provincia e quanto pericoloso sia operare delle distinzioni sociologiche nell'ambito dei gruppi dirigenti municipali"; (M. Torelli, *Studi Miscellanei* 10 [Seminario di Archeologia e Storia dell'Arte greca e romana dell'Università di Roma], 1963–64, p. 80n45).

Trimalchio's character and his attitudes underwent no detectable major changes—as those believe who argue for his "metamorphosis" from trader into a landed proprietor, self-sufficient and absentee, and believe in his simultaneous and serious identification of himself with men of senatorial standing and values, even going so far as to ape "upper-class distrust of philosophers" on his tombstone. His social and cultural pretensions must be seen in proper perspective, as the secondary and self-indulgent affectations of a man whose principal energies were directed towards accumulating material weath. To lay excessive emphasis upon Trimalchio's landed wealth is to confuse him with the Younger Pliny, to forget that he simultaneously derived revenues from his trading activities and his lands; in short, it is to attach major significance to some passages but to ignore or to underestimate the value of many others, the importance to which it has been the major purpose of these pages to establish. Thereby, it is hoped, we have come to be better acquainted with Petronius' Trimalchio, who differs from the diverse Trimalchiones whom we meet in the writing of recent social and economic historians. Petronius' *libertus* was a rich trader and landowner, with diversified lucrative interests, living near a busy Roman port, and the symbols to which he attaches chief importance are not those of show but of substance: his zodiacal sign, cancer, that of the merchant (39.8); his patron deity, Mercury, protector of traders (29.3, 67.7, 77.4); and his household gods: Gain, Luck, and Profit (60.8).

6

The Freedmen of Puteoli and Ostia
in Imperial Economy and Society

Trimalchio's vast wealth, and his status superior to that of other freedmen, owed something to his own acquisitive capacities and something to his patron's backing. But it derived especially from the lucrative opportunities offered by a major port, with close links to a fertile and productive hinterland. As part of the attempts to establish Trimalchio's multiple sources of wealth and his attitudes, we have occasionally referred to epitaphs of freedmen from the Roman ports of Puteoli and Ostia:[1] the inscriptions from these cities, nonideological records of the activities of actual persons, provided documentary counterweights to what might otherwise have seemed the colorful literary extravagance of Petronius. But the use of these inscriptional parallels raises, in turn, the question of how representative they may be of the activities of freedmen in these ports; and there remains the further question of whether Trimalchio, or other documented and actual freedmen, were unusual or typical in their independence, in their ability to pursue profits in their own right, rather than acting as representatives of their patrons.

An analysis of the function of nonimperial freedmen from the Roman ports of Puteoli and Ostia in the first two centuries will enable us to test some of the major conclusions of the last chapter in actual urban settings. It is intended also as an historical case study, for the epitaphs and dedications of freedmen dominate the surviving inscriptions from these cities: taken in the aggregate this body of evidence—for all its often recognized limitations—yields considerable information as to the types and extent of the freedmen's wealth and hence forms the basis of our knowledge of their collective impact on the local economies. It also provides indices of status, the freedmen's position in local soci-

1. See above, Chapter 5, notes 25, 33, 47.

eties, and their prospects for eventual assimilation into the ruling class: which factors promoted, which impeded upward social mobility? We want especially to try to measure—despite earlier studies, despite gaps in our evidence, and despite methodological problems which encumber the path to definitive answers—to what degree a freedman's lucrative activities and other interests were subject to a patron's control, to what degree they were pursued more independently, and to consider the probable consequences for the cities of the predominant patterns of interaction between freedmen and their patrons.

The first section below contains preliminary remarks on the points of convergence and of disparity between Ostia and Puteoli, and an explanation for the choice of the main evidence for this study, inscriptions of the seviri Augustales. In sections II and III the various indices of the wealth and standing of the local Augustales are discussed, together with special problems concerning the upward social mobility of the sons of freedmen. In section IV, various patterns of relationship between freedmen and patrons are reviewed, and a predominant pattern proposed for Augustales. Three major implications of these findings are set forth in a brief conclusion.

I

To widen the geographical focus of this study to include the freedmen of two cities provides a broader base from which to work towards historical conclusions. Ostia and Puteoli (figures 16, 17, 19) commend themselves to common treatment. They were the major Italian ports in the West under the Empire, and exhibit numerous parallels and congruities—in their institutions, in their economy, and in their social structure. Not surprisingly, *navicularii* were among the earliest of the organized *collegia* in both cities; *embaenitarii*, a class of boatmen whose precise functions remain obscure, are attested only in these ports; one of the distinctive inscribed glass flasks, depicting the coastline and monuments of Puteoli, where they were manufactured, has turned up in a tomb at Ostia.[2] The large numbers of men of slave

2. *Navicularii: NdSc.* 1927, p. 325 (Puteoli, from the Flavian amphitheater); *CIL* XIV, 3603, with Meiggs, *RO²*, p. 276 (Ostia, Augustan Age); *embainitarii:* Cic. *Ad Fam.* 8.1.4 (*embaeneticam facere*) with the references of SB, *Fam.* 1 *ad loc.* (p. 384); glass flasks: *NdSc.* 1909, p. 209 (Ostia); for the entire series—eight are now known— see most recently J. Kolendo, "Parcs à huitres et viviers à Baiae sur un flaçon en

descent who lived and worked in these commercial centers is reflected not only by the numbers of their inscriptions, but by the high proportions of citizens enrolled in the tribe Palatina, which under the Empire tends to replace the cities' old tribes.[3] The earliest known magistrates in Palatina, we now know, held office at Puteoli already by the reign of Nero, and at Ostia only slightly later.[4]

There are, to be sure, major differences between the cities, among them their different rhythms and rates of growth. Puteoli established her position as Italy's major commercial port well before Ostia, where the greatest period of prosperity came in conjunction with the construction of the imperial harbors. Puteoli's geographical position in the Campanian region, amid the early hellenized population of the Bay of Naples, contrasts with that of Ostia, at the Tiber mouth, in close proximity to Rome, and often therefore a mirror of major historical developments in the capital. Many more Ostians than Puteolans entered the senatorial and equestrian orders of Rome, beginning with the late Republic;[5] the Roman upper classes directly experienced Puteoli rather through their villa society and other interests on the Bay of Naples, discussed above in Chapter 4.

Puteoli's closest foreign trading ties were with Egypt, the cities of Asia Minor, the East; Ostia looked west, beyond Gallia Narbonensis to Spain and to North Africa. Puteoli's attachment to the fertile and productive hinterland, the *ager Campanus*, facilitated interdepen-

verre," *Puteoli: Studi di Storia Antica* 1 (1977), pp. 108–127; K. S. Painter, "Roman Flasks with Scenes of Baiae and Puteoli," *Journal of Glass Studies* 17 (1975), pp. 54–67; S. E. Ostrow, "Problems in the Topography of Roman Puteoli" (Ph.D. diss., University of Michigan, 1977), pp. 51–150.

3. On Puteoli's tribe (Falerna) see "Puteoli," *RE* 23 (1959), 2042; L. R. Taylor, *The Voting Districts of the Roman Republic*, MAAR 20 (Rome 1960), p. 323; *JRS* 64 (1974), p. 117n100; Ostia: Meiggs, *RO²*, p. 190.

4. L. Cassius Cerealis (Puteoli): J. H. D'Arms, "Tacitus, *Annals* 13.48 and a New Inscription from Puteoli," in B. Levick, ed., *The Ancient Historian and His Materials, Essays in Honour of C. E. Stevens* (Farnborough 1975), pp. 155–165; C. Cartilius Sabinus (Ostia): F. Zevi, *Epigraphica* 30 (1968), pp. 88ff; Meiggs, *RO²*, pp. 584–585; cf. *AJP* 97 (1976), pp. 390–391.

5. For Ostian senators and equestrians, see Meiggs, *RO²*, pp. 192–193, 196–197, 199, 206–208; for Puteoli, see *JRS* 64 (1974), p. 115 and nn. 91, 92, to which should be added the *praefectus praetorio* Sex. Cornelius Repentinus (whose inscription, dated to 175, will soon be published by G. Camodeca), and possibly also Ti. Claudius Quartinus, the Trajanic senator (*PIR²* C, 990).

dence between trade and agriculture, whereas the land near Ostia was less suited to profitable farming.[6] The enormous disparities between the extent and preservation of the archaeological remains in the two cities (figures 16, 17) do not encourage a study of their common features; scholars have tended to discuss the cities separately, or, if together, by adapting a chronological scheme which emphasizes Ostia's gradual replacement of Puteoli as a major imperial port.[7]

New archaeological discoveries, however, which have begun to be incorporated into historical research, reveal that Ostia's commercial importance began earlier, and that of Puteoli endured longer, than was earlier believed.[8] In fact, the arguments for study of the parallels between these urban centers are strong ones. From the Age of Augustus, when the ports, the chief economic arteries, assumed new importance in communications with and exploitation of the provinces, there are clear signs that the emperors viewed developments at Puteoli and Ostia reciprocally, in complementary terms. The need to make imperial provisions for reception, storage, and distribution of imported grain explains why both cities were organized, probably under Augustus, into *regiones*, why officials of the *annona*, some with simultaneous responsibilities in both cities, continue to be associated with Puteoli and Ostia through the second century, and why imperial procurators, responsible for upkeep and administration of the imperial harbors, are attested from the time of Claudius through the fourth century.[9] The

6. On the agricultural wealth of the *ager Campanus*, see M. W. Frederiksen, *PBSR* n.s. 14 (1959), pp. 112ff; on local interdependence of trade and agriculture, see *JRS* 64 (1974), p. 121. Ostia: Meiggs, *RO*[2], pp. 9, 263–270.

7. Cf., e.g., T. Frank, *ESAR* 5, p. 132; Rostovtzeff, *SEHRE*[2], pp. 162ff (with p. 610n25); Meiggs, *RO*[2], pp. 60–61; G. Barbieri, in *IV Miscellanea Greca e Romana*, 1st. ital. stor. ant. (Rome 1975), p. 310.

8. For an excellent brief resumé of work at Ostia between 1960 and 1972, see Meiggs, *RO*[2], pp. 578–593; cf. M. Cébeillac-Gervasoni and F. Zevi, "Revisions et nouveautés pour trois inscriptions d'Ostie," *MEFR* 88 (1976), pp. 607–637. For Puteoli, see J. H. D'Arms, "Puteoli in the Second Century of the Roman Empire: A Social and Economic Study," *JRS* 64 (1974), pp. 104–124.

9. *Regiones*: G. Camodeca, "L'ordinamento in *regiones* e i *vici* di Puteoli," *Puteoli: Studi di storia antica* 1 (1977), pp. 62–98, has produced the first comprehensive study for Puteoli and accepts an Augustan date (p. 84); at Ostia, a third century inscription refers either to five *regiones* or to the fifth *regio* (*CIL* XIV, 352 = *ILS* 6149); the division must have occurred much earlier. *Annona*: *JRS* 64 (1974), pp. 104–105. *Procuratores portus*: Meiggs, *RO*[2], pp. 298–300; J. H. D'Arms, *PdP* 27 (1972), pp. 255ff (an equestrian *procurator portus Puteolanorum*; for his date, probably not later than 326, see now G. Camodeca, p. 66n18).

first such Ostian procurator was a freedman of Claudius who also served as prefect of the fleet at Misenum.[10] It was probably he who engineered the transport of Gaius' mammoth obelisk carrier from Puteoli to Ostia and sank it there to form the foundation of the harbor's lighthouse.[11] Claudius' establishment of cohorts of *vigiles Puteolis et Ostis* derives from similar concern for protection of merchandise bound for Rome, as does Nero's revival of a scheme, originally conceived by Julius Caesar, for the construction of a waterway, navigable by quinquiremes, from lake Avernus, the westernmost extension of Puteoli's port, to the Tiber mouth.[12] Under Vespasian, sailors assigned to the imperial fleet petitioned the emperor *ab Ostis et Puteolis*, and the cemeteries of Ostia and Portus contained tombs belonging to members of the Misene fleet.[13] Antoninus Pius' attention to the *annona* and to Italian harbors, attested by his biographer, is confirmed at Ostia and Puteoli by numismatic and inscriptional evidence.[14]

Such examples of parallelism show that satisfactory maintenance of port installations, with the complexity of engineering involved, and the administration of shipping, posed problems too great for the towns themselves to resolve. Imperial supervision and control were thus required. Puteoli and Ostia, in short, were both commercial ports and imperial ports, and this fact, although it amply justifies a study of their common features, can also be a complicating factor in a study which focuses on freedmen: it will not always be clear whether the prominence in both cities of certain freedmen stems from their own involvement, and that of their nonimperial patrons, in commercial and manufacturing ventures, or whether that prominence reflects, rather, an emperor's

10. *CIL* XIV, 163 (= *ILS* 1533), Claudius Optatus, *Aug. libertus;* a man of the same name was *praefectus classis Misenensis* under Claudius (Plin. *NH* 9.62); they are presumably the same man: cf. *PIR*[2] C, 946; Meiggs, *RO*[2], p. 299.

11. Gaius' obelisk carrier: Plin. *NH* 16.201–202; foundation of the Claudian lighthouse: O. Testaguzza, *Portus* (Rome 1970), pp. 105–120.

12. *Vigiles* under Claudius: Suet, *Claud.* 25.2. Caesar's plan: Plut. *Caes.* 58.10; Suet. *Claud.* 20.1, on which see Meigg's *RO*[2], pp. 53–54. Nero's scheme: Tac. *Ann.* 15.42. 2–4, on which see *RBN*, pp. 97–98; also Meiggs, *RO*[2], pp. 57–58. The extension of the commercial harbor of Puteoli to Lake Lucrinus shortly after the Augustan Age has been convincingly demonstrated by F. Castagnoli, "Topografia dei Campi Flegrei," *Atti dei Convegni Lincei* 33 (Rome 1977), pp. 65–70.

13. Suet. *Vesp.* 8.3 (*classiarii*); *CIL* XIV, 233–243; H. Bloch, *NdSc.* 1953, pp. 276–277 (no. 39) (Misene sailors).

14. SHA *Ant. Pius* 8.2–3; *CIL* X, 1640, 1641; Meiggs, *RO*[2], commentary on pl. xviii c: cf. *PdP* 27 (1972), p. 261.

direct administrative intervention. For example, the C. Avianii were members of the local aristocracies of both Puteoli and Ostia in the first years of the Empire:[15] since C. Avianii are not attested in higher echelons of imperial administration, it is reasonable to suppose that these families forged private trading ties which involved both ports, also that their local freedmen furthered these. But as regards *liberti* of the Julio-Claudian Turranii, also known in both cities,[16] similar inferences are more hazardous, since C. Turranius was prefect of Egypt under Augustus, and *praefectus annonae* under Tiberius: how far local Turranii were engaged in furthering imperial, rather than private enterprises, or how far imperial and private interests went forward in combination, it is not possible to measure.[17]

Caution, then, will be required; often we can speak only of probabilities, not certainties, in dealing with the freedman sample. In what follows possible ambiguities are reduced to a minimum, since the focus is not upon the freedmen members of the *familia Caesaris*, but rather on the prominent nonimperial Ostian and Puteolan *liberti*, principally those designated Augustales or seviri Augustales (hereafter collectively Augustales).[18] The local evidence for them is substantial, especially at Ostia, where 114 are known from epitaphs (these include 19 unpublished texts), 270 from the late second and early third century registers

15. Above, Chapter 2, section I.

16. At Puteoli, an unpublished inscription of early Julio-Claudian date was prepared by Turrania, freedwoman of C. Turranius, for herself, her husband C. Turranius C. l. Posidonius, and four other named freedmen; and a later M. Turranius Hermonicus is known (*SIG* 817; cf. *RBN*, p. 152); at Ostia, an M. Turranius was *IIvir* in the Augustan Age (*CIL* XIV, 375), and the family name may also be partially preserved in the Ostian Fasti of 14 (Meiggs, *RO*², pp. 201–202); later members of the *gens* are commonly Q. Turranii, who are found among the *fabri tignarii* (*CIL* XIV, 160), and the Augustales (XIV, 4563.5; Appendix, no. 113). Hereafter, all Ostian and Puteolan Augustales listed in the Appendix will be cited by number (= no.); arabic numerals have been used for Ostians, Roman numerals for Puteolans.

17. Turranius: Stein, *RE* 7A (1948), 1441–42; for the dates of his posts, see P. A. Brunt, *JRS* 65 (1975), p. 142. The degree to which Ostia and Puteoli were anomalous in social and economic terms will repay further study; see the suggestive questions raised by G. W. Houston, "The Administration of Italian Seaports during the First Three Centuries of the Roman Empire," in *Seaborne Commerce*, p. 166.

18. The simpler term has been adopted as a matter of convenience, since at Ostia the freedmen were originally Augustales, their title subsequently changed to seviri Augustales (for the date and significance of the change in title, see presently Meiggs, *RO*², pp. 218–221; I hope to discuss the problem more fully elsewhere); in Puteoli, they are designated merely Augustales. See also the Appendix.

of their members; there is in addition archaeological evidence for their buildings. At Puteoli the Augustales were divided into at least two *centuriae* (that need not mean that there were in fact as many as 200 members), and some thirty names are known. (Part I of the Appendix is an up-to-date list of all known Ostian and Puteolan Augustales.)

Furthermore, the Augustales are the freedmen group most likely to provide answers to the social and economic questions posed at the outset of this chapter. It is clear from even a cursory reading of the more than three thousand inscriptions from cities and towns in the Roman West that collectively the *liberti* who held the title "Augustalis" were the wealthiest and most prominent freedmen in the towns. Like *equites* in Rome—whose titulature they reflect—Augustales had their own section of special seats at games and spectacles, and their own insignia of office; they owned their own buildings; they are associated with games in honor of the *princeps* and collectively made cash donations to their municipalities; they, like members of the *ordo decurionum* paid entry fees, *summa honoraria*, upon adlection; the *ordo Augustalium* is regularly listed after the *ordo decurionum* and before the plebs in municipal decrees and other official enactments.[19] One consequence of the inauguration of the institution under Augustus was that a *libertus* could now be invested with his own form of *dignitas* in a city or town where, because born in slavery, he was blocked by the Visellian law from membership in the local governing council.[20] *Libertina nobilitas*: the phrase aptly captures the ambiguities of the standing of the Augustales in the imperial cities and towns.[21]

All this has become clearer in recent years, now that emphasis is shifting away from the Augustales as a religious institution exclusively: in the standard early monographs on Puteoli and Aquileia and in books

---

19. On all this, see A. von Premerstein, "Augustales," *Dizionario epigrafico* 1 (1895), pp. 824ff; F. Mourlot, *Essai sur l'histoire de l'Augustalité dans l'empire romain* (Paris 1895); L. R. Taylor, "Augustales, Seviri Augustales, and Seviri: A Chronological Study," *TAPA* 45 (1914), pp. 231ff; *JRS* 14 (1924), pp. 158ff.

20. A. D. Nock, "*Seviri* and *Augustales*," *Ann. de l'Institut de Philol. et d'Hist. Orientales* 2 (1933–34), p. 635 (= Z. Stewart, ed., *A. D. Nock, Essays on Religion and the Ancient World* [Oxford 1972], p. 354). Visellian law of 23: *Cod. Iust.* 9.21.1.

21. Nock (above, note 20), p. 635 (= p. 354), was the first modern scholar, so far as I know, to employ the phrase, but for the verbal collocation cf. *CIL* XIV, 2298 (= *ILS* 1949), of Tiberian date: *Libertinus eram, fateor; sed facta legetur / patrono Cotta nobilis umbra mea.*

on freedmen, Augustales occupy a place in chapters on religion and cult.[22] Scholars are now taking an interest in their levels of wealth and social standing.[23] But there has been no attempt before now to anchor discussions of Augustales to discrete and particular urban contexts, or to define the relative position of these freedmen in imperial economy and society by reference to the various patterns of their interaction with their patrons.

II

The surviving inscriptions, particularly epitaphs, of individual Augustales demonstrate that at Puteoli and Ostia they were integrally connected with the commercial and manufacturing elements of the local economies—either directly, or through their contacts with the professional *collegia*, the members of which practiced specialized trades. Among Puteolan Augustales in commerce we find two *negotiatores* in different articles of trade, and a seagoing *navicularius*;[24] the economic activities of others can be guessed from their position as treasurer of a boatman's association or as a patron of shippers.[25] Manufacturers include a *purpurarius*, *marmorarius*, and a *vascularius;* an *argentarius* is also known.[26] Among Ostian Augustales one *negotiator* and one *navicularius* declare their direct involvement in commerce, five their interests in banking;[27] and twenty-three record, normally after their title "Augustalis," their presidencies or other offices in the professional *collegia*: eight were presidents of the builders' association (the *fabri tignarii* were the richest of Ostia's *collegia*, numbering 352

22. See e.g. Dubois, *PA*; A. Calderini, *Aquileia romana* (Milan 1930). "The subject of emperor worship naturally leads to the Augustales." That comment, by Duff (*Freedmen*, p. 133), typifies the early approach to the subject.

23. It is symptomatic of the shift in emphasis that in M. Clavel and P. Lévêque, *Villes et structures urbaines dans l'occident romain* (Paris 1971), Augustales are discussed in a socio-economic context under the rubric "les bourgeoisies urbaines," and in Meiggs, *RO²*, they appear in the chapter on the people. See further R. Duthoy, "La fonction sociale de l'Augustalité," *Epigraphica* 36 (1974), pp. 134–154, and now in *ANRW* II (Principat), 16.2 (Berlin 1978), pp. 1254–1309, esp. p. 1305.

24. No. III; M. Claudius Tryphon (unpublished), no. XI; no. X.

25. No. VIII; no. XXII.

26. No. XIII; no. IV; M. Claudius Tryphon (unpublished), no. XI.

27. *Negotiator*: no. 87; *navicularius*: A. Licordari, *Rend. Acc. Linc.* 29 (1974), pp. 313–314; bankers: no. 49; A. Egrilius Polytimus (unpublished), no. 51; M. Lucceius Hermes (unpublished), no. 76; A. Licordari, *Rend. Acc. Linc.* 29 (1974), pp. 313–314; no. 92.

members at full strength);[28] others are discovered holding positions of responsibility among associations of the shipbuilders, grain measurers, Adriatic shippers, wine importers, or the various *corpora* which provided ferry services.[29] Since the percentages of known Augustales who indicate their lucrative activities in the epitaphs are 28 percent and 26 percent at Puteoli and Ostia respectively, we are working with evidence sufficient to hypothesize that these activities are broadly representative of those of the group as a whole; indeed, the distinctive flavor of these port cities is best sensed by a reading of the epitaphs of these very freedmen.

Several indices help us to measure how profitable such practices might be. Two Ostian Augustales established capital foundations of HS 40,000 and HS 50,000 respectively, for *sportulae* for their members and for the town's decurions.[30] The latter sum is one-half the required property qualification for magistrates in municipalities; at Ostia itself it is equalled by only one other capital fund, donated by a member of the governing class.[31] A Puteolan Augustalis reconstructed a basilica in marble, apparently at his own expense.[32] By the time of Domitian, treasurers of the Ostian Augustales, of whom there were annually no fewer than four and at times as many as eight, paid HS 10,000 for the privilege of holding that office, and in addition to these sums, one Ostian *curator* contributed ten pounds of silver to his town, and a *viritim* cash donation as well.[33] How far this pattern held true also at Puteoli is not possible to judge, though there too *curatores* are attested, one of whom held office for forty-five years.[34]

Size of tomb plots and the tomb decoration—when known; there is no evidence from Puteoli—can also be a helpful economic indicator. The Ostian tomb of L. Marrius Aquila, an early Augustalis whose

28. No. 13; no. 33; no. 69; *CIL* XIV, 5345; no. 49; no. 95; no. 103; no. 11. On the *fabri tignarii* see Meiggs, *RO*[2], pp. 319–321, 330–331; for an up-to-date list of the presidents, see A. Licordari (above, note 27), pp. 322–323.

29. No. 67; no. 22; no. 4; no. 27; no. 42; no. 108; no. 81; Q. Aquilius (unpublished), no. 12.

30. No. 60; no. 117; *CIL* XIV, 431; on which see Duncan-Jones, *ERE*, p. 285; Meiggs, *RO*[2], p. 221.

31. *CIL* XIV, 353 = *ILS* 6148; see also Duncan-Jones, *ERE*, p. 176 (no. 672). Not surprisingly, the donor was himself a freedman, L. Fabius Sp. f. Eutychus, who rose to the presidency of the builders: Meiggs, *RO*[2], p. 211; *AJP* 97 (1976), pp. 400–401.

32. *CIL* X, 1838.

33. Meiggs, *RO*[2], p. 218; cf. *ILS* 7812. Donation of silver: no. 42.

34. *Curatores:* no. XVI, no. VII; forty-five years: no. XIV.

affluence is attested also by other evidence, measured 2400 square Roman feet.[35] We must allow for the possibility that large plots were more readily available, and less costly, in the early Empire; but in the second century the magnificent tombstone of a rich officer in the association of Adriatic shippers included a plot of 2100 square feet; and in the early years of the third century an enclosure of 1920 square feet is known.[36] In all, thirty-two Ostian Augustales have indicated the size of their burial spaces. The 1240 square feet which enclosed the earthly remains of L. Rennius Platanus and his dependents is fairly typical of the tomb plots of the Ostian Augustales, and exceeds by more than 400 square feet that of a representative sample of other Ostian freedmen.[37]

The epitaphs, further, provide evidence for Augustales' simultaneous involvement in multiple economic pursuits. Some freedmen list two or more professions (the Puteolan [figure 20] and Ostian discussed above),[38] or offices in more than one *collegium*: a Puteolan was patron of both *navicularii* and *utricularii*, while at Ostia men were simultaneously officers of the grain measurers and the *codicarii*, whose function was to transport food supplies up the Tiber to Rome; of the builders and boat builders; or of the builders and wine traders.[39] Another Ostian was both a *negotiator* in wine and a *navicularius*, holding office in the *collegium* of the Adriatic shippers.[40] It is occasionally possible to trace the multiple interests of other Augustales more indirectly, through coincidences of their names with those of members of certain Ostian *collegia*.[41] We should know still more about the possible combination

35. No. 79.

36. *FA* 8 (1956), p. 272, no. 3680; Meiggs, *RO*², p. 276 (Adriatic shipper); no. 103 (third century evidence).

37. L. Rennius Platanus (unpublished), no. 96. The largest attested Ostian plot is that of the Augustalis C. Novius Trophimus (no. 86): 290 feet across the front, extending *in agro* for two and one-half *iugera*. For large burial spaces of freedmen not Augustales, cf. *CIL* XIV, 730, 736, 5026. For a first attempt to exploit such evidence as this, see M. Cébeillac, *MEFR* 83 (1971), pp. 39ff.

38. Above, Chapter 5, section II, and note 25.

39. Puteolan: no. XXII; *mensores frumentarii* and *codicarii*: no. 22, not noticed by Meiggs, who however observes elsewhere that the two professional groups are joined together in other evidence (*RO*², p. 293); builders and boatbuilders: no. 69; builders and wine-traders: *Rend. Acc. Linc.* 29 (1974), pp. 313–314.

40. *CIL* VI, 9682.

41. E.g., the M. Cornelii associated with the *corpus lenunculariorum: AJP* 97 (1976), pp. 399–400; or the Q. Plarii associated with the *fabri navales: NdSc.* 1953, pp. 282–285 (no. 43).

of freedmen's trading activities if more tombs survived of the type illustrated by one of those at Isola Sacra, where twin terracotta plaques represent, respectively, a harbor tugboat in action and a grain mill in operation: Ti. Claudius Eutychus, the deceased, was presumably active in both of these trades (figures 21, 22).[42]

Some Augustales pursued profits over distances, employing numerous dependents to carry out their aims. Wine importers from Rome did business side by side with Ostian importers: the Augustalis L. Carullius Felicissimus, who had trading connections with both groups, employed a freedman who must often have been on the road.[43] Membership in the Augustales of two towns in close geographical proximity implies trading interests of regional, not merely local significance: Puteolans are found holding offices simultaneously at Cumae, Naples, and Venafrum, whereas two Ostians were Augustales at Tusculum as well as in their home city.[44] Collocation in the texts of names of cities widely dispersed implies a more complex network of commercial organization. The funeral monument of Q. Capito Probatus Senior is in Lyon, his *patria*, but he was Augustalis both at Lugdunum and Puteoli, and a resident of Rome; we know, too, of a patron of several groups of Gallic traders, who was treasurer of the Puteolan Augustales.[45] This evidence is suggestive of the widespread trading tentacles of others who, like Probatus, declare themselves to be *navicularii marini*.[46] A *negotiator ex Hispania citeriore* came to Ostia, enriched himself in trade with the place he had left, and became respectably established in his new surroundings.[47] The existence at Ostia of a corporation of *navicularii maris Hadriatici* implies an organized system of distant commercial exchange which is confirmed by recent archaeological discoveries at Ostia; it was by such means as this that A. Caedicius Successus amassed his wealth.[48]

42. H. Thylander, *Inscriptions du port d'Ostie* (Lund 1952), vol. 1, p. 64 (A 61); Meiggs, *RO*[2], notes on pl. xxviii.

43. No. 27; Meiggs, *RO*[2], pp. 282–283.

44. Cumae: no. VIII; Naples: no. III; Venafrum: no. XXX; Tusculum: no. 67, no. 106.

45. Probatus: no. X; the patron: no. XXII.

46. No. X.

47. No. 87.

48. The new evidence, which includes a magistrate of Vicetia domiciled at Ostia, is presented and analyzed by M. Cébeillac-Gervasoni and F. Zevi, *MEFR* 88 (1976), pp. 610–611; A. Caedicius Successus (unpublished), no. 19.

The Ostian grave of the A. Manlii includes an A. Manlius Ɔ. l. Putiolanus (*sic*).[49] The reciprocal commercial relationships between Ostia and Puteoli are difficult to visualize, even though voyages by sea between the two ports were regular and were completed in just over two days, as Philostratus confirms;[50] the linkages must normally be plotted through the inscriptions of small men whose names recur in both ports, and the hazards of inferences based on coincidences of nomenclature are notorious. But the recent publication of an Ostian epitaph illustrates what must have been a common phenomenon: the deceased declares, "[*Natus eg*]*o in patriam, Puteolana stirpe creatus, selecta mihi domus est Ostia felix.*"[51] C. Domitius Primus also records his experiences in both regions.[52] Those have a flavor more hedonistic than lucrative, but the mention of members of the *gens Messia* on his inscription helps to establish the Ostian ambience of another epitaph found in Puteoli[53] which implies that the Ostian pursued commercial interests in both ports.

In freedmen's epitaphs, the deceased normally provided for "freedmen, freedwomen, and their descendants." The formula is too generic to illustrate employment patterns precisely, but it does confirm in a general way the established Roman practice: freedmen employed freedmen of their own to carry out their objectives.[54] That a man was actually employed by a freedman *patronus* is patent in those cases where the *libertus* commemorates a former master who was active in commerce and manufacture (we have one Puteolan example and four from Ostia),[55] or in those, far more frequent, where the *patronus* makes provision to include specifically named freedmen and *vernae*, personal slaves born in the household, in his own burial space. At Ostia C. Tuccius Eutychus mentions ten freedmen by name;[56] in nine other texts the numbers range from five to one. These include one freedman dependent who is specifically commended as an *adiutor abstinens*,[57]

49. *CIL* XIV, 1305.

50. Philos. *Vit. Apoll.* 7.16.

51. G. Barbieri, "Una nuova epigrafe d'Ostia e ricerche sugli acrostici," *IV Miscellanea greca e romana*, Ist. ital. stor. ant. (Rome 1975), pp. 301ff.

52. *CIL* XIV, 914.

53. *CIL* X, 2735.

54. Cf. above Chapter 2, section III; Chapter 5, section II, and note 30.

55. Puteoli: no. VIII; Ostia: no. 65, no. 86, no. 27, no. 15.

56. No. 110.

57. A. Egrilius Primigenius Minor (unpublished), no. 52.

a man with four named freedmen and three wards,[58] and the monument of the affluent L. Calpurnius Chius, who names two freedmen, two *vernae* subsequently freed, and one *verna* who was still a slave at the time the monument was inscribed.[59] The practice of freeborn Ostians in both respects helps to place the activities of our freedmen in perspective: one magistrate, P. Aufidius Fortis, is commemorated by four freedmen; another freeborn Ostian provides for four *liberti* on his tomb.[60] But the Augustalis A. Livius Chryseros received a monument from five freedmen who give their names.[61] As regards these employment patterns, no clear line separates prominent freedmen from members of the ruling class.

III

The prominence of the *ordo Augustalium* within these cities ought to be reflected also by individual careers, and again several indices assist evaluation of social standing. *Ornamenta decurionatus* were reserved for wealthy and prominent freedmen whose background in slavery prohibited them from holding local magistracies. Three instances are attested at Ostia: one man was an imperial freedman who had been *procurator annonae*; the second, M. Licinius Privatus, was a donor of HS 50,000 to the city treasury; the third, also a president of the builders, was a president of the Augustales.[62] Second, the voting by the governing council of a public funeral was a mark of distinction which a city magistrate and benefactor, like P. Lucilius Gamala, might expect as a matter of course: it is far more unusual to find freedmen similarly honored, but Augustales received the privilege at Ostia.[63] Third, whereas the highest offices within *collegia* were regularly held by members of the Augustales, patrons of these associations were normally drawn from the senatorial and equestrian orders of Rome. This fact places the significance of T. Testius Helpidianus' patronate of an Ostian ferry service in considerably higher relief.[64]

58. A. Egrilius Polytimus (unpublished), no. 51.

59. No. 22.

60. *CIL* XIV, 4621 (Aufidius Fortis); No. 74.

61. No. 71.

62. Meiggs, *RO*[2], p. 514; and see now *AJP* 97 (1976), p. 411.

63. Gamala: *CIL* XIV, 375. Augustales: no. 100; possibly also Q. Vergilius Marianus (*NdSc.* 1953, p. 303, no. 71: see *AJP* 97 [1976], p. 410).

64. Senatorial and equestrian patrons: *CIL* XIV, 246, 247; the reasons for the association of such notables with Ostia, though obscure (cf. Meiggs, *RO*[2], p. 316),

For social patterns, the marriage ties of Augustales are perhaps most instructive. From Ostia there are three examples[65] in which freedmen married women who were freeborn, and hence, presumably, their social as well as their juridical superiors. But the sample is small. A different and more valuable index is available. Thirty-eight of 113 Ostian Augustales known from the epitaphs, and 9 of 30 Puteolans, mention their wives by name. In 21 Ostian instances, better than half of the cases, and in two-thirds of the Puteolan examples, the *nomen gentilicium* of the wife is different from that of the Augustalis.[66] Yet from random samplings of hundreds of other freedmen's inscriptions from both cities, more than 90 percent of husbands and wives bore the same *nomen gentilicium*. Here is proof that in both ports, significant numbers of Augustales forged marriage ties outside of the *familia* in which they had labored as slaves, and that they were able to do so in far greater proportion than the other freedmen from these cities. These findings have further implications, to be discussed below.

It is well known that whereas the freedman was legally prohibited from holding local magistracies, a freeborn son was not: parental pride in a son's achievement, or a son's ascent to a level of superior status, are reflected in inscriptions on both tombstones and funerary altars in the Roman West. What was the rate of upward social mobility? The relevant inscriptional evidence from the Italian ports of Ostia and Puteoli was first analyzed nearly fifty years ago, when one scholar concluded that by the second half of the second century approximately one-third of the members of the ruling class in such cities were the sons of freedmen; her figure was 25 percent for an inland city like Beneventum.[67] In recent years, interest in the problem has revived, with no agreement reached. Two analyses of the same evidence from Beneventum produce widely divergent conclusions,[68] and the broader

---

may be economic: see below, Chapter 7. T. Testius Helpidianus: no. 108; his status is, surprisingly, ignored in a recent comprehensive study of patrons of *collegia*: G. Clemente, "Il patronato nei *collegia* dell'impero romano," *Studi Class. Orient.* 21 (1972), pp. 201–206.

65. Q. Aquilius (unpublished), no. 12; no. 17; no. 48.

66. See Appendix, Part II.

67. M. L. Gordon, "The Freedman's Son in Municipal Life," *JRS* 21 (1931), pp. 65–77.

68. 8%: H. W. Pleket, "Sociale stratificatie en sociale mobiliteit in de romeinse keizertijd," *Tijdschrift voor Geschiedenis* 84 (1971), pp. 215–251, esp. p. 244; 25 percent: P. W. Garnsey, "Descendants of Freedmen in Local Politics: Some Criteria,"

socio-economic significance of the conclusions are equally divergent: high percentages have been used to support the notion of a peaceful "penetration" of the ruling class in municipalities by men of servile descent;[69] low percentages confirm a view of Roman imperial cities as places where leadership was monopolized, "generation after generation," by a narrow circle.[70] The Ostian and Puteolan information is unlikely, in itself, to resolve such wide disparities; but some of it is new, and a fresh assessment may help to define more clearly the terms of the discussion, by highlighting problems of method which deserve to be made explicit.

The first need is to distinguish individual unambiguous cases of advancement from the ambiguous ones, the next to suggest criteria by which ambiguous cases may be interpreted. At Puteoli N. Naevius Vitulus, at Ostia Cn. Sergius Priscus, C. Silius Nerva, and P. Attius Silianus were all Augustales' sons who achieved magistracies or priesthoods; the cases are unambiguous because the freedman father and his successful son are mentioned in the same texts.[71] Similarly unambiguous is the statement in the inscription honoring the Ostian freedman M. Licinius Privatus that he was "father and grandfather of councillors, father of Roman knights."[72]

On the other hand, when an Augustalis is named in one inscription, and a local notable with the same praenomen and *nomen gentilicium* is known from another text, and there are further no internal or other indicators as to the precise dates of the two inscriptions, the relationship between the two men is ambiguous. The freedman may be the father of the magistrate, but he may also be his freedman: this was certainly the relationship between the Ostian Augustalis Sex. Avienus Nico and a similarly named decurion, since the latter's inscription mentions both men.[73] What criteria, then, may be used to determine the relationship, at Puteoli, between the Augustalis L. Plutius Euty-

---

in *The Ancient Historian and His Materials, Essays in Honour of C. E. Stevens* (Farnborough 1975), pp. 167–180, esp. 178.

69. M. L. Gordon (above, note 67), p. 65.

70. MacMullen, *RSR*, pp. 97–101; q.v. also for excellent formulation of the complex issues.

71. No. XXV; no. 97; no. 100; no. 14; cf. the unpublished example of the P. Celerii discussed by Meiggs, *RO²*, p. 205.

72. *CIL* XIV, 374 (= *ILS* 6165).

73. *CIL* XIV, 4623; cf. *CIL* XIV, 4562, 3 col. II, line 20, discussed in *AJP* 97 (1976), pp. 396–397.

chio and L. Plutius L. f. Pal. Phoebus, who made a dedication to Trajan in 112;[74] or, at Ostia, that between the Augustalis P. Ostiensis Thallus and P. Ostiensis Macedo, *Pontifex Volcani* at the end of the first century?[75] At Ostia, the problem is one of considerable proportions: we know the names of 114 Augustales from the epitaphs, and those of 134 local notables from the Augustan Age and later. In 42 cases, better than 30 percent of our surviving sample, there is a coincidence of Augustales' praenomina and nomina with those of members of the governing class. How many of these were the forbears, how many the freedmen, of notables?

Criteria can hardly be said to be definitive, but some guidelines may nevertheless be suggested. As a preliminary, however, certain statistics from the epitaphs themselves, which count cumulatively against mobility, should be considered. Some successful sons of freedmen reached only the threshold of local office before their death—at Ostia, typical appointments are to preliminary posts in the priesthood of Vulcan.[76] Others died young (attested ages are nineteen, fourteen, twelve, and eight).[77] In at least some cases we must allow for the possibility that the honors awarded were *post mortem*, and were atypical, a special gesture of consolation (*solacium*) by the *decuriones* who may have anticipated resulting benefactions from the freedman father.[78] Freeborn sons of freedmen died before any office is attested for them: the phrase *parentes superstites* recurs.[79] Five Augustales name only daughters in their epitaphs, and fourteen mention no children at all.[80] It is hard to

74. No. XXVII; cf. *CIL* X, 1633.
75. No. 88; the name of Macedo, who must have been descended from a public slave, is known from the Fasti; see Meiggs, *RO*[2], pp. 204–205.
76. P. Attius Silianus, *praetor sacris Volcani faciundis*, predeceased his freedman father: no. 14; A. Fabius Felicianus died after the aedileship in the cult, at age 19 (*CIL* XIV, 351); another praetor died during his fifth year: *CIL* XIV, 306 (= *ILS* 6143); for the cult and the preliminary offices, see Meiggs, *RO*[2], pp. 177–178.
77. *CIL* XIV, 351 (death at age nineteen, on the threshold of office); *CIL* XIV, 400, 401 (an *eques* who died at age fourteen); *CIL* XIV, 341 (= *ILS* 6144) (an *eques* who died in his thirteenth year); *CIL* XIV, 793 (an *ingenuus* who died before his ninth year).
78. *CIL* XIV, 321: a public funeral for an eighteen year old, *decurionum decreto decurio allectus*; cf. also *CIL* XIV, 353, 4642: a public funeral for C. Domitius Fabius Hermogenes, *in solacium Fabi patris*—and the father was a *libertus*. For other examples, cf. Gordon (above, note 67), p. 67.
79. *CIL* XIV, 400, 401, although this fourteen year old had already been designated *equo publico*.
80. Daughters: C. Agrius Felix (unpublished), no. 5; Clodius Lucrio, no. 36;

know how much weight one ought to assign to such facts as these, especially since we have no way of establishing the death rate in these port cities, where the population was fluid and cosmopolitan and the urban density pronounced.[81] Collectively, these factors must have constituted some kind of impediment to the upward mobility of the descendants of freedmen, and must therefore count as a negative valence in individual ambiguous cases.

There are three types of case in which we have no scope for inferring whether the relationship between individuals was one of paternity or patronage. In the first type, the combination of the initial names of freedmen is particularly common: C. Julius and P. Aelius are imperial names; L. Pomponius is undistinctive.[82] A second class of names is difficult owing to the well-known Ostian tendency for patterns of nomenclature to cluster and repeat themselves, especially within the *collegia*.[83] The M. Cornelii associated with the *lenuncularii tabularii* are a particularly instructive illustration of the hazards in identifying persons who happen to be homonymous; and consequently the connection between the Augustalis M. Cornelius Epagathus, and a similarly named decurion and Roman knight cannot be specified.[84] Third, we must often remain similarly agnostic about patterns of relationship

---

C. Iulius Rammius Eutychus, no. 65; L. Marrius Aquila (unpublished), no 79; C. Similius Philocyrius, no. 103. No children: T. Annius Victor, no 9; P. Aelius Agathemerus (unpublished), no 2; Q. Aeronius Antiochus, no. 4; C. Baebius Eucharistus, no. 17; D. Nonius Hermes, no. 83; C. Novius Trophimus, no. 86; Q. Plarius Herclianus (unpublished), no. 90; L. Pomponius Celsus, no. 91; L. Publicius Eutyches, no. 92; L. Rennius Platanus (unpublished), no. 96; C. Silius Iucundus, no. 101; C. Statilius Crescens Crescentianus, no. 106; Cn. Villius Hilarus, no. 118; L. Voluseius Dius, no. 119.

81. As Meiggs notes (*RO²*, p. 233), Ostia must have been particularly vulnerable to epidemics, but only one death is explicitly ascribed to *dira pestis* (*CIL* XIV, 632). Galen reports that doctors at Ostia and Portus informed him of their more unusual cases: this seems to imply a close working relationship between professionals, and mutual respect (Galen [Kühn] xviii, 348). For urban density, see Meiggs, *RO²*, pp. 533–534 (arguments for a population of between 50,000 and 60,000 in the Antonine Age); pp. 585–586 (focusing on the problem of the accommodation for slaves). For repercussions at Ostia of the famous plague which occurred under Marcus Aurelius, there is no evidence known to me: see in general J. F. Gilliam, "The Plague under Marcus Aurelius," *AJP* 82 (1961), pp. 225–251.

82. Nos. 62, 63, 64, 65 (C. Iulii); no. 2 (P. Aelius); no. 91 (L. Pomponius: cf. the name of the *IIvir* of 145, Meiggs, *RO²*, p. 512).

83. F. H. Wilson, *PBSR* 13 (1935), pp. 65–66; cf. Meiggs, *RO²*, p. 323.

84. Augustalis: no. 42; Decurion: *CIL* XIV, 341; see further *AJP* 97 (1976), pp. 399–400.

in certain of Ostia's most prominent families. Ten Augustales are A. Egrilii.[85] The family is one of the best known and influential in early imperial Ostia; it produced eight known *duoviri* between 6 and 146, and figured prominently in Roman government by the time of Hadrian; its freedmen are known by the scores, distributed throughout the most important *collegia*.[86] Or the A. Livii, who held Ostia's chief magistracies in 105 and 146; their known freedmen number more than forty; six of these were Augustales.[87] Where there are enough instances of the name to study onomastic patterns in some detail, and where there is dated evidence indicating a wide chronological distribution among examples, hypotheses about relationships between any one Augustalis and any one magistrate are especially ill-advised.

On the other hand, these last named cases present a special opportunity as well as challenge, precisely because of the frequency of their occurrence; and onomastic patterns can assist in establishing direct linear descent. Recent prosopographical work on the A. Livii may serve as a case in point. The grandmother of P. Nonius P. f. Pal. Livius Anterotianus, decurion and knight, was a Livia, and it has now been established that his grandfather was A. Livius Anteros, Augustalis; though the upward mobility of the family required three generations, it was compressed within a narrow time span, between the early 140s and 170.[88] The Augustalis L. Florius Euprepes, we now know, was grandfather of the homonymous *duovir* of 251, as was Q. Veturius Socrates of the other *duovir* of that year.[89]

Moreover, the son of this last freedman, Q. Veturius Felix Socrates, was a decurion.[90] When combinations of names are unusual, or the cognomina of magistrates are Greek, hellenized, and regularly associated with freedmen, or the magistrate's tribe is Palatina, or finally,

85. Nos. 46–55.

86. See in general Meiggs, *RO*[2], pp. 502–507; pp. 583–584, with many revised conclusions in the light of F. Zevi, *MEFR* 82 (1970), pp. 279ff.

87. For the magistrates of the family, see Meiggs, *RO*[2], p. 202; I count forty three humble A. Livii among the Ostian *sepulchrales*. Unlike the A. Egrilii, however, they are not found distributed among the Ostian guilds, and no illustrious A. Livii are found in Rome. Augustales: nos. 68–74.

88. Augustalis: no. 69. His descendant, adopted by a P. Nonius: A. Licordari, "Considerazioni sull'onomastica ostiense," *L'onomastique latine*, Centre national de la recherche scientifique (Paris 1977), pp. 242–243; *AJP* 97 (1976), p. 402.

89. Euprepes: *CIL* XIV, 4562.2, line 11; his descendants: *AJP* 97 (1976), p. 393. Q. Veturius Socrates: no. 117; See *AJP* 97 (1976), pp. 395–396.

90. Q. Veturius Q. f. Felix Socrates: no. 117; cf. *AJP* 97 (1976) pp. 395–396.

the cognomen of a magistrate has been made respectable, the possibility of a paternal connection or linear relationship between the bearers is greatly increased.[91] L. Combarisius Vitalis, who held all the Ostian offices in the Severan period, was in Palatina, and the name is rare at Ostia; even if the Augustalis L. Combarisius Hermianus was not his father, the magistrate's nomenclature has a suspiciously servile flavor.[92] As does that of Cn. Haius Pudens, councillor of Puteoli: Cn. Haius Doryphorus the Augustalis and *purpurarius* is likely to have been a forbear.[93] The Augustales of Ostia dedicated a statue after 211 to L. Licinius L. f. Pal. Herodes; this and the *duovir*'s tribe have led one scholar to postulate a background in slavery.[94] A L. Licinius Blastus, in fact, was a high official among the local Augustales in 196: chronological considerations, and other indicators, suggest that he was the parent of Herodes.[95] A freedman father was named Moschus at Puteoli; his son, a decurion, bore the cognomen Vitulus: it is a fair surmise that there were close family ties, at Ostia, between the Augustalis Cn. Sergius Anthus and [Cn.] Sergius Florus, the *duovir* of 53.[96]

Employing such criteria as these, we can be reasonably certain that in other comparable cases[97] the local notables were descendants of local freedmen, and that the ambiguous cases of L. Plutius Phoebus and P. Ostiensis Macedo mentioned earlier in this section are resolvable: both will have been the descendants of freedmen.

In the end, the limitations of our evidence, which consists entirely of individual examples, are a strong impediment to expressing any general conclusions in statistical terms. On balance the results seem to suggest that "the freedman's son and grandson in municipal life" was a historical phenomenon of genuine importance in these imperial

91. For a recent attempt to exploit such criteria, with positive results, see P. W. Garnsey (above, note 68), pp. 169–178.

92. Vitalis: *CIL* XIV, 335; Hermianus: no. 37.

93. Pudens: *CIL* X, 1786; Doryphorus: no. XIII; see further *JRS* 64 (1974), p. 110.

94. Meiggs, *RO*[2], p. 210.

95. *CIL* XIV, 4562.1, line 9; on which see *AJP* 97 (1976), p. 393.

96. Puteoli: no. XXV, on which see *JRS* 64 (1974), pp. 110–111; Ostia: no. 97 (which demonstrates that at least one son of Anthus, Cn. Sergius Priscus, reached the threshold of local office). Cn. Sergius Florus: Meiggs, *RO*[2], p. 517.

97. The fragmentary Egrilii of no. 53 are probably members of the same family; cf. also nos. 55 (other A. Egrilii), 81 (cf. *CIL* XIV, 4553, M. Marii), 112 (cf. the Ostian Fasti for 145, P. Turranii), 114 (L. Valerii). Observe also the magistrate of *CIL* XIV, 390, 391; what was his relationship with no. 85 (P. Nonius Zethus)?

ports, that the prospects for the sons of Augustales were especially favorable, and that the actual cases of such assimilation were far more numerous than are the surviving unambiguous examples which attest it. Were this not so, especially in the second century, Tacitus could hardly make a senator say, in the time of Nero, that many *equites*, even many senators, were the descendants of slaves.[98] But to place the problem for these cities in proper perspective its overall dimensions need to be outlined: the proportion of Augustales in the major ports— Ostia, Puteoli, Aquileia—with praenomina and nomina the same as those of members of the governing class, is approximately one-third at Ostia; elsewhere the ratios are considerably lower. If the surviving samples faithfully reflect the historical situation—and in our records of both Augustales and local notables there are of course many lacunae—one implication for the local societies is of some interest: while the governing class and the leading freedmen formed overlapping circles, not all Augustales were freedmen of notables, nor did they all feed into the governing class. This finding is best elucidated in a different context, that of the predominant patterns of interaction between these local freedmen and their patrons.

IV

As we have seen, the Ostian and Puteolan Augustales were both economically active and socially respectable, at least to a considerable degree. The social and economic significance of manumission in these cities may now be analyzed. How far did the escape from slavery enable these freedmen to become genuinely free to pursue their money-making and other activities, and how far did former masters continue to exercise control? Trimalchio inherited from his master, was encouraged to accumulate wealth, and was able to transmit it to his heirs; what of the Augustales in these ports? The questions are more easily asked than answered, but their importance for the present study is large. If the freedmen who were active in the commercial and manufacturing ventures here described were predominantly promoting, as personal representatives, the interests of their former masters, profits must have remained predominantly under the patron's control; this in turn ought to have favored, in these cities, the continuing domination of a relatively few powerful families, who not only controlled the means of production and the distribution of articles of trade, but also continued

98. Tac. *Ann.* 13.27.

to reserve for themselves the powers and privileges of local office. If, on the other hand, freedmen or a substantial number of freedmen operated in an atmosphere of independence, accumulating wealth either separately from or in competition with their patrons, one anticipates a different set of social consequences, including a more open governing class, whose composition was socially more heterogeneous. One scholar has asserted that "a weakening of class barriers is to be expected in a trading city";[99] another has claimed that "the extensive commercial use of freedmen tended to assist the domination of a few large families."[100] The two propositions are incompatible when cities are commercial in character; which better fits the actual historical situations in the ports?

We have reviewed in earlier chapters the legal provisions and social conventions according to which an ex-slave continued to provide services for his former master,[101] and this must also have been a frequent practice in the ports. Freedmen Sex. Fadii appear at Ostia, one of them an Augustalis; they were in all probability planted there by their rich patron, a Gallic shipper, and their function will have been to watch over the cargoes of his Spanish wine which was en route to Rome.[102] When Augustales are mentioned with other members of the *familia* in the epitaphs of their former masters or when we have other means of knowing that they were buried within their patrons' family tombs, it is probably safe to infer the continuing dependence of the freedman after manumission.[103] C. Prastina Pacatus Messallinus, the Antonine consul, has a rare and distinctive name which is seldom found outside Rome except among small freedmen in Puteoli and Ostia, where he had property:[104] these *liberti* were probably advancing the interests of their patron, not acting independently. Augustales with

99. Meiggs, *RO*², p. 230 (describing conditions in second century Ostia).

100. M. W. Frederiksen, *PBSR* n. s. 14 (1959), p. 111 (the historical context is the late Republican and Julio-Claudian period).

101. Above, Chapter 2, section III; Chapter 5, section II, and refs. in note 30.

102. Ostian Sex. Fadii: *CIL* XIV, 994–996; cf. also *CIL* VI, 17651, 26537. The Augustalis: *CIL* XIV, 4563.5, line 49; for the shipper, Sex. Fadius Secundus Musa, see H. de Villefosse, "Deux armateurs narbonais," *Mem. Soc. Nat. Antiq. France* 74 (1914), pp. 153–180; see further T. Frank, *JRS* 27 (1937), pp. 72–79; Meiggs, *RO*² p. 289. For further discussion, see below, Chapter 7, section I.

103. E.g., the A. Caesennii, freedmen of L. Fabricius L. f. Caesennius Gallus: *CIL* XIV, 354, with the discussion in *AJP* 97 (1976), pp. 391–393.

104. *PIR* P, 686 (*cos. ord.* 147); for his Ostian connections, see Hanslik, *RE* 22 (1954), 1721; *CIL* XV, 2189 (*praedia* at Ostia), *CIL* XIV, 4557, with Wickert's com-

small or humble burial places, provided by their wives or other relatives, may have been acting independently—but this seems immaterial, if their assets were in fact as small as they appear to be.[105]

"Dependent" and "independent" are, however, relative terms, and hardly precise; and our problem is complicated by the fact that descriptions of freedman/patron relationships in modern works tend to be "patron-oriented"; either the ex-slave's functions are imagined as remaining essentially the same as those which he performed as a slave, or, at the other end of the spectrum, *liberti* are conceived as performing more responsible tasks, but tasks imposed by the patrons, primarily to the patron's economic (and other) advantage.[106]

In fact, in marked contrast with those patrons who continued to control their freedmen by retaining them in personal service or by promoting them to more responsible posts within the *familia*, other masters made provision for testamentary manumission of their slaves, often with accompanying legacies; the frequency of this practice suggests that *libertini orcini*,[107] freedmen of the deceased, formed a substantial group. We may also envisage another, whose patrons were still alive but had voluntarily relinquished the authority which, by law and by custom, they were entitled to exercise over *liberti*. Together, the two groups comprise a pool of candidates which, theoretically at least, might make up a category of independent freedmen. That, again theoretically, the category might be a substantial one is suggested by legal evidence. Passages from the *Digest* indicate a wide range of possible patterns of interaction between *patronus* and *libertus*—from situations

---

ments *ad loc.*; XIV, 4571 f II 4; XIV, 1505–1507, and especially *CIL* XIV, 4562.6 line 18: one of the *quinquennales* of the seviri Augustales in 228. Puteoli: *CIL* X, 2888. The man's full name was C. Ulpius Pacatus Prastina Messallinus: W. Eck, *RE*, suppl. 14 (1974), 478 (discussed further below, chapter 7, section I).

105. E.g., nos. 46, 84, 93.

106. Cf. F. H. Wilson, *PBSR* 13 (1935), p. 66: "Many slaves were manumitted, not as a reward for past services, but in order to enable them to hold more responsible posts in the service of their late masters"; Meiggs, *RO*[2], p. 224 (freedmen managing shops "and the main profits would go to the patron"). Although Keith Hopkins has recently argued that Roman slaves' purchase of their freedom was "very common," his emphasis too is upon the masters and the economic incentives which led them to manumit; he implies the existence of, but does not actually discuss, a category of independent freedmen—a group considerable in size (*Conquerors and Slaves* [Cambridge 1978], pp. 123 ff, 129–132).

107. *Orcini* is the technical term for persons freed upon the death of the testator: persons freed by testament (*manumissio testamento*) were considered as belonging to Orcus, to the realm of the dead.

in which a slave's freedom was conditional upon his guarantee to serve his master as *procurator*, to ones in which freedmen actually competed as rivals with their patrons in business affairs and were provided with protective legal sanctions.[108] *Institores* are a class of business managers whose wide ranging transactions, attested in legal sources, would repay a special study.[109] One aspect of the distinction drawn in the legal texts between *institores* and *procuratores* was that the former had authority to make contracts with third parties which bound both themselves and also their principals, whereas the latter, who were more like household servants, had not. And *institores* could conduct business *inside* the sphere of the *praepositio*, on the principal's account and with results which bound the principal, whereas *procuratores* may not have had such rights—although they could certainly possess their own *familia*, and a business which was financially separate from that of the principal.[110] In other words, a freedman acting as a patron's business representative enjoyed considerable latitude and discretion in conducting his affairs— a latitude entirely compatible with pursuing interests of his own. *Liberti* might enter into private partnerships (*societates*[111]): a legal text reveals two co-freedmen (*colliberti*) joining together in pursuit of profits, with their patron uninvolved in the partnership.[112]

108. Freedom conditional upon serving former masters as procurators: Ulp. *Dig.* 40.2.13 (manumission conditional on magistrate's assent); cf. 40.4.17.1, 40.5.41.15. Freedmen as business rivals: *Dig.* 37.14.2: *Liberti homines negotiatione licita prohiberi a patronis non debent.* Cf. *Dig.* 37.15.11; 37.14.18, and especially *Dig.* 38.1.45: *Libertus negotiatoris vestiarii an eamdem negotiationem in eadem civitate et eodem loco, invito patrono, exercere possit?* [*Scaevola*] *respondit, nihil proponi, cur non possit.* On such economic competition, see further L. Juglar, *Quomodo per Servos Libertosque Negotiarentur Romani* (Paris 1902), pp. 68–70.

109. For the *actio institoria*, for persons who managed businesses on land on behalf of a principal, cf. *Dig.* 14.3.1ff; for the *actio exercitoria*, by which a principal was bound by his business manager (usually the *magister navis*), cf. *Dig.* 14.1.1ff; and see in general A. Berger, *Encyclopedic Dictionary of Roman Law* (Philadelphia 1953), s.v. *exercitor*.

110. *Dig.* 14.3.5.10—a distinction which survived for centuries, before being overturned by Papinian in the Severan period: see *Dig.* 17.1.10.5; M. Kaser, *Das römische Privatrecht*[2], 1 (Munich 1971), p. 608; 2, p. 107n55, with refs. For the implications for freedmen, see the important study by P. W. Garnsey, "Independent Freedmen and the Economy of Roman Italy under the Principate," forthcoming in *Klio* 63 (1981).

111. Above, chapter 2, section III, and notes 104–105; see further, for the legal texts, L. Juglar (above, note 108), chap. 4, "De Societate inter Patronum Libertumque," pp. 70–74.

112. *Dig.* 17.2.71.1.

Since there is no Latin phrase for "independent freedman," the problems in recognizing such individuals are formidable. In our inscriptions we cannot even make clear distinctions between a freedman who was self-employed and one who was employed by another; therefore, a search for ex-slaves who were working simultaneously in their own and in another's interests—we may suspect that such situations comprised the majority—is bound to end in frustration. Yet, given the profitability of commercial and manufacturing ventures during these early centuries of the Empire, all historians today would probably concede that independent freedmen existed. The debate is principally over numbers: were they many, or too few to make an impact on the economy and society? Most are committed to the latter view.[113] But the debate has taken a new turn, now that Garnsey has proposed two rough criteria by which an independent freedman can be identified: substantial wealth and positions of responsibility.[114] Garnsey argued primarily on a general level and was concerned to show that earlier negative conclusions had been reached largely on an intuitive basis; he did not test his criteria by applying them systematically to groups of freedmen about whom something is known in detail.

Herein lies the chief interest of the previous two sections of this study, where we presented the various indices of freedmen's wealth and standing and examined them in two defined urban contexts. We saw, first, that entrance fees, treasurers' fees, and the expenses of benefactions guaranteed that membership in the Augustales was economically beyond the reach of most persons in the cities' work force; second, that these men discharged official functions in the *collegia*;[115] and third, that a high proportion of the wives of Augustales came from *familiae* different from their own, which implies a social and financial condition permitting freedom of choice. Moreover, as many as five Augustales were commemorated by their own freedmen.[116] Such men, the proper conduct of whose businesses required the employment of representatives or agents in distant places, and whose own patrons are not named, clearly operated independently.

113. See, e.g., P. Veyne, "Vie de Trimalcion," *Annales E.S.C.* 16 (1961), pp. 224ff; J. Andreau, *Les affaires de monsieur Jucundus* (Rome 1974), pp. 165ff; MacMullen, *RSR*, pp. 100–105.
114. P. W. Garnsey (above, note 110).
115. Above, section II.
116. Above, section III.

Studies of the form of economic organization in commercial and manufacturing ventures, studies in which the emphasis is on the distribution of certain articles of trade, rather than as here, on the persons engaged in their production and distribution, help us to advance the argument still further. This new work shows that in the lamp business and the production of *terra sigillata*, branch firms were established in places far removed from the original centers of production, and that the branches, while related to one another, operated with a high degree of independence.[117] That is to say, whether the focus be articles traded or the traders of articles, conclusions are converging, and beginning to suggest that in commerce and manufacture, the system of economic organization was more complex, the network of relationships more loosely coordinated than were those common and natural in agricultural production. The financing, manufacture, transport, distribution and marketing of goods were not separate and unrelated processes, but nonetheless occurred across distances which often required the services of independent affiliates rather than those of personal employees under direct control.

Finally, there are those cases in which a freedman, a man of standing, commemorates, or is commemorated by, a man with no discernible family ties with the deceased; the relationship between the two is either left unspecified or defined in terms of friendship. No patrons are named and we are therefore invited to speculate upon the character of the relationship between the deceased and his friend. That they may have been mutually involved in acquisitive pursuits seems a strong possibility, particularly in the light of the finding, discussed above, that relationships with lucrative dimensions tend to be expressed in terms of friendship. Moreover, since *societates* technically terminated on the death of any partner, and a man might be simultaneously active in a number of partnerships, partners (if mentioned on tombstones at all) will appear primarily as friends or heirs of the deceased. Four Ostian examples are interesting in this respect,[118] while at Puteoli one man (figure 20) describes himself as "a friend and heir" of an Augustalis

117. W. V. Harris, "The Organization of the Roman Terracotta Lamp Industry," to appear in *JRS* 70 (1980); he emphasizes that "Roman society and law provided the framework on which a system of branch workshops could be built."

118. Nos. 19, 48, 72, 101. In the last text, future bonds between C. Silius Iucundus and Ti. Claudius Vitalis (who shared a common tomb) appear to be corroborated by *CIL* XIV, 281: a C. Silius C. f. Vitalis.

who had trading interests so highly diversified that, without business associates, it would have been impossible to pursue them.[119]

V

Taken in the aggregate, these and other indicators suggest that a clear majority of the Augustales named in our texts belonged to the category of independent freedmen, in the sense of "independent" employed here: a freedman released from the restricting controls of a former master and his *familia*, and in a position both to accumulate wealth in commercial and manufacturing ventures where success depended upon his own capacities, contacts, and initiative, and to establish and maintain social relationships which were largely of his own choosing. Some of these were the *liberti* of local notables: a detailed prosopographical study of the Ostian A. Egrilii and A. Livii might be expected to provide a useful test of the hypothesis that the freedmen of powerful local families would themselves be in an especially favorable position to achieve independence. Others, however, were the ex-slaves of patrons who stood outside the governing class: the fact that the names of two-thirds of local notables were not repeated among the Augustales suggests that decurions recruited colleagues and successors from a sizeable pool, not only from their own sons and relatives, but also from among families of comparable standing who had migrated to the ports from elsewhere, the process of their elevation to high office being speeded by the mechanism of adoption.[120] These conclusions carry three larger implications, which extend beyond Puteoli and Ostia to a somewhat more distant horizon.

First, the parallels between these actual freedmen, who were juridically, economically, and socially independent of their patrons, and Trimalchio are obvious and close: they suggest that the independent freedman was not as exceptional as he has sometimes been made to appear. The numbers of such men in the two port cities, and their interurban network of interests and contacts, is a clear sign that the

---

119. M. Claudius Trypho (unpublished): No. XI.

120. For the composition of Ostia's governing class, Meiggs, *RO*^{2}, chap. 10 pp. 189–213, is fundamental; on that of Puteoli, see *JRS* 64 (1974), pp. 104–124. Patterns of adoption require a special study; for preliminary remarks, see *AJP* 97 (1976), p. 392 (Ostia); for developments at Pompeii, see P. Castrén, *Ordo Populusque Pompeianus* (= Act. Inst. Rom. Finl. 8) (Rome 1975), pp. 99–100.

group as a whole counted for something in imperial urban centers, to a degree which it is easy to underestimate, if the history of these cities be conceived solely in terms of the local aristocracies and the changing rhythms of their fortunes.

Second, the pattern of independence of freedmen from patrons provides the key to one structural aspect of the institution of the Augustales itself, and also helps to account for the vitality of the institution in the economically active cities of the Roman West through the second century. Many individual Augustales had no patrons, but were often the patrons of other freedmen. In the same way, the institution as institution differs from all *collegia* in that, like the other *ordo* of the city, patrons played no part in their organization—but Augustales are themselves sometimes found acting as patrons of the various *collegia*.[121] In effect, socially and economically, the institution of the Augustales functioned for the independent *liberti* as did the institution of the *familia* for other, less fortunate freedmen: it provided not only social solidarity, but also economic cohesion. In their lavish new Ostian headquarters (figure 23), built during the reign of Marcus Aurelius,[122] and built to last, there was space for the 300 members to banquet, to sacrifice, to undertake acts of corporate munificence. There was opportunity, also, to exchange shipping information derived from various ports, to share news of market rates and property values, to learn of current developments in the building trade, in the ferry services, in naval construction and the other specialized *collegia* where, as individuals, Augustales discharged professional functions, and to sift and synthesize these reports through common discussion in a common meeting place. "Sea captains, traders, and supercargoes from all towns furthered commercial relations, and could be found in exchanges . . . of every port, discussing with one another world markets and the state of trade—mutual interest in the traffic of the Empire [welded the merchants] together into a distinct social group—every

121. There are references still to the *ordo Augustalium* in 182 (no. 60), and in the early third century (*CIL* XIV, 373; for the date, see Meiggs, *RO*², p. 210). The latter inscription, a dedication by the *ordo Augustalium* to L. Licinius Herodes, is the exception which proves the rule: Herodes is referred to, not as patron, but as *optimus civis*. It was long thought that the *fabri tignarii* at Ostia also lacked patrons; but see now Meiggs *RO*², p. 320, with the "revisions," p. 595 *ad loc.* Augustalis as patron of a *collegium*: no. 108 (cited above, section III, note 64).

122. G. Calza, *NdSc.* 1941, pp. 196ff; Meiggs, *RO*², pp. 220–221.

town had a merchants' exchange meeting daily."[123] This is a description of conditions in the preindustrial trading cities in the new world in 1742—Antigua, London, Bristol, Boston, New York, Philadelphia, and Charleston—but despite the exuberance, the distance from Roman imperial society, and the different resonances, there are features and characteristics in common—above all in common with the Augustales, drawn by shared interests into communal association.

Third and finally, it may be tentatively suggested that the findings of the present study have implications for the social structure of Puteoli and Ostia as a whole, possibly also for the cities elsewhere, where prevailing conditions facilitated the accumulation of wealth by multiple means and facilitated its diffusion among different sectors of the population. Whether the freedmen of local notables who had released them from positions of dependence, or the freedmen of others who were outside the local ruling elites, many Augustales, both individually and as an institution, were patronless: this suggests that, collectively, the Augustales constituted a group apart from the city's governing class, rather than one subordinate to it. If this is so, we shall be better prepared, in future studies of Roman cities, to discern more richness and complexity of texture in the social fabric, to identify elements of both continuity and diversity, and to visualize a gradual process of social change in which a nucleus of influential families which dominated the towns under the early Empire became less conspicuous as the fortunes of others, more heterogeneous in geographical and social origin, rose with the outset of the Flavian period. The growth in numbers and importance of the Augustales themselves is a reflection, at an institutional level, of these more general historical developments. With new and better evidence it may someday be possible to demonstrate what can be only provisionally suggested here, that the Augustales are better visualized as standing by the side of, rather than beneath, the cities' governing classes, and that the social structure of some Roman ports is more accurately described as a continuum than as a hierarchy.

123. C. Bridenbaugh, *Cities in the Wilderness: The First Century of Urban Life in America, 1625–1742* (Oxford paperback, 1971; first published 1938), pp. 339–340.

7

Attitudes, Conduct,
and Commercial Organization
in the Early Empire

In the three case studies which make up the final chapters of this book, we analyzed, in carefully defined contexts, the attitudes and money-making activities of some early imperial notables, and more early imperial freedmen. Although wider implications were traced in outline in the final sections of the chapters, these were essentially empirical studies, with rather austere limitations; they did not—nor were they intended to—lead to final paragraphs of broad generalization, in which the defining characteristics and essential structures of imperial economy and society were set forth and summed up as a whole. Hence it may be useful, in conclusion, to seek to relate some of the organizational features of Roman Republican commerce, described in earlier chapters, to the changed conditions of the early Roman Empire.

As a preamble, those economic conditions themselves may be briefly and somewhat panoramically reviewed. The Roman Empire, prodigious in size (map 1), became a monetary unit in the sense that the denarius was everywhere recognized; exchanges in kind were both few and exceptional. Imperial Rome itself was a city almost wholly dependent upon outside trade, and so was bound to concern itself at all levels—governmental and private—with the importing of its needs. Other cities, including those discussed in these pages, were important trading centers; still others—it is enough to peruse the pages of Strabo or Pausanias—were incidentally important for emporia, and even rural Roman towns functioned as markets for the inhabitants of the nearby productive countryside. These rural producers thus had access to money, to the men who specialized in its handling, and to products of urban manufacture. Goods got about: by land, over a comprehensive network of roads (the high costs and inefficiency of Roman land transportation ought not to be exaggerated, as recent studies are beginning to show); by sea, in sophisticated and durably constructed commercial ships, their passages facilitated by the uniform currency and the low customs duties which prevailed throughout the imperial ports. The movers of these goods—luxury products, government supplies, but also less exotic manufactured items—were predominantly the mass of *negotiatores* and *mercatores* whom we find mentioned in inscriptions: most of these men practiced highly diversified trades and only a relatively small number *distinguish* themselves by being traders in more things than one. While I have omitted some and oversimplified other features of what was in fact a far more complicated economic system, these generalizations may help to provide a clearer sense of what I take to be the Empire's characteristics, and help to indicate what Rome had in common with, and in what ways it was distinctive from, other preindustrial economies.[1]

After the annexation of Egypt Alexandrian traders who hailed Augustus at the port of Puteoli left no doubt as to their dependence on the emperor, freely acknowledging that it was "owing to him that they made a living, sailed the seas, enjoying both freedom and fortune."[2] How far, to what degree, in what forms, were the social arrangements which characterized commercial enterprises in the late Republic able to survive under the principate, when one man held the principal power and authority? Above all, what place remained for continued private initiatives, furthered through the *familia*, *clientela*, and *ami-*

1. For recent general appraisals of the Imperial economy, see Duncan-Jones, *ERE*, pp. 1–13; Keith Hopkins, *Conquerors and Slaves* (Cambridge 1978), pp. 15–18; F. De Martino, *Storia economica di Roma antica* 2 (Florence 1980), pp. 217ff. For the view of economic relations between town and countryside adopted here, see J. H. D'Arms, "Rapporti socio-economici fra città e territorio nella prima età imperiale," *Antichità Altoadriatiche* 15 (1979), pp. 549–573; Keith Hopkins, "Economic Growth and Towns in Classical Antiquity," in P. Abrams and E. A. Wrigley, eds., *Towns in Societies* (Cambridge 1978), pp. 35–77; see too the important discussion of G. Pucci, in *DdArch*. 9–10 (1976–1977), pp. 631–647. For the changing conception of the itensity of land transport, see P. W. Garnsey, "Economy and Society of Mediolanum under the Principate," *PBSR* n.s. 44 (1976), pp. 13–27; Hopkins, "Economic Growth," pp. 47–48. Technology of commercial ships: see the refs. collected in Chapter 1 above, note 33. Customs duties (varying usually between 2 percent and 5 percent): S. J. de Laet, *Portorium* (Bruges 1949), p. 242. My conceptions of the standing of independent *negotiatores*, of the scope of their activities, and of the character of their markets, differ substantially from those sketched by (e.g.) A. H. M. Jones in "Ancient Empires and the Economy: Rome," (first publ. 1970), reprinted in P. A. Brunt, ed., *The Roman Economy* (Oxford 1974), pp. 124–129, 137–139.

2. Suet. *Aug.* 98: *per illum se vivere, per illum navigare, libertate ac fortunis per illum frui.*

citia, in a world where both the materials and the means of production and distribution were increasingly under state control, and were dominated by a new kind of *familia*, new clients, and new friends—the personal appointees and lesser functionaries of the emperor?

Some major changes, in fact, have already been described above: the increasing number of new senators whose *patria* was in the provinces, and the emperor's taking on increased responsibility for administration of the major ports, the chief economic arteries. Imperial control and regulation of the money supply, of mines, of the grain trade; of the building industry with its timber, bricks and tiles; of the marble quarries, that source of "prestige" material *par excellence*; the steady accretions, also, through bequests and confiscations, to the emperor's landed estates; the establishment of lucrative equestrian procuratorships, which some men found to be an easier path to riches than the senatorial career; the growth and steady encroachments of the imperial bureaucracy at the expense of the autonomy (including fiscal) of the cities and towns—these are, of course, frequently treated themes of Roman imperial economic history.[3] In relation to these the attitudes and behavior of private individuals will inevitably seem to some to be of minor, even marginal, consequence.

Yet, precisely because of the encroachments of the state at the expense of both private individuals and groups, historians need to be alert to such private initiatives as continued to exist, in order to sense more keenly the social realities, including tensions, of the imperial system. Moreover, the boundary between public and private, in commercial ventures, is at times a fine one, not always easily discerned or defined: the Alexandrian traders owed much to Augustus, yet their words have an unmistakably independent ring, inappropriate, one might surmise, for state employees; furthermore, imperial administrators and private *negotiatores* could be active simultaneously, with interests which overlap and converge.[4] A comprehensive treatment of all the forms of private initiative will not be attempted here; but a brief

3. Provincial senators: above, Chapter 4, section IV; imperial ports: Chapter 6, section I. For private initiative in the imperial grain trade, see the refs. below, note 81; for personal profits from building, see the discussions of Cn. Domitius Afer and of M. Rutilius Lupus below, with notes 22 and 51; for the private sector's considerable role in the marble trade, see now J. B. Ward-Perkins, "The Marble Trade and its Organization," in *Seaborne Commerce*, pp. 325–336. On the Emperor's wealth, see F. Millar, *The Emperor in the Roman World* (Ithaca, N.Y. 1977), pp. 133–201.

4. Above, Chapter 6, section I.

and illustrative review of certain of the main themes developed in earlier chapters will indicate areas where further research may prove productive.

I

In his treatise on peace of mind, the Younger Seneca, alert to the hazards which beset political life under the Julio-Claudian emperors, asserted grimly that inherited wealth (*patrimonium*) was the single greatest source of human misery, worse even than death, pain, fear, or desire.[5] Wealthy members of the governing class indeed had good reason to fear the greed of acquisitive *principes*: when Tacitus cites as remarkable the fact that one nonagenarian senator never incurred the ill-will of any emperor, despite his possession of extraordinary riches (*praecipuae opes*), he was illustrating an exception which proved the rule.[6] Dangers were real; they represent one major difference between the conditions of the late Republic and those of the early principate. All the same, there is nothing to show that the sense of peril substantially altered upper-class attitudes to wealth or, more precisely, succeeded in blunting the desire to acquire riches. The doctrines of *De Tranquillitate Animi* represent one pole of Seneca's thinking; those, however, of *De Vita Beata* accord rather better with Seneca's personal experience, and we are introduced in that work to a *sapiens* with *amplae opes*, including a *domus splendida*.[7]

"Good is the smell of profits, from whatever source derived"; "money should be sought first; virtue after cash."[8] Roman senators, of course, do not espouse or endorse such vulgar maxims. Instead, the morally

---

5. Sen. *Tranq An.* 8.1: *Transeamus ad patrimonia, maximam humanarum aerumnarum materiam.* On Seneca's independence from his principal source at this point in the work, an indication that he wrote with current historical developments very much in mind, see M. T. Griffin, *Seneca: A Philosopher in Politics* (Oxford 1976), p. 314.

6. Tac. *Ann.* 13.30.4: *At L. Volusius egregia fama concessit, cui tres et nonaginta anni spatium vivendi praecipuaeque opes bonis artibus inoffensa tot imperatorum malitia fuerunt.*

7. Sen. *Vit. Beat.* 23.1; 25.1. On Seneca's range of views on the subject of wealth, and for *De Tranquillitate Animi* and *De Vita Beata* as representing extreme positions (the latter most closely in accord with the evidence from Seneca's own life) see Griffin (above, note 5), pp. 303–311.

8. Juv. *Sat.* 14.204–05: *Lucri bonus est odor ex re / qualibet*; Hor. *Ep.* 1.1.53–54: *O cives cives quaerenda pecunia primum est: / virtus post nummos.* Cf. also Juv. *Sat.* 1.110–13.

approved ways of acquiring wealth continue to receive a special emphasis. Tacitus' allusion in one obituary notice to *magnae opes innocenter partae*, his juxtaposition, in another, of *praecipuae opes* and *bonae artes*, are conscious echoes of the Republican aristocratic sentiment discussed at the beginning of Chapter 2.[9] Diligence (*industria*) and thrift (*parsimonia*) are the standard terms used to signal the ways by which a fortune should be increased, honorably and respectably: frequent references in imperial authors recall the sections of Cicero's *De Officiis* reviewed above.[10] And again as in an earlier age, commerce is first among the forms of wealth to be singled out for moral censure. Seneca inveighs against energetic trading, mining, and other pursuits as forms of *avaritia*.[11] Tacitus condemned as sordid huckstering the seaborne trading ventures in which a scion of the late Republican nobility was actively engaged.[12] Apollonius of Tyana, according to Philostratus, reduced a noble young Spartan to tears of shame, by pointing out the depravity of his betraying a distinguished family tradition of land-owning to belong instead "to the ill-starred breed of traders and shippers, who secrete themselves in the hold of a ship and think of nothing but cargoes and petty bills of lading."[13]

The laws prohibiting senators from owning commercial ships were still in force in the early third century.[14] Discussions of an individual senator's ability or inability to accumulate wealth were not thought

9. Tac. *Ann.* 4.44.1 (Cn. Cornelius Lentulus): *Ann.* 13.30.4 (quoted above, note 6). Cf. the funeral eulogy of L. Caecilius Metellus delivered in 221 B.C.: above, Chapter 2, section I, and note 2. The Tacitean parallels with this eulogy were observed also by Harris, *WIRR*, p. 67n3.

10. E.g., Sen. *Ira* 1.10.2 (*industria*): cf. *Ben* 2.27.1 and *Ep. Mor.* 101.2; *Tranq. an.* 11.3; *Vit. Beat.* 23.2. For *parsimonia* in Tacitus see, e.g., *Ann.* 3.55.4 (*domestica parsimonia* ascribed to *novi homines* from the provinces). The word may be applied to cities (*provincialis parsimonia*; Massilia, *Agr.* 4.3) as well as to persons (*longa parsimonia*: L. Volusius Saturninus, *Ann.* 14.56.1). Cf. Cic. *de Off.* 1.92, 2.87, discussed above, Chapter 2, section I.

11. Sen. *Ira* 3.33.4; *Brev. Vit.* 2.1; 7.7; *Const. Sap.* 9.2; *Ben.* 2.17.1–2; 6.38.4; *Ep. Mor.* 4.10–11; see further Griffin (above, note 5), p. 298. For variations on the theme that *avaritia* was Rome's prevailing vice, cf. Hor. *Sat.* 1.4.26; 1.1.23–26; *Ep.* 1.10.30; Seneca also notes the popularity of *sententiae* of Publilius Syrus on the theme (*Ep. Mor.* 108.8). Cf. Vitr. 1.7, for the view that philosophy's most important contribution to the architect is to free him from *avaritia*.

12. Tac. *Ann.* 4.13.2 (on C. Sempronius Gracchus): see above, Chapter 1, section I, and note 8.

13. Philos. *Vit. Apoll.* 4.32, cited also by MacMullen, *RSR*, p. 100; the passage is replete with conventional prejudices.

14. Scaev. *Dig.* 50.5.3, on which see above, Chapter 1, section I, and note 17.

suitable subjects, Tiberius declared, for airing in meetings of the senate.[15] Under Augustus, exiles were not to own more than one ship of
a capacity of one thousand amphorae, or two ships drawn by oars; they
were to possess no more than twenty freedmen or slaves, or to have a
patrimonium of more than HS 500,000.[16]

Yet the need for such restrictions should alert us, as in the case of
others already examined, to the behavior which actually prompted
them. The combined reference in the last passage to ships, freedmen,
and wealth is highly suggestive; equally suggestive is the fact that
the rich nonagenarian whose vast riches, according to Tacitus, were
"acquired by honorable means" was none other than L. Volusius
Saturninus, whose family's diverse economic activities, including
commercial, were exposed in Chapter 3. Would the "sordid huckstering" of C. Sempronius Gracchus, one wonders, be on record at all, had
the man not been called into court on an entirely different pretext?
Would we know of Dio Chrysostom's revenue-producing shops in Prusa
unless, during a crisis in the city, Dio had been called upon to answer
the charge of building for private profit rather than for the public
good?[17]

In fact, relying largely upon the social mechanisms examined earlier—the extended *familia*, *clientela*, and claims of *amicitia*—Roman
aristocrats continued to exploit economic opportunities, especially and
conspicuously linked with the provinces, without compromising their
dignitas. And again as in the late Republic, the combined importance
of tradition, convention, and the law remained considerable in influ-
encing aristocrats to assume an indirect role in commercial operations.
The Younger Pliny, a man intensely conscious of his own dignity, did
not actually buy slaves himself, preferring to enlist the help of a
"friend," a *vir municipalis* of Comum: yet the consular troubled to
inspect his newly acquired possessions, and was not embarrassed to
publicize the fact. Since it was a part of upper-class etiquette for a rich

15. Tac. *Ann.* 2.37–38.

16. Cass. Dio 56.27.3, on which see Rougé, *OCM*, p. 464.

17. L. Volusius Saturninus: Tac. *Ann.* 13.30.4, quoted above, note 6; cf. his *longa parsimonia* (*Ann.* 14.56.1). For the continuity of the family and the multiplicity of the sources of its wealth, see above, Chapter 3, section III. Tacitus on C. Sempronius Gracchus: quoted above, Chapter 1, note 8. The shops of Dio Chrysostom: *Or.* 46.9, on which see C. P. Jones, *The Roman World of Dio Chrysostom* (Cambridge, Mass. 1978), p. 24.

man to pretend that he was not really well-to-do, the character and degree of senators' involvement in money-making ventures usually resist precise documentation. We are often dependent upon the tone of a passage or upon nuance in attempting to reconstruct prevailing attitudes; at times, one can do no more than ask suggestive questions.[18] Nonetheless, in order to make progress, historians must be prepared to try to investigate actual cases.

Under Augustus, there are the Nonii Asprenates, whose name on lead ingots establishes the existence of mining interests in Spain;[19] there is also T. Statilius Taurus (*cos*. II, 26), who may have exported lumber from Dyrrachium to Rome, where his amphitheater, constructed in the Campus Martius, was built in large part by the family's own freedmen, who are prominent in the building trade.[20] Slightly later, M. Valerius Messalla Barbatus owned property in Puteoli which included granaries.[21] Cn. Domitius Afer (*cos. suff*. 39) and his adopted

18. Pliny, the *vir municipalis*, and slaves: Plin. *Ep*. 1.21.2, on which see W. V. Harris, "Towards a Study of the Roman Slave Trade," in *Seaborne Commerce*, p. 132. For wealthy senators' claims that they were men of moderate means, see Plin. *Ep*. 2.4.3: *Sunt quidem omnino nobis modicae facultates*, with the comments of Duncan-Jones, *ERE*, p. 18, and n. 4. The difficulties in extracting detailed information from imperial literature about the sources of wealth of upper-class Romans are typified by the case of Fronto. In his voluminous correspondence he says little about his property, still less about the sources of his income, and yet he was a rich man. His apparent attitude towards his wealth was one of indifference; "as a topic of correspondence it holds no interest for him." See Edward Champlin, *Fronto and Antonine Rome* (Cambridge, Mass. 1980), p. 25. Tacitus is scarcely more forthcoming: see R. Syme, *Tacitus* (Oxford 1958), p. 448. Dio of Prusa claimed not to have been wealthy—yet his estates included pasturelands, vineyards, and arable; he may have been a money-lender; and he paid HS 200,000 for a piece of land near the public baths of the city, building colonnades and retail shops at the site: *Or*. 46.6ff, on which see Jones (preceding note), pp. 6–7.

19. C. Domergue, *Arch. Esp. Arq*. 29 (1966), pp. 41ff; 32 (1969), pp. 159ff, cited also by M. W. Frederiksen, *JRS* 65 (1975), p. 167.

20. For Taurus and Dyrrachium, see *PIR* S, 615 with *CIL* III, 605; for Dyrrachium as a source of timber cf. Rostovtzeff, *SEHRE²*, p. 639n64; p. 650n96 (though R. Meiggs has expressed to me his doubts as to whether timber was being exported from such a distance at so early a date). For the amphitheater, see Cass. Dio 51.23, Suet. *Aug*. 29. The presence of freedmen of the family among the *fabri tignarii* of Rome, and their significance for the family's sources of wealth, have been observed by J. H. More, *The Fabri Tignarii of Rome* (Ph. D. diss., Harvard University, 1969), pp. 126–129.

21. Above, Chapter 4, notes 17, 24; it should be noted that the reference to a *horreum* indicates that the *praedia* were in all probability urban holdings; cf. in general *RE* VIIIA (1955), 129, no. 259; *PIR* V, 88.

sons initiated and developed the serious manufacture of bricks before
40.[22] Those who would hesitate to call this "a 'heavy industry' in the
modern sense" must then invent terminology which describes more
appropriately an enterprise that rapidly came to control most of the
brick production of Italy and remained in the hands of the same family
for a century and a half;[23] those who regard brickmaking as an exception, merely an extension of agriculture and therefore acceptable activity for members of the Roman governing class, will then be obliged
to broaden the category of the exceptional to include other stamped
products of *figlinae*, such as pottery and lamps.[24] C. Sallustius Pas-
sienus Crispus (*cos.* II, 44) possessed a private fortune of HS 200
million, the eleventh largest known under the principate.[25] How much
of this derived from slave trading at Ephesus, where the consul came
to be *patronus* of those *qui in statario negotiantur*,[26] and would Pas-
sienus have permitted such blatant advertisement of the common interests between himself and slave dealers had Ephesus been much
closer to Rome? There are the Hordeonii Flacci, who moved from the
manufacturing center of Capua to the port of Puteoli in the late Republic and produced a Roman consul by the end of Nero's reign.[27]

Palfurius Sura was removed from the senate by Vespasian: the family's amphorae, bricks, and tiles have long been known from evidence
from Istria; they are now known also at Ostia.[28] Many members of the

22. *PIR*[2] D, 126; *CIL* XV, 979–983; H. Bloch, *I bolli laterizi e la storia edilizia
romana* (Rome 1947), pp. 336–337. See now T. Helen, *Organization of Roman Brick
Production* (= Ann. Acad. Sc. Fenn. Diss. Hum. Litt. 5) (Helsinki 1975), pp.
100–102 (but I am not persuaded that the *dominus* regularly mentioned on stamps
was uninterested in brick production); cf., for the chronology of the family's *figlinae
doliare*, M. Steinby, "La cronologia delle figlinae doliare urbane," *Bull. Comm. Arch.
Com. Roma* 84 (1974), pp. 37ff.
23. H. Bloch, *HSCP* 56–57 (1947), p. 2.
24. Cf. the oft-cited pronouncement of T. Frank, (*Economic History of Rome*[2]
[Baltimore 1927], p. 230), "brickmaking is practically the only industry at Rome in
which the aristocrat does not hesitate to display his connections with the profits of a
factory." But observe the objections of T. P. Wiseman, *Mn.* 4th ser., 16 (1963),
p. 276.
25. Duncan-Jones, *ERE*, p. 344, with refs. *ad loc.*; cf. *PIR* P, 109.
26. Keil, *Forschungen in Ephesos* 3, nos. 25, 26 (A.D. 42 or 43); cf. W. V. Harris,
"Towards a Study of the Roman Slave Trade," in *Seaborne Commerce*, p. 130.
27. J. H. D'Arms, "Tacitus, *Hist.* 4.13 and the Municipal Origins of Hordeonius
Flaccus," *Historia* 23 (1974), pp. 497–504.
28. Palfurius Sura, senator: scholiast on Juv. 4.53, cf. Suet. *Dom.* 13.1, Cass. Dio
68.1–2. Distribution of amphorae: C. Panella, *Studi miscellanei* 16, *Ostia*, vol. 2,
Baths of the Swimmer (Rome 1968–1969), pp. 127ff.

familia of A. Caesennius Gallus, suffect consul before 82, were buried in the same tomb at Ostia; what does this imply as to the economic interests of the consul himself?[29] The name of C. Aquillius Proculus appears on a Roman anchor found near Punta Licosa, in Lucania.[30] We should like to know this man's connection with the homonymous consul of 90 and with the later decurion of Puteoli;[31] we should like still more to be able to clarify the nature and extent of his maritime interests. The Sulpicii Galbae, of ancient and impressive lineage, owned commercial warehouses in Rome before their elevation to the principate;[32] later, the consul Q. Tineius Sacerdos Clemens owned Roman repositories where his dependents—assuredly not the consul himself—found lessees for "grain space, lock-up space, close storage, safes, column-safes and space for safes."[33]

At Aquileia, freedmen facilitated the distribution—not only in north Italy—of the jars of wine and oil which came from the estates of C. Laecanius Bassus (*cos. suff.* 40),[34] and of T. Caesernius Macedo, suffect consul at the outset of the reign of Antoninus Pius.[35] Earlier, at Ostia, freedmen of the A. Egrilii are found in quantity, either in the trading *collegia* or, more interestingly, since the consular A. Egrilii held important Roman treasury posts, acting as financiers, *coactores argentarii*.[36] Coastal Minturnae was the city of origin of L. Burbuleius

29. On *CIL* XIV, 354, the epitaph of the Ostian notable L. Fabricius Caesennius Gallus, see *AJP* 97 (1976), pp. 391–393. On the family and origins (Tarquinia?) of A. Caesennius Gallus, see R. Syme, *JRS* 67 (1977), pp. 45–46.

30. P. A. Gianfrotta, "Ancore 'romane': Nuovi materiali per lo studio dei traffici marittimi," in *Seaborne Commerce*, p. 112, and cf. the same author's earlier study, "Un ceppo di C. Aquillio Proculo," *Rivista di Studi Liguri* 40 (1974, publ. 1979), pp. 100–102.

31. Consul: *PIR*² A, 999; decurion: *CIL* X, 1786.

32. For the *horrea Sulpicia* see G. Rickman, *Roman Granaries and Store Buildings* (Cambridge 1971), pp. 171–172.

33. Bruns, *FIRA* 3, 145b; J. A. Crook, *Law and Life of Rome* (London 1967), p. 228. Q. Tineius Sacerdos Clemens (*cos.* 158): *PIR* T, 165; A. Degrassi, *I Fasti consolari dell' impero romano* (Rome 1952), *sub anno*.

34. *PIR*² L, 30, where the frequent finds of stamped amphorae at Tergeste, Pola, Aquileia, Patavium, Vercellae, and Rome (also in Noricum and Pannonia) are emphasized, as well as the presence of family freedmen in the ports. His warehouse in Val S. Pietro is known: see G. Alföldy, *Noricum* (London 1974), p. 112, with refs. collected in n52 (p. 317)

35. T. Caesernius Statius Quinctius Macedo Quinctianus: *PIR*² C, 182; and see above, Chapter 4, section IV.

36. F. Zevi, "Nuovi documenti epigrafici sugli Egrilii ostiensi," *MEFR* 82 (1970), pp. 279ff; Meiggs, *RO*², pp. 583–584: "That the Egrilii drew their wealth from trade

Optatus Ligarianus, the Hadrianic consular; as *curator rei publicae* he discharged his duties in three ports: Terracina, Ancona, and Narbo.[37] What was the relationship between his professional maritime expertise and the private sources of his wealth?

L. Cuspius Pactumeius Rufinus (*cos.* 142) once asked the oracle at Didyma how to extract an oath from his own *naukleros*; that this rich Pergamene was involved in maritime commercial enterprises seems clearly indicated.[38] The name of C. Ulpius Prastina Pacatus Messallinus, the Antonine consul, is seldom found outside Rome except among freedmen in Ostia and Puteoli, and his Ostian freedmen were probably either shippers or men who provided transport service in Ostia's harbor; the consul's wealth may have been largely invested in land, but at least a part of what he had to invest derived originally from trade.[39] C. Fulvius Plautianus' origins were humble, and his fortune modest, until he was advanced and enriched by Septimius Severus, his fellow townsman and patron. Part of his newly acquired wealth derived from the marble trade: consignment notes, inscribed on blocks from the quarries, prove that it was at the order of Plautianus that the stone arrived to adorn the forum of his native Leptis Magna.[40]

It is important to clarify the cumulative significance of the evidence just presented. Eighteen early imperial notables, with highly diversified lucrative interests, have been put on parade; not unlike their late Republican counterparts,[41] their freedmen or others of lower status are normally found marching in front of them, carrying the actual banners of trade. Collectively, they should not tempt us to return to

---

and commerce rather than land receives support from the addition in unpublished inscriptions of two bankers, *coactores argentarii*, among the freedmen of the family in addition to the one already known." Cf. above, Chapter 6, section III, and notes 85, 86.

37. L. Burbuleius Optatus Ligarianus: *PIR*² B, 174; for his *cura* cf. *CIL* X, 6006 (= *ILS* 1066); newly discussed by J. C. Fant, *Curatores Rei Publicae in the Roman Empire*, Ph.D. dissertation, University of Michigan, 1976.

38. *Anth. Pal.* 14.72, on which see L. Robert, *CRAI* (1968), pp. 598–599. For Rufinus, see *PIR*² C, 1637, and G. W. Bowersock, *Greek Sophists in the Roman Empire* (Oxford 1969), pp. 60–61, 86; his first *nomen gentilicium* is incorrectly reported by H. Pleket, *Tijdschrift voor Geschiedenis* 84 (1971), p. 246n155.

39. See above, Chapter 6, section IV, with refs. in note 104.

40. *IRT* 530, with the comments of Reynolds and Ward-Perkins *ad loc.* (pp. 142–143); q.v. also for the date (between 202 and 205).

41. Above, Chapter 3, section III.

Rostovtzeff's vision of a society for which "the main source of large fortunes was commerce." Rather, a diversity and multiplicity of private economic pursuits was undoubtedly the normal rule, a multiplicity which the increasing interdependence between "landed" and "commercial" activities, and increasing exploitation of the provinces, helped to foster.[42] But the fact that imperial senators continued to realize such profits, and continued to realize them through such social mechanisms, is one small additional sign that the principate was built upon the institutions and values of the late Republic.

Emperors might augment a senator's *dignitas* and often did; yet titles and honors, as senators themselves were quick to point out, added nothing to the *patrimonium*.[43] What of the attitudes and activities of the *equites*, those who avoided *sumptuosa dignitas*[44] and preferred a life outside the senate? In earlier chapters examples were assembled of late Republican worthies who declined senatorial careers, motivated in part by the hopes of making money; and we detected, in the conventional senatorial language which describes such *equites*, occasional traces of self-conscious and disingenuous posturing.[45] Cicero made room in *De Officiis* for a generous-minded description of men like Atticus: persons who neither held high office nor philosophized but, preferring a life of leisure, devoted themselves instead to the accu-

42. Rostovtzeff's vision: *SEHRE*[2], p. 153, discussed above in Chapter 1, section II. Multiplicity of economic activities: Above, Chapter 5, section II, with notes 21–25; Chapter 4, section III with note 43; Chapter 3, sections I (Vestorius), III (Lucceii); Chapter 2, section I; cf. the phrasing in Philos. *Vit. Soph.* 605 (describing Damian of Ephesus): αὐτός τε πλούτῳ ποικίλῳ καὶ πολυπρεπεῖ κατεσκευασμένος. See further, on the increasing interdependence of "landed" and "commercial" pursuits, G. Pucci, *DdArch* 9–10 (1976–77), pp. 639ff; and, more generally, H. Pavis d'Escurac, "Aristocratie sénatoriale et profits commerciaux," *Ktema* 2 (1977), pp. 339–355, which however would have profited from closer attention to individual cases.

43. Sen. *De Ira* 3.31.2. We may compare the grandson of the orator Hortensius, who pleaded for subventions for his sons in Tiberius' presence, arguing that owing to changing times he had been unable either "to receive or acquire money" (*pecuniam . . . accipere vel parare,* Tac. *Ann.* 2.37.5). On senators' petitions (successful and unsuccessful) to emperors for buttressing the *patrimonium*, see the examples collected by F. Millar, *The Emperor in the Roman World* (Ithaca, N.Y. 1977), pp. 297–298.

44. Plin. *Ep.* 2.4.3; cf. 6.32.1: *ratio civilium officiorum necessitatem quandam nitoris imponit.* See further A. Stein, *Der Römische Ritterstand* (Munich 1927), p. 190–191.

45. See above, Chapter 3, section III, notes 52–56; Chapter 5, section III and refs. collected in note 77.

mulation of large fortunes (they must be prepared, of course, to put their riches at the disposal of their highly-placed political friends).[46]

Echoes and resonances of such attitudes continue to be audible, despite the altered structures of the principate. There is Seneca's younger brother who believed that equestrian procuratorships offered a shorter road to riches than possession of senatorial rank.[47] When Fronto, requesting an equestrian post for Appian, assured Antoninus Pius that Appian was not seeking the honor out of "desire for the salary of a procurator," he makes it clear that such salaries were normally a serious inducement.[48] Columella, who held an equestrian post, was contemptuous of those who grasp for senatorial offices and thereby waste away their patrimony; he directed his readers instead to the building up of wealth in the one conspicuously sure (and honorable) way: through agricultural pursuits.[49] Here the sense of the distance between the more overtly acquisitive equestrian ethos and that of the senator is strikingly conveyed; it finds corroboration in the contrasting mentalities presented by the two Plinies, the one equestrian, the other senatorial. Pliny the procurator, possessed of a sharp business sense, had attitudes on many subjects which contrasted with those of his consular nephew, a man obsessed with rank and standing. Their respective comments on *negotiatores* are symptomatic. The elder Pliny speaks of *nostri negotiatores*, a sign that he regarded them as neither a separate nor a pariah class. In contrast, when the Younger Pliny describes, in a letter full of literary allusions and self-congratulation, his generous behavior towards certain *negotiatores* (middlemen who bought his wine crop 'on the vine' in the hopes of selling at a scarcity price which failed to materialize), the sense of social distance is unmistakable.[50]

Attested behavior of certain highly placed equestrians is the best

46. Cic. *De Off.* 1.92, on which see above, Chapter 2, section II, notes 7–8, and Chapter 3, section II, notes 44–48.

47. Tac. *Ann.* 16.17.3, discussed above in Chapter 5, section III, note 76.

48. Front. *Ad Ant. Pium* 9 p. 262, 264 Haines: *Non . . . procuratoris stipendii cupiditate optat adipisci hunc honorem.*

49. Colum. 1 *praef.* 10, on which see Stein (above, note 44), pp. 199–200.

50. *Nostri negotiatores*: Plin. *NH* 6.140,149. The nephew's posture: Plin. *Ep.* 8.2. The Elder Pliny's "keen business sense" has been noticed by R. Syme, "Pliny the Procurator," *HSCP* 73 (1969), pp. 201ff, 224. Despite the nephew's carefully cultivated attitude of indifference to profits, attentive reading of the letters reveals how financially astute he was: the subject would repay further study. For hints, see Syme, *Tacitus*, p. 84.

guide to their acquisitive attitudes. M. Rutilius Lupus, prefect of the grain supply before 111 and *praefectus Aegypti* from 113–117, was also a major figure in the brick industry; both an owner of brickyards and a producer, he must be credited with introducing the use of dated stamps in buildings in the capital. Lupus' public career was no impediment to private gain, but actually created fresh opportunities for profits—and these he astutely exploited. This is shown, among other ways, by the concentration of his bricks in granaries and markets at Ostia, where M. Rutilius Lupus cannot fail to have acquired influential local connections during his tenure of office as *praefectus annonae*.[51]

Not all men of the requisite census were eager for procuratorial and other equestrian posts; *otium* continues, in a number of identifiable cases, to be preferred to *honores*, whether senatorial or equestrian. Maecenas' withdrawal to private life constituted the grand *exemplum* here: allusions in Propertius and Tacitus, as well as those in Petronius,[52] suggest that Maecenas made a public speech or some other symbolic gesture of refusal, and that the gesture was sufficiently memorable to be repeated later when others declined to pursue honors—Sallustius Crispus is a case in point.[53] To be sure, the changed conditions of the principate give the old equestrian formula a heightened political significance. Imperial patronage and the control of salaried equestrian appointments made it the more noticeable when an eligible worthy opted for *quies*, and made it the more important, therefore, when an *amicus principis* urged such a man to go into the senate, for him to have his answer ready.

Honesta quies,[54] under the Empire, was a formula broad enough to

51. On all this, see the discussion by H. Bloch, "The Serapeum of Ostia and the Brick-Stamps of 123 A.D.," *AJA* 63 (1959), pp. 235–237, with refs. The identification of the equestrian official and the brickyard owner has been generally accepted, most recently by P. Setälä, *Private Domini in Roman Brick Stamps of the Empire*, Ann. Acad. Sc. Fenn. 10 (Helsinki 1977), pp. 177ff, q.v. also for the view that Lupus was the producer (*officinator*) as well as the owner of the land on which the bricks were made (*dominus*). These works supersede the entry in *PIR* R, 173.

52. Prop. 3.9; Tac. *Ann.* 3.30.7; 14.53.3 (Maecenas adduced as precedent in Seneca's retirement speech before Nero). Petronius: see above, Chapter 5, section III, notes 66–70.

53. Tac. *Ann.* 3.30.4: *Atque ille, quamquam prompto ad capessendos honores aditu, Maecenatem aemulatus sine dignitate senatoria multos triumphalium consulariumque potentia anteiit.* Cf. A. Stein (above, note 44), p. 196–197.

54. R. Syme, "The Colony of Cornelius Fuscus: An Episode in the *Bellum Neronis*," *AJP* 58 (1937), pp 7–8; cf. also the same author's remarks in *Tacitus* (Oxford 1958),

cover a multitude of cases, and a variety of motives. Much more is usually implied than a single-minded interest in the pursuit of profits: Cornelius Fuscus' desire, in renouncing a senatorial career, was *quies*, not *quaestus*.[55] Nevertheless, lucrative activities are a part of what is implied by the formula, as was true also with *honestum otium*, under the Republic. Arrianus Maturus, *Altinatium princeps*, Minicius Macrinus of Brixia, Terentius Junior, even Cornelius Fuscus in his early days, were all conspicuously wealthy men;[56] and, as Syme has suggested, in their habits and tastes they are unlikely to have differed greatly from other acquisitive *viri boni et locupletes* of Narbonensis and Transpadane Gaul.[57]

II

Adapting traditional social mechanisms to the changed structures and conditions of the principate, Roman aristocrats and other notables continued to realize substantial increments to their *patrimonia* in ventures which included forms of commerce and manufacture. Those who occupy the foreground in these enterprises, freedmen, subsenatorial and subequestrian inhabitants of the cities and towns of the Empire, could also be men of standing and reputation, while pursuing profits over great distances and employing numbers of their own dependents to carry out their aims. This will not seem surprising, now that we have become better acquainted with seviri Augustales, both fictional and actual, in cities such as Puteoli and Ostia but also Lugdunum, Arelate, and Aquileia.[58] They were freedmen, but also wealthy, respectable,

p. 684. See Plin. *Ep.* 1.14.5, with the comments of A. N. Sherwin-White (*The Letters of Pliny*, Oxford, 1966) *ad loc.* (pp. 118–119).

55. Cf. Tac. *Hist.* 2.86.3, where Grotius attempted to alter the reading of the manuscript from *quietis cupidine* to *quaestus cupidine*. Despite the convincing demonstration of R. Syme, *AJP* 58 (1937), pp. 7–8, Grotius' conjecture continues to surface in scholarly works: see MacMullen, *RSR*, p. 200n95.

56. Arrianus Maturus: Plin. *Ep.* 3.2.2.: *Caret ambitu: ideo se in equestri gradu tenuit, cum facile posset ascendere altissimum.* Minicius Macrinus: Plin. *Ep.* 1.14.5: *Honestam quietem . . . ambitioni . . . praetulit.* Terentius Junior: *Ep.* 7.25.4; Cornelius Fuscus: Tac. *Hist.* 2.86.3. See further A. Stein (above, note 44), p. 201, and Sherwin-White (above, note 54) *ad loc.*

57. R. Syme, "Pliny the Procurator," (above, note 50), p. 224; *AJP* 58 (1937), p. 8: "This predilection for *honesta quies* is not likely to have been of rare occurrence among the opulent families of Northern Italy."

58. See above, Chapter 6, *passim*; and, for the diversified economic pursuits of freedmen *navicularii* at Arles, cf. M. Christol, "Remarques sur les naviculaires

and able to realize their diverse economic objectives with a considerable degree of independence (figure 23). Libertine status, in many of these cases, seems to have posed no severe impediment to good standing in their native cities and towns. L. Licinius Secundus, freedman of L. Licinius Sura who was three times consul, was an Augustalis and a very big fish in the coastal Spanish cities of Tarraco and Barcino: private citizens, *collegia*, and municipalities were profuse with their gratitude for his benefactions, and eager to curry favor.[59]

Under the Empire, the functional equivalents of men like C. Vestorius of Puteoli, whose multiple business enterprises were discussed in Chapter 3,[60] are now to be found in widely disparate parts and places. "Honorable on his father's side, and his mother had equal renown; good and upright, a man beloved by all, from whose tongue as he spoke to the Celts persuasion flowed"—this man was not a senatorial orator or a sophist but a Syrian trader, who carried his wares to distant Lugdunum.[61] Another man, an independent grain trader famous in Rome, Tuscany, and Umbria, thanked Fortune in dignified hexameters which emphasize their author's good repute, good faith, and "that sense of shame which is more potent than (mere) riches."[62]

Roman jurists recognized that far-flung independent business enterprises were a reality: a passage in the *Digest* refers to "men who have overseas business in remote parts of the world, managed by slaves and by freedmen."[63] From Narbo came Sex. Fadius Secundus Musa, of the tribe Papiria, a rich Gallic shipper, widely honored for his benefactions as local magistrate.[64] His name and those of other Sex. Fadii are found on many amphorae at Monte Testaccio near the ware-

d'Arles," *Latomus* 30 (1971), pp. 643–663. For the so-called "Navarch of Cavenzano" (Aquileia), see now M. José Strazzulla, *Antichità Altoadriatiche* 15 (1979), p. 344.

59. See *ILS* 1952, 6956, and, for many more texts, cf. *AE* 1957, 26. For discussion, see R. Syme, *HSCP* 73 (1969), p. 232n119; for L. Licinius Sura (*cos.* III, 107), see *PIR²* L, 253.

60. Above, Chapter 3, section I.

61. C. P. Jones, "A Syrian in Lyon," *AJP* 99 (1978), pp. 336–353.

62. *CIL* XIV, 2852 = *ILS* 3696 (T. Caesius Primus, A.D. 136). M. Junius Faustus, *mercator frumentarius* (*CIL* XIV, 4142), is equally substantial and comparably independent. For other signs of independence, cf. SHA, *Alex. Sev.* 33.

63. *Dig.* 40.9.10: *Saepe enim de facultatibus suis amplius, quam in his est, sperant homines. Quod frequenter accidit his, qui transmarinas negotiationes et aliis regionibus, quam in quibus ipsi morantur, per servos atque libertos exercent.*

64. *CIL* XII, 4393 (A.D. 149), on which see M. Clavel and P. Lévêque, *Villes et structures urbaines dans l'occident romain* (Paris 1971), pp. 324–327.

houses on the Tiber. The shapes and sizes of the jars prove that they were carrying Spanish oil from Baetica both to Gaul and to Rome; and at nearby Ostia Sex. Fadii also appear, probably planted in the port to facilitate the passage of Fadius' cargoes through Ostia to Rome.[65] Such persons—one might include some of the many members of the *gens Barbia*, whose trading tentacles spread far beyond their native Aquileia, or the potters Ateii[66]—who are freeborn, politically powerful, with geographically extended and well-organized shipping concerns, are very much a part of the more heterogenous, even motley, social fabric of the first two centuries of the Roman Empire (figure 2).

Damian, the famous sophist of mid-second century Ephesus (figure 24), is a perfect representative of an age in which status, sources of wealth, and attitudes were in ferment and resist easy compartmentalization.[67] His ancestors were local notables, and Damian himself never attained senatorial rank, yet he married the daughter of a *clarissimus vir* and their five children either became consuls or married consuls in the Severan period. His immense wealth was of multiple and variegated character: lands under cultivation, urban property, a sophist's fees, residences in the suburbs—but also holdings on the coast where merchant vessels could safely dock and put out again to sea. There was nothing acquisitive or mean spirited, Philostratus insists, about Damian: he supported the poor, remitted lecture fees, and spent lavishly on the public buildings of Ephesus. Yet he bought much productive land and planted fruit-bearing trees on all of it, and he had the foresight and initiative to convert a seaside property into a series of artificial islands, harbor installations, and docking facilities for cargo

65. For Ostia, see above, Chapter 6, section IV, with refs. in note 102; for the Spanish origin of the products, see T. Frank, "Notes on Roman Commerce," *JRS* 27 (1937), pp. 72–79. For other shipping activities of Musa, see Rougé, *OCM*, p. 250.

66. J. Šašel, "Barbii," *Eirene* 5 (1966), pp. 117–137; for the presence of the *gens* in Puteoli, see J. H. D'Arms, "Rapporti socio-economici fra città e territorio nella prima età imperiale," in *Antichità Altoadriatiche* 15 (1979), pp. 571–572. A new Barbia is now attested at Misenum, married to a Dalmatian attached to the imperial naval base: M. Borriello and A. D'Ambrosio, *Baiae-Misenum* (= Forma Italiae, reg. 1, vol. 14) (Florence 1979), p. 116. See further, on the Barbii, S. Panciera, *Vita economica di Aquileia in età romana* (Aquileia 1957), pp. 96–99. For the potters Ateii, with branches at Arezzo, Pisa, Lyon, and in Campania, see G. Pucci, *DdArch*. 7 (1973), p. 286; cited also by Garnsey, *Klio* 63 (1981).

67. On what follows, see Philos. *Vit. Soph.* 605–606; Rostovtzeff, *SEHRE*², p. 149; *PIR*² F, 253 (T. Flavius Damianus), with the stemma, p. 178; G. W. Bowersock, *Greek Sophists in the Roman Empire* (Oxford 1969), pp. 27–28.

ships, thereby deriving personal advantage from Ephesus' importance as a major commercial center.[68] In the Ephesus of Damian's day—as often elsewhere—senatorial and provincial dignity were not irreconcilable alternatives but could coincide and converge; landed and commercial wealth could be simultaneous and complementary assets; public generosity and a concern for status could be compatible with efficient management of assets and a keen interest in profits.[69]

Modern historians' inclination to view the ventures of private, unillustrious *negotiatores* as small in scale and rudimentary in organization stems from two factors: the low status of the practitioners, and the silence of their tombstones as to the existence of partners or associates. Concerning status, enough already has been said; as regards associates, partnerships were normally of short duration, and references to *institores* are mostly confined to the legal texts.[70] The concept of agency, moreover, was never systematically developed in Roman jurisprudence.[71] Rather, business relationships were often expressed in Rome in the language of friendship (*amicitia*), and persons besides aristocrats had *negotia* which were expedited by helpful "friends."

Epitaphs, when viewed in this light, no longer appear so economically uninformative. A seller of goatskins in Rome described himself as *semper communis amicis*;[72] another *negotiator*, who hoped to become rich through trade, complained that "he was deceived by hope, and by many friends";[73] we may compare the freedman *negotiator*

---

68. For increased pressure on existing port facilities at Ephesus under Antoninus Pius, resulting from intense commercial traffic in the harbor, observe the edict at Ephesus of the proconsul for Asia in 146–147, L. Antonius Albus, ordering importers of wood and of marble not to overload the pylons of the port: L. Robert, "Lettres byzantines," *Journal des Savants* (1962), p. 35; H. Wankel, *Die Inschriften von Ephesos* pt. 1a (Bonn 1979), pp. 140ff (no. 23). For silting problems which were chronic at the harbor of Ephesus, see G. E. Bean, *Aegean Turkey*[2] (London 1979), pp. 131–132.

69. Cf. MacMullen, *RSR*, p. 118; "The Romans indeed acknowledged a goddess called Money (*pecunia*); but some of them were blinder devotees than others, and her cult was tributary to another, *Status* (Philotimia)." Such a formulation does not prepare us for men like Damian, holders of heterogeneous attitudes.

70. Above, Chapter 6, section IV, note 109; see further H. J. Loane, *Industry and Commerce of the City of Rome* (Baltimore 1938), pp. 147ff.

71. See, e.g., J. A. Crook, *Law and Life of Rome* (above, note 33), pp. 206–207, and especially M. Kaser, *Das römische Privatrecht*[2] (Munich 1971), pp. 605ff, 608ff.

72. *ILS* 7542.

73. *ILS* 7519: L. Licinius M. f. Pol. Nepos . . . *qui negotiando locupletem se speravit esse futurum; spe deceptus erat et a multis, bene meritus, amicis.* (The translation of this text in MacMullen, *RSR*, p. 100, is misleading.)

mentioned in the *Satyricon* who, when his business partnership was in trouble, found himself bereft of friends.[74] By properly exploiting the declaration of friendship, in inscriptions, between persons known to be traders—we made initial attempts of this kind in our discussion of Augustales (figure 20)[75]—it ought to be possible to establish more securely particular economic connections, among families and across distances, and to begin to glimpse also some of the social realities which lie behind such friendship claims. For the Latin vocabulary of friendship conveniently glides over differences in status;[76] to permit oneself to be designated "friend" need not imply full social equality— as Cicero knew full well when he manumitted Tiro and became his *amicus*.[77] In Puteoli C. Erucius Faustus names P. Annius Eros as *amicus*,[78] but in their social, as well as in their professional, relationships we can be certain that Eros was the "senior partner," for he was a freedman of P. Annius Plocamus, an influential and well-connected trader, whose dependents reached the eastern Egyptian desert, and who may be the same man as the Annius Plocamus who farmed the taxes of the Red Sea early in the reign of Claudius.[79]

74. Pet. *Sat.* 38.13: *Sociorum olla male fervet, et ubi semel res inclinata est, amici de medio.*

75. Above, Chapter 6, section IV.

76. See above, Chapter 2, section III, and notes 114–116, and, for some highly suggestive observations, cf. Peter White, "*Amicitia* and the Profession of Poetry in Early Imperial Rome," *JRS* 68 (1978), pp. 74–92, esp. p. 82: "I know of no generic name for the relationship, standing on the same plane as *amicitia*, which draws attention to the aspect of dependence or dominance. In Roman society the attachment of one person to another was termed and regarded as *amicitia*, whether or not the 'friends' were equals."

77. Cic. *Ad Fam.* 16.16.1, quoted above in Chapter 2, note 115. For the varied statuses of the Younger Pliny's "friends," see White (preceding note), p. 80.

78. *CIL* X, 2389.

79. A slave of P. Annius Plocamus signed his name in a cave on Berenice road in the eastern Egyptian desert in A.D. 6: D. Meredith, "Annius Plocamus: Two Inscriptions from the Berenice Road," *JRS* 43 (1953), pp. 38–40, q.v. also for the identification with the Annius Plocamus of Plin. *NH* 6.84. For an eastern trader to have dependents in the port of Puteoli is precisely what one might have expected. See now M. G. Raschke, "New Studies in Roman Commerce with the East," *ANRW*, II (Principat), 9.2 (Berlin 1978), p. 644, who supposes "two successive generations of Annii Plocami active in Egypt." For a P. Annius Seleucus in Puteoli or the vicinity in 40, cf. F. Sbordone, *RAAN* n.s. 51 (1976), p. 146 (the *gentilicium* is of course widely diffused, and hence the exact connections between these P. Annii must remain uncertain); we also know of a Puteolan *duovir* of Tiberian date (unpublished), Annius Maximus. Cf. in general *PIR*[2] A, 676; and, for the Annii of Puteoli, *JRS* 64 (1974), pp. 107–109.

Finally, in discussing late Republican *negotiatores*, it was noted that they might form coherent groups of permanent residents in a city, and act in organized ways out of common interest.[80] Under the Empire the early development in major cities of *collegia "quibus coire licet,"* the special privileges granted to *navicularii* by Claudius and others, and the developing character of the institution of the Augustales[81] all indicate that organized groups of traders continued to enjoy a certain latitude and freedom of action. To be sure, it is only infrequently that we are able to find them exerting considerable pressure on the central government, and, in a typically Roman way, relying on highly placed and influential patrons to further their special interests.

For just this reason, a constellation of information about *thurarii* and *unguentarii* under Nero has a special interest. A certain C. Popillius Primio, a dealer in ointments, aromatics, and pepper, dedicated a tablet in gratitude to the last Julio-Claudian emperor.[82] It was also in Nero's reign that the entire Seplasia—the district in Capua famous for the production of aromatics and unguents—accused a *publicanus* before the consuls for exacting import duties which were excessive.[83] From Popillius' gratitude, it appears as though Nero took steps to satisfy the *thurarii* and *unguentarii*, and there is a hint of this in a passage of Tacitus, where Nero is represented as considering a major change in fiscal policy, the abolition of customs duties altogether.[84] Clearly, then, the *thurarii* had powerful patrons. The family of the L. Faenii and their dependents, known from inscriptions, specialized in the trade in cosmetics; they are found importing Capuan wares to

80. See above, Chapter 2, section I.

81. Claudius' measures: Gaius, *Inst.* 1.32c: cf. Suet. *Claud.* 18.4–19. For a new formulation of the importance of groups of *collegia* in the early Empire, see G. E. Rickman, "The Grain Supply," in *Seaborne Commerce*, pp. 271–272; q.v. also for the view that "the growth in importance of the *collegia* for state purposes . . . [was] inherent in the measures concerning privileges for grain shippers and grain merchants." The theory of J. P. Waltzing (*Étude historique sur les corporations professionelles chez les romains* [Louvain 1895–1900], vol. 2, pp. 42ff), that to be a member of a *collegium* associated with the *annona* constituted no automatic right to privileges, needs modification in the light of Rickman's findings. For fresh assessments of the considerable place of private initiative in commerce in grain under the Empire, see now the papers by Rickman (above, pp. 261–275) and by L. Casson, "The Role of the State in Rome's Grain Trade," in *Seaborne Commerce*, pp. 21–33.

82. *CIL* VI, 845.

83. Plin. *NH* 33.164.

84. Tac. *Ann.* 13.50.

the capital,[85] in Puteoli,[86] on Ischia,[87] as far away as Lugdunum;[88] two more of them are designated *thurarii* on a large and costly marble epitaph (figure 25) currently in Rome.[89] Since the name is not widely diffused, particular interest attaches to L. Faenius Rufus, *praefectus annonae* in 55 and designated, along with Tigellinus, *praefectus praetorio* in 62:[90] here, we may legitimately surmise, is the highly placed equestrian *patronus* who helped to press the traders' case. Had L. Faenius Rufus also a financial interest in the trade in unguents, taking a share of profit in return for his patronage and possibly also for his capital risk? If so, the fragmentary and small-scale efforts of the humble Faenii known from inscriptions appear at once more integrated, organized, and economically substantial.[91]

III

When, both at the outset of these concluding paragraphs and elsewhere in this study, we attempted to document the commercial and manufac-

85. *CIL* VI, 5680, 9932.

86. *CIL* X, 1962 = *ILS* 7615 (for the date, Augustan, cf. *Röm. Mitt.* 93 [1978], pp. 299–300); *AJA* 2 (1898), p. 380 (no. 17); *AE* 1973, no. 153 (where, however, the cognomen should be read as Eumenes, as T. Renner will soon show).

87. *CIL* X, 6802.

88. *CIL* VI, 9998.

89. L. Faenius Polybius and L. Faenius Celadus; the inscription (figure 25), presently visible in the epigraphical collections of the Terme museum in Rome, once stood on the Via Appia near Bovillae: see G. M. de Rossi, *Bovillae* (= Forma Italiae, reg. 1, vol. 15), Florence 1979, p. 286. For earlier discussions of the L. Faenii, see H. J. Loane, *Industry and Commerce of the City of Rome* (above, note 70), p. 143; M. W. Frederiksen, *PBSR* n.s. 14 (1959), p. 111; for the organization of other dealers in incense and unguents, cf. H. Pavis d'Escurac, *Ktema* 2 (1977), pp. 347ff; S. Treggiari, *Florilegium* (1979). pp. 70–72.

90. Tac. *Ann.* 13.22.1.; 14.51.5; cf. *PIR*[2] F, 102, The man's lucrative interests are further suggested by the existence of *horrea Faeniana* in Rome: *CIL* VI, 37796, on which see *AJP* (1909), p. 158.

91. The point needs emphasis in the light of Keith Hopkins' recent discussion of small-scale manufacturing units in the Roman world ("Economic Growth and Towns in Classical Antiquity," in P. Abrams and E. A. Wrigley, eds., *Towns in Societies* [Cambridge 1978], p. 53). Most manufacturing units in preindustrial economies are small; "what matters are the number and size of the exceptions, and whether there was any system by which a host of small producers, each engaged in one stage of production, was integrated by the activities of capitalistic entrepreneurs, who took a share of the profits in return for their effort and capital risk." Hopkins concludes that "there is only slight evidence that such integration did take place in the Roman world, and it seems probable that . . . the roles and institutions of integrating fragmented piece workers were never highly developed." (ibid., p. 53). The economic function of patrons in Roman trading organizations needs closer examination.

turing interests of senators, the trail descended directly to less distinguished associates—freedmen and other dependents—who were
directly involved in lucrative enterprises; when at the end we considered
the lowly Faenii, the trail instead rose upward and ended with a prefect
of the praetorian guard. One of the chief purposes of these pages has
been to demonstrate precisely this, that the organization of commerce
and manufacturing in the Roman world crossed easily back and forth
over boundaries of status, involving men at very different social levels.
Partnerships existed, and within them persons could function in specialized roles; duties, liabilities, obligations, and expectations came
to be more precisely labelled and defined, as is proved by the growing
body of civil law; and much depended upon a man's particular rank and
station. At the same time, however, the Romans flexibly adjusted and
extended the boundaries of traditional relationships—those of the *familia*, of *clientela*, of *amicitia*—in ways which gave these terms new
meaning, and gave commercial organization new dimensions. That
freedmen and friends in Roman society could often be the functional
equivalents of the partners and agents familiar to us from more evolved
social systems should be no more surprising than the fact that when
partners in the *commende* and *compagnie* of medieval Italy describe the
nature of their relationship, they often had recourse to the vocabulary
of family and of friendship.[92]

Nevertheless—and it has been one of the aims of this book to show
this also—"functional equivalents" are not the only important feature
in Roman commercial organization. Attitudes are equally significant,
along with the conduct which is often their clearest expression. As we
have seen, Roman upper-class authors tend to ignore their own lucrative
activities and those of other respectable men, or else to describe them
obliquely, as though they were something else. This obliqueness in fact
turns them into something else. Cicero's attitude toward income-
producing property at Puteoli was not the same as Vestorius', and Pliny's
attitude toward his slaves at Comum was not the same as that of his local
friend.[93] Senators are separated by an ethos—the amalgam of back-

---

92. See Iris Origo, *The Merchant of Prato* (London 1957), p. 108; excerpts from the
private correspondence of Francesco di Marco Datini show "that the tie between
partners should be as close as a family one, a truly fraternal bond." Datini declared
to a man who had been his partner for more than twenty years that the bond between
two partners could be closer and more secure than any family tie. "One sees brothers
betray each other every day; but good friends do not do so" (ibid., p. 109).

93. Cicero: above, Chapter 3, note 54; Pliny: above, note 18.

ground, education, political experience, social convention, *dignitas*—from the values of men of inferior rank. Values help to determine conventions, and these in turn fundamentally affect the substance of experience—in the commercial as well as in other spheres. The differences between the transactions conducted by persons of different standing in Roman society go beyond, but also partially reflect, one astute observer's reaction to transactions in the Bedesten, the great domed hall of the bazaar in sixteenth century Constantinople. Gain and trade, this writer opined, are like wild birds, but the courtesy and politeness with which they are practiced can domesticate them, can radically change their character. [94]

Discussing commercial associations in his magisterial survey of the Mediterranean world in the late sixteenth century, Braudel observed that "the usual pattern was the family firm at both upper and lower level, and short-term associations that were rarely renewed"; he appreciated also the importance of genealogical research, which can "shed much light on the network of marriages, family-ties, friendships and partnerships. [95] The pertinence of these remarks to a student of Roman society is patent and requires no elaboration. Still more recently, however, an historian of the medieval Islamic world, in a study of the commercial correspondence of traders of the Cairo Geniza (950–1250), [96] has drawn a distinction which may help the Roman historian to view his evidence in still clearer perspective, to locate Roman commercial organization more precisely along a continuum whose two theoretical extremes are the exceedingly informal and the highly defined. He observes that on the northern and western shores of the Mediterranean in the eleventh and twelfth centuries, the Italian merchant "lived and breathed in a world of contracts, of partnerships, agencies, commissions and loans; his status was that of a senior partner, a junior partner, or a factor; the structure of his commercial relationships was clear, defined, and very well labeled."[97] In contrast, the predominant and no less effective form of commercial association revealed in the Geniza documents was ex-

94. The observation of Evliya Çelibi is quoted in H. Sumner-Boyd and J. Freely, *Strolling through Istanbul*[2] (Istanbul 1973), p. 172.

95. F. Braudel, *The Mediterranean and the Mediterranean World in the Age of Philip II*, vol. 1, English edition (New York, 1972), p. 445.

96. Avrom L. Udovitch, "Formalism and Informalism in the Social and Economic Institutions of the Medieval Islamic World," in A. Banani and S. Vryonis, Jr., eds., *Individualism and Conformity in Classical Islam* (Wiesbaden 1977), pp. 61–81.

97. Udovitch (preceding note), p. 74.

tremely informal, without specific shape or content; the essential feature was one in which merchants were friends, undertaking the execution of favors for colleagues without any prospect of financial remuneration for themselves; the element of personal guarantee assured that informal commercial cooperation remained effective. Features common to both of these systems have been described in the preceding pages; while no precise calibrations are possible, I hope I have made a case for my belief that Roman commercial organization lay somewhere between these two extremes.

APPENDIX. AUGUSTALES OF PUTEOLI AND OSTIA

BIBLIOGRAPHY

INDEX

Appendix.
Augustales of Puteoli and Ostia

Puteoli

I. P. Aemilius Conon (X, 1870 = *ILS* 8300)
II. Q. Aemilius Helpidephorus (X, 1790 = *ILS* 6332)
III. M. Antonius Trophimus (X, 1872)
IV. A. Arrius Chrysanthus (X, 1873 = *ILS* 6331)
V. P. Avius Celer (X, 1551)
VI. P. Avius Gallinatus (X, 1551)
VII. Q. Aurelius Hermadion (X, 1567)
VIII. L. Caecilius Dioscorus (*NdSc*. 1897, p. 12 = *ILS* 6339)
IX. C. Caesonius Eudiaconus (X, 1874 = *ILS* 6330)
X. Q. Capito Probatus (XIII, 1942 = *ILS* 7029)
XI. M. Claudius Trypho (unpublished) (figure 22)
XII. Cn. Cornelius (X, 1875)
XIII. Cn. Haius Doryphorus (X, 540)
XIV. Q. Insteius Diadumenus (X, 1877 = *ILS* 6329)
XV. C. Iulius Didymus (X, 1878)
XVI. C. Iulius Glaphyrus (X, 1574 = *ILS* 266)
XVII. C. Iulius Victor (X, 1879)
XVIII. C. Laecanius Philumenus (*NdSc*. 1902, p. 381)
XIX. L. Lollius Zotio (X, 1882)
XX. M. Manlius Epaphroditus (X, 1883)
XXI. T. Marcius Taurus (X, 1884)
XXII. C. Marius (XIII, 1960)
XXIII. M. Marius M. l. Pothus (unpublished)
XXIV. C. Minatius Bithus (X, 1885 = *ILS* 5882 = *AE* 1950, 86)
XXV. N. Naevius Moschus (X, 1807)
XXVI. C. Nautius C. l. Felix (unpublished)
XXVII. L. Plutius Eutychio (X, 1888)
XXVIII. Sex. Patulcius Apolaustus (X, 1886)

XXIX. Cn. Pollius Victor (X, 1574 = *ILS* 226)

XXX. Sex. Publicius Bathyllus (X, 1889)

XXXI. Cn. Saenius Cn. l. Faustus (unpublished)

XXXII. C. Tantilius Hyla (X, 1574 = *ILS* 226)

XXXIII. Q. Valerius Salutaris (X, 690)

Ostia

1. M. Acilius Modestus (XIV, 287)
2. P. Aelius Agathemerus (unpublished, inv. no. 8224)
3. P. Aemilius Leo (XIV, 288)
4. Q. Aeronius Antiochus (XIV, 4140 = *ILS* 6155)
5. C. Agrius Felix (unpublished; inv. no. 1052)
6. L. Annius Felix (XIV, 4617)
7. T. Annius Lucullus (XIV, 33)
8. T. Annius Ostiensis (XIV, 291)
9. T. Annius Victor (XIV, 293)
10. ? Antonius ? (XIV, 295 = *ILS* 6157)
11. L. Antonius Peculiaris (XIV, 297)
12. Q. Aquilius ? (unpublished; inv. no. 11336)
13. L. Aquillius Modestus (XIV, 299)
14. P. Attius Felicio (*NdSc.* 1953, p. 289, no. 50)
15. T. Aurelius Eutyches (XIV, 305)
16. C. Baberius Cerialis (XIV, 4141)
17. C. Baebius Eucharistus (*Bollettino d'Arte* 33 [1948], p. 127)
18. L. Cacius Cinnamus (XIV, 308; *Scavi di Ostia* 3, p. 45)
19. A. Caedicius Successus (*Fasti Arch.* 8 [1956], p. 272, no. 3680)
20. C. Calpetanus Trofimus (*NdSc.* 1953, p. 290, no. 51)
21. D. Calpurnius Primigenius (XIV, 420)
22. L. Calpurnius Chius (XIV, 309)
23. L. Caltilius Epagathus (*NdSc.* 1953, p. 290, no. 52)
24. L. Caltilius Hilarus (XIV, 310)
25. ? Carminius ? (XIV, 313)
26. L. Carullius Epaphroditus (XIV, 316 = *ILS* 6161)
27. L. Carullius Felicissimus (XIV, 318 = *ILS* 6162)
28. ? Cassius ? (unpublished; inv. no. 6662)
29. Q. Catinius Eliodus (XIV, 319)
30. Ti. Claudius Arrianus (XIV, 386)
31. Ti. Claudius Cerialis (XIV, 329)
32. Ti. Claudius Urbanus (XIV, 330)
33. Ti. Claudius ...orus (XIV, 4633, 4725 a, b; inv. no. 8472)
34. C. Clodius ? (*NdSc.* 1941, p. 205)

35. P. Clodius Flavius Venerandus (XIV, 4318)
36. ? Clodius Lucrio (XIV, 331)
37. L. Combarisius Hermianus (XIV, 333)
38. L. Combarisius Hesperion (XIV, 4562, 1, 8)
39. ? Considius Hermes (XIV, 4669)
40. C. Cornelius Isochrysus (XIV, 339)
41. L. Cornelius Av.... (XIV, 336)
42. M. Cornelius Epagathus (XIV, 8 = *ILS* 6154)
43. Sex. Cornelius Eutychus (XIV, 338)
44. ? Cornelius Nicephorus (XIV, 4639)
45. M. Cossutius Protus (unpublished; inv. no. 16654)
46. A. Egrilius Callistio (XIV, 345)
47. A. Egrilius Faustus (unpublished; inv. no. 8011)
48. A. Egrilius Hermes Galatanus (XIV, 4663)
49. A. Egrilius Hilarus (*NdSc*. 1953, p. 291, no. 53)
50. A. Egrilius Leontius (XIV, 4559)
51. A. Egrilius Polytimus (unpublished; inv. no. 8226)
52. A. Egrilius Primigenius Minor (unpublished; inv. no. 1028 a)
53. A. Egrilius Onesimus (XIV, 4641)
54. A. Egrilius Primitivus (XIV, 4645)
55. A. Egrilius ? (XIV, 4644)
56. L. Faecenius Apollonius (XIV, 355)
57. M. Graecinius Dama (XIV, 4650)
58. A. Granius Acestes (XIV, 361)
59. A. Granius Atticus (XIV, 360 = *ILS* 6160)
60. P. Horatius Chryseros (XIV, 367 = *ILS* 6164)
61. Sex. Horatius Chryserotianus (XIV, 367 = *ILS* 6164)
62. C. Iulius Evangelus (XIV, 461, with Wickert's addition, p. 615)
63. C. Iulius Karus (XIV, 369)
64. C. Iulius Pothus (XIV, 5322)
65. C. Iulius Rammius Eutychus (*NdSc*. 1953, p. 292, no. 55)
66. M. Iulius Chrysophorus (unpublished; inv. nos. 19865, 11683)
67. L. Lepidius Eutychus (XIV, 372 = *ILS* 6158)
68. A. Livius Agathangelus (XIV, 4655)
69. A. Livius Anteros (XIV, 4656, plus inv. nos. 7364, 8221)
70. A. Livius Callistus (XIV, 381)
71. A. Livius Chryseros (*NdSc*. 1941, p. 203)
72. A. Livius Strato (XIV, 380 = *ILS* 8149)
73. A. Livius ? (XIV, 12)
74. M. Livius Nico (XIV, 358; cf. *Scavi di Ostia* 3 [1958], p. 156)
75. L. Lorenus Maximus (*Boll. d'Arte* 33 [1948], p. 127)
76. M. Lucceius Hermes (unpublished; inv. no. 8485)

77. L. Marcius ? (unpublished; inv. no. 6636a, b)
78. T. Marcius Chrysostomus (XIV, 461; cf. Wickert's addition, p. 615)
79. L. Marrius Aquila (unpublished)
80. L. Marrius Moderatus (XIV, 383)
81. M. Marius ? (XIV, 5328, 5327)
82. C. Mundius Felix (XIV, 4559)
83. D. Nonius Hermes (XIV, 392)
84. P. Nonius Helius (XIV, 389)
85. P. Nonius Zethus (XIV, 393, 394, 395)
86. C. Novius Trophimus (XIV, 396 = *ILS* 8346)
87. L. Numisius Agathemerus (XIV, 397)
88. P. Ostiensis Thallus (XIV, 290))
89. C. Papirius ? (unpublished, inv. no. 6636 a, b)
90. Q. Plarius Herclianus (unpublished; inv. no. 11342)
91. L. Pomponius Celsus (*NdSc*. 1953, p. 295, no. 59)
92. L. Publicius Eutyches (XIV, 405 = *ILS* 7512)
93. L. Publicius Onesimus (XIV, 406)
94. M. Quintilius ? (unpublished; inv. no. 8216)
95. L. Rennius Philodoxus (XIV, 407)
96. L. Rennius Platanus (unpublished)
97. Cn. Sergius Anthus (XIV, 412 = *ILS* 6142)
98. Cn. Sergius ? (XIV, 411)
99. ? Sergius ? (unpublished; inv. no. 6700))
100. C. Silius Felix (XIV, 415)
101. C. Silius Iucundus (XIV, 416)
102. C. Silius Mo.... (XIV, 417)
103. C. Similius Philocyrius (XIV, 418)
104. L. Spurius Fortunatus (XIV, 420)
105. L. Spurius Theophanes (XIV, 420)
106. Cn. Statilius Crescens Crescentianus (XIV, 421 = *ILS* 6159)
107. C. Tannonius Sabbatius (XIV, 4559)
108. T. Testius Helpidianus (XIV, 425 = X, 542 = *ILS* 6170)
109. C. Tuccius Beryllus (XIV, 427)
110. C. Tuccius Eutychus (XIV, 427)
111. ? Tuccius C. l. Malchio (XIV, 428)
112. P. Turranius (XIV, 1517)
113. Q. Turranius ? (*Epigrafica* 1, 1938–39, p. 37 = *AE* 1940, 65)
114. L. Valerius ? (XIV, 4671)
115. Q. Varius Secundus (XIV, 4293)
116. Q. Veturius Felicissimus (XIV, 431, 461)
117. Q. Veturius Socrates (XIV, 431)

118. Cn. Villius Hilarus (XIV, 436)
119. L. Voluseius Dius (XIV, 439 = *ILS* 6156)

PART II. WIVES OF AUGUSTALES

Puteoli

II. Q. Aemilius Helpidephorus	= Aemilia …ina
III. M. Antonius Trophimus	= Iulia Irene
VIII. L. Caecilius Dioscorus	= Caecilia Marciana
XI. M. Claudius Trypho (figure 20)	= Maria Quarta
XII. Cn. Cornelius ….	= Antonia Lentybiane
XV. C. Iulius Didymus	= Lollia Nereis
XXI. T. Marcius Taurus	= Cornelia Abascentilia
XXV. N. Naevius Moschus	= Naevia Saturnina
XXVIII. Sex. Patulcius Apolaustus	= Pomponia Chrysis
XXX. Sex. Publicius Bathyllus	= Urulneia Modesta
XXXIII. Q. Valerius Salutaris	= Valeria Tryfena

In seven of eleven treatable cases, husband and wife bore different *gentilicia*, a percentage of .636.

Ostia

1. M'. Acilius Modestus	= Acilia Quarta
4. Q. Aeronius Antiochus	= Aninia Anthis
6. L. Annius Felix	= Laberia Hilara
9. T. Annius Victor	= Annia Anthis
10. ? [A]ntonius ?	= Marcia Hilara
11. L. Antonius Peculiaris	= Antonia Soteris
12. Q. Aquilius ?	= Nonia M. f. Faustina
13. L. Aquillius Modestus	= Decimia Sp. f. Prisca
14. P. Attius Felicio	= Silia Helene
17. C. Baebius Eucharistus	= Cassennia L. f. Calliste
22. L. Calpurnius Chius	= Cornelia Ampliata

26.	L. Carullius Epaphroditus	= ? Eutychia
30.	Ti. Claudius Arrianus	= Mundicia Felicissima
31.	Ti. Claudius Cerialis	= Claudia Primilla
37.	L. Combarisius Hermianus	= Combarisia Onesime
39.	? Considius Hermes	= Statia Procula
40.	C. Cornelius Isochrysus	= Silia Tyrannis
46.	A. Egrilius Callistio	= Cominia Secundina
48.	A. Egrilius Hermes Galatanus	= Vettia Q. f. Severa
49.	A. Egrilius Hilarus	= Egrilia Iustina
51.	A. Egrilius Polytimus	= Iunia Aphrodite
53.	A. Egrilius Onesimus	= ? Daphne
63.	C. Iulius Karus	= Nonia Damalis
65.	C. Iulius Rammius Eutychus	= Iulia Euvennia
70.	A. Livius Callistus	= Livia Antigone
72.	A. Livius Strato	= Livia Eutychia
74.	M. Livius Nico	= Salinatoria Aucta
75.	L. Lorenus Maximus	= Annia C. f. Primilla
76.	M. Lucceius Hermes	= Lucceia Materna
77.	L. Marcius ?	= Papiria ?
83.	D. Nonius Hermes	= Nonia Heraclia
84.	P. Nonius Helius	= Nonia Synthrophia
85.	P. Nonius Zethus	= Nonia Pelagia
86.	C. Novius Trophimus	= Novia Synerusa
87.	L. Numisius Agathemerus	= Numisia Mercatilla
90.	Q. Plarius Herclianus	= Nasennia Charitine
91.	L. Pomponius Celsus	= Furia Maximilla
93.	L. Publicius Onesimus	= Publicia Afrodite
96.	L. Rennius Platanus	= Egrilia A. l. Quarta
100.	C. Silius Felix Maior	= Silia Fausta
102.	C. Silius Mo....	= ? Sabina
103.	C. Similius Philocyrius	= Similia Philete
106.	Cn. Statilius Crescens Crescentianus	= Statilia Atalante
110.	C. Tuccius Eutychus	= Tuccia Elate
118.	Cn. Villius Hilarus	= Modia Gemnis
119.	L. Voluseius Dius	= Iulia Thais

In three of the above cases (nos. 26, 53, 102) the *gentilicium* of the wife is unknown; eight other texts (nos. 16, 18, 24, 79, 88, 92, 99, 111) have not been included because the relationship between man and woman remains unclear. Wives therefore bear *gentilicia* different from husbands in twenty-three out of forty-three treatable cases, a percentage of .535. In three cases in which the *gentilicia* of the couple are distinct, the combined *praenomen* and *gentilicium* of the husband, and the *gentilicium* of the wife, are also attested among the families of Ostia's governing class (nos. 22, 51, 90).

A. Caedicius Successus (no. 19), has been omitted from this list; despite Meiggs, *RO*², p. 276, the woman named in line 6, Pontulena Pyrallis, must be the wife not of Successus but of A. Iulius Epagathus (*amori eius*).

Bibliography

I have included in this bibliography principally the books and articles frequently cited in the foregoing pages and, secondarily, some works mentioned only once or twice which have special importance for the main themes discussed in this book. Articles in standard works of reference are omitted, except for a few of particular significance in *RE*, as are editions and collections of ancient evidence and handbooks.

André, J. M., *Otium dans la vie morale et intellectuelle romaine* (Paris 1966).

Andreau, J., "Remarques sur la société pompéienne," *DdArch*. 7 (1973), pp. 213-254.

———— *Les affaires de Monsieur Jucundus*, Collection de l'École française de Rome 19 (Rome 1974).

———— "M. I. Finley, la banque antique et l'école moderne," *Ann. Sc. Norm. Sup. Pisa*, 3rd ser., 7 (1977), pp. 1129-52.

———— *Le dernier siècle de la république romaine et l'époque augustéenne* (Strasbourg 1978).

Archi, G. G., ed., *Pauli Sententiarum Fragmentum Leidense* (Leiden 1956).

Astin, A. E., *Cato the Censor* (Oxford 1978).

Badian, E., *Publicans and Sinners* (Ithaca, N.Y. 1972).

———— "Marius' Villas: The Testimony of the Slave and the Knave," *JRS* 63 (1973), pp. 121–132.

Baldacci, P., "*Negotiatores* e *mercatores frumentarii* nel periodo imperiale," *Rend. Ist. Lombardo* 101 (1967), pp. 273–291.

Baldwin, B., "Trimalchio's Domestic Staff," *Acta Classica* 21 (1978), pp. 95–106.

Benoit, F., *L'épave du grand Congloué à Marseille*, *Gallia*, supp. 14 (Paris 1961).

Bloch, H., *I bolli laterizi e la storia edilizia romana* (Rome 1947).

———— "The Roman Brick-Stamps Not Published in Volume XV, 1 of the *Corpus Inscriptionum Latinarum*," *HSCP* 56–57 (1947), pp. 1–128.

———— "The Serapeum of Ostia and the Brickstamps of 123 A.D.," *AJA* 63 (1959), pp. 225–240.

Bodei Giglioni, G., "Pecunia fanatica: l'incidenza economica dei templi laziali," *Riv. Stor. Ital.* 89 (1977), pp. 33-76.

Boëthius, A., and Ward-Perkins, J. B., *Etruscan and Roman Architecture* (London 1970).

Bowersock, G. W., *Augustus and the Greek World* (Oxford 1965).

———— *Greek Sophists in the Roman Empire* (Oxford 1969).

———— *"The Social and Economic History of the Roman Empire* by M. I. Rostovtzeff," *Daedalus* 103 (1974), pp. 15–23.

Braudel, F., *The Mediterranean and the Mediterranean World in the Age of Philip II*, English ed. (New York 1972), 2 vols.

Bridenbaugh, C., *Cities in the Wilderness: The First Century of Urban Life in America, 1625–1742* (Oxford 1971; first published 1938).

Broughton, T. R. S., *The Magistrates of the Roman Republic* (New York 1951–52), 2 vols.

———— "Comment," in *Second International Conference of Economic History: Aix 1962* (Paris 1965), pp. 150–162; reprinted in R. Seager, ed., *The Crisis of the Roman Republic* (Cambridge 1969), pp. 118–130.

———— "Some Notes on Trade and Traders in Roman Spain," in J. A. S. Evans, ed., *Polis and Imperium, Studies in Honour of E. T. Salmon* (Toronto 1974), pp. 11–30.

Brown, F. E., *Cosa: The Making of a Roman Town*, Jerome Lectures, 13th ser. (Ann Arbor 1980).

Brunt, P. A., "The *Equites* in the Late Republic," in *Second International Conference of Economic History: Aix 1962* (Paris 1965), pp. 117–149; reprinted in R. Seager, ed., *The Crisis of the Roman Republic* (Cambridge 1969), pp. 83–115.

———— *Italian Manpower 225 B.C.–A.D. 14* (Oxford 1971).

———— "Aspects of the Social Thought of Dio Chrysostom and of the Stoics," *Proc. Camb. Phil. Soc.* n.s. 19 (1973), pp. 9–34.

———— "The Administrators of Roman Egypt," *JRS* 65 (1975), pp. 124–147.

——— "Two Great Roman Landowners," *Latomus* 34 (1975), pp. 619–635.

Bugno, L. V., "M. Barronio Sura e l'industria della porpora ad Aquino," *Rend. Acc. Linc.* 26 (1971), pp. 685–695.

Calderini, A., *Aquileia romana* (Milan 1930).

Camodeca, G., "L'Ordinamento in *regiones* e i *vici* di Puteoli," *Puteoli: Studi di storia antica* 1 (1977), pp. 62–98.

Carandini, A., ed., *Instrumentum domesticum di Ercolano e Pompei* (Rome 1977).

Carandini, A., and Settis, S., *Schiavi e padroni nell' Etruria romana* (Rome 1979).

Carrington, R. C., "Studies in the Campanian *villae rusticae*," *JRS* 21 (1931), pp. 110–130.

Cassola, F., *I gruppi politici romani nel III secolo a.C.* (Trieste 1962).

——— "Romani e Italici in Oriente," *DdArch.* 4–5 (1970–71), pp. 305–329.

Casson, L., "New Light on Maritime Loans," *Eos* 48.2 (1956), pp. 89–93.

——— "Harbour and River Boats of Ancient Rome," *JRS* 55 (1965), pp. 31–39.

——— "The Role of the State in Rome's Grain Trade," in *Seaborne Commerce*, pp. 21–33.

Castagnoli, F., "Topografia dei Campi Flegrei," in *I Campi Flegrei nell'archeologia e nella storia*, Atti dei convegni Lincei 33 (Rome 1977), pp. 41–79.

——— "Installazioni portuali a Roma," in *Seaborne Commerce*, pp. 35–42.

Castrén, P., *Ordo Populusque Pompeianus, Polity and Society in Roman Pompeii*, Acta Instituti Romani Finlandiae 8 (Rome 1975).

Cébeillac, M., "Quelques inscriptions inédites d'Ostie, de la république à l'empire," *MEFR* 83 (1971), pp. 39–125.

Cébeillac-Gervasoni, M., and Zevi, F., "Revisions et nouveautés pour trois inscriptions d'Ostie," *MEFR* 88 (1976), pp. 607–637.

Champlin, E., *Fronto and Antonine Rome* (Cambridge, Mass. 1980).

Christol, M., "Remarques sur les naviculaires d'Arles," *Latomus* 30 (1971), pp. 643–663.

Cipolla, C. M., "The Italian 'Failure,'" in F. Krantz and P.M. Hohenberg, eds., *Failed Transitions to Modern Industrial Society:*

Renaissance Italy and Seventeenth Century Holland (Quebec 1975), pp. 8–10.

Clavel, M., and Lévêque, P., *Villes et structures urbaines dans l'occident romain* (Paris 1971).

Clemente, G., *I Romani nella Gallia meridionale* (Bologna 1974).

—— "Il patronato nei *collegia* dell'impero romano," *Stud. Class. Orient.* 21 (1972), pp. 201–226.

Coarelli, F., "Classe dirigente romana e arti figurative," *DdArch.* 4–5 (1970–71), pp. 241–265.

—— "Architettura e arti figurative in Roma, 150–50 a.C.," in P. Zanker, ed., *Hellenismus in Mittelitalien*, Abh. Akad. Wiss. 97 (Gottingen 1976), pp. 21–51.

—— "Public Building in Rome between the Second Punic War and Sulla," *PBSR* n.s. 45 (1977), pp. 1–23.

Connor, W. R., *"Homo Lucrans?"*, *Arion* n.s. 1 (1973–74), pp. 731–739.

Cotton, H. M., "Cicero, *Ad Familiares* XIII, 26 and 28: Evidence for *Revocatio* or *Reiectio Romae/Romam?*" *JRS* 69 (1979), pp. 39–50.

Crawford, M. H., "The Early Roman Economy, 753–280 B.C.," in *L'Italie préromaine et la Rome républicaine*, *Mélanges offerts a J. Heurgon*, Collection de l'Ecole Française de Rome 27 (Rome 1976), pp. 197–207.

Crook, J. A., *Law and Life of Rome* (London 1967).

Daniela Conta, G., "Peschiere marittime nel mondo romano," in G. Schmiedt, ed., *Il livello antico del Mar Tirreno* (Florence 1972), pp. 215–221.

D'Arms, J. H., *Romans on the Bay of Naples* (Cambridge, Mass. 1970).

—— "A New Inscribed Base from 4th Century Puteoli," *PdP* 27 (1972), pp. 255–270.

—— "*CIL X*, 1792: A Municipal Notable of the Augustan Age," *HSCP* 76 (1972), pp. 207–216.

—— "Puteoli in the Second Century of the Roman Empire: A Social and Economic Study," *JRS* 64 (1974), pp. 104–124.

—— "Tacitus, *Hist.* 4.13 and the Municipal Origins of Hordeonius Flaccus," *Historia* 23 (1974), pp. 497–504.

—— "Notes on Municipal Notables of Imperial Ostia," *AJP* 97 (1976), pp. 387–411.

—— "Rapporti socio-economici fra città e territorio nella prima età imperiale," *Antichità Altoadriatiche* 15 (1979), pp. 549–573.

D'Arms, J. H., and Kopff, E. C., eds., *Roman Seaborne Commerce: Studies in Archaeology and History*, MAAR 36 (Rome 1980).

De Franciscis, A., "La villa romana di Oplontis," in B. Andreae and H. Kyrieleis, eds., *Neue Forschungen in Pompeji* (Recklinghausen 1975), pp. 9–38.

Degrassi, A., "Aquileia e l'Istria in età romana," in *Studi Aquileiesi offerti a G. Brusin* (Aquileia 1953), pp. 55–85.

de Laet, S. J., *Portorium* (Bruges 1949).

De Martino, F., *Storia economica di Roma antica* (Florence 1980), 2 vols.

de Villefosse, H., "Deux armateurs narbonais," *Mem. Soc. Nat. Antiq. de France* 74 (1914), pp. 153–180.

Dubois, C., *Pouzzoles antique*, Bibliothéque des Écoles Françaises d'Athènes et de Rome 98 (Paris 1907).

Duff, A. M., *Freedmen in the Early Roman Empire* (Oxford 1928).

Duncan-Jones, R. P., *The Economy of the Roman Empire: Quantitative Studies* (Cambridge 1974).

——— "Scaurus at the House of Trimalchio," *Latomus* 32 (1973), pp. 364–367.

——— "Giant Cargo-Ships in Antiquity," *CQ* n.s. 27 (1977), pp. 331–332.

Duthoy, R., "La fonction sociale de l'Augustalité," *Epigraphica* 36 (1974), pp. 134–154.

——— "Les *Augustales*," *ANRW* II (Principat) 16.2 (Berlin 1978), pp. 1254–1309.

Eck, W., "Die Familie der Volusii Saturnini in neuen Inschriften aus Lucus Feroniae," *Hermes* 100 (1972), pp. 461–484.

Finley, M. I., "Archaeology and History," *Daedalus* 100 (1971), pp. 168–186.

——— *The Ancient Economy*, Sather Classical Lectures, vol. 43 (Berkeley 1973).

——— ed., *Studies in Roman Property*, Cambridge University Research Seminar in Ancient History (Cambridge 1976).

——— "The Ancient City: From Fustel de Coulanges to Max Weber and Beyond," *Comp. Stud. Soc. Hist.* 19 (1977), pp. 305–327.

Frank, T., *Economic History of Rome*, 2nd ed. (Baltimore 1927).

——— "Notes on Roman Commerce," *JRS* 27 (1937), pp. 72–79.

——— *An Economic Survey of Ancient Rome*, vol. 1 (Baltimore 1933), vol. 5 (Baltimore 1940).

Frederiksen, M. W., "Republican Capua: A Social and Economic Study," *PBSR* n.s. 14 (1959), pp. 80–130.

——— "Puteoli," *RE* 23 (1959), 2036–60.

——— "Theory, Evidence, and the Ancient Economy," *JRS* 65 (1975), pp. 164–171.

Friedländer, L., *Petronii Cena Trimalchionis*, 1st ed. (Leipzig 1891), 2nd ed. (Leipzig 1906).

Frier, B. W., "Cicero's Management of His Urban Properties," *CJ* 74 (1978–79), pp. 1–6.

Gabba, E., "Riflessioni antiche e moderne sulle attività commerciali a Roma nei secoli II e I a.C.," in *Seaborne Commerce*, pp. 91–102.

Gagé, J., *Les classes sociales dans l'empire romain* (Paris 1974).

Garnsey, P. W. "Descendants of Freedmen in Local Politics: Some Criteria," in B. Levick, ed., *The Ancient Historian and His Materials, Essays in Honour of C. E. Stevens* (Farnborough 1975), pp. 167–180.

——— "Economy and Society of Mediolanum under the Principate," *PBSR* n.s. 44 (1976), pp. 13–27.

——— "Urban Property Investment," in Finley, *Property*, pp. 123–136.

——— "Independent Freedmen and the Economy of Roman Italy under the Principate," *Klio* 63 (1981).

Gatti, C., "Le ville marittime italiche e africane," *Rend. Ist. Lombardo* 91 (1957), pp. 285–305.

Gaudemet, J., *Institutions de l'antiquité* (Paris 1967).

Gianfrotta, P. A., "Ancore 'romane': Nuovi materiali per lo studio dei traffici marittimi," in *Seaborne Commerce*, pp. 103–116.

Gilliam, J. F., "The Plague under Marcus Aurelius," *AJP* 82 (1961), pp. 225–251.

Giordano, C., "Su alcune tavolette cerate dell'agro murecine," *RAAN* n.s. 41 (1966), pp. 107–121.

——— "Nuove tavolette cerate Pompeiane," *RAAN* n.s. 45 (1970), pp. 211–231.

——— "Nuove tavolette cerate Pompeiane," *RAAN* n.s. 46 (1971), pp. 183–197.

——— "Quarto contributo alle tavolette cerate Pompeiane," *RAAN* n.s. 47 (1972), pp. 311–318.

Goldthwaite, R. A., "The Florentine Palace as Domestic Architecture," *The American Historical Review* 77 (1972), pp. 977–1012.

Gordon, M. L., "The Freedman's Son in Municipal Life," *JRS* 21 (1931), pp. 65–77.

Griffin, M., *Seneca, A Philosopher in Politics* (Oxford 1976).

Gruen, E. S., *The Last Generation of the Roman Republic* (Berkeley and Los Angeles 1974).

Habicht, C., "Zwei neue Inschriften aus Pergamon," *Istanbuler Mitteilungen* 9–10 (1959–60), pp. 109–127.

Harris, W. V., *War and Imperialism in Republican Rome, 327–70 B.C.* (Oxford 1979).

——— "The Organization of the Roman Terracotta Lamp Industry," *JRS* 70 (1980), pp. 126–145.

——— "Towards a Study of the Roman Slave Trade," in *Seaborne Commerce*, pp. 117–140.

Gummerus, H., "Industrie und Handel," *RE* 18 (1916), 1381–1535.

Hatzfeld, J., *Les trafiquants italiens dans l'orient hellénique* (Paris 1919).

Hawthorn, J. R., "The Senate after Sulla," *G&R* 9 (1962), pp. 53–60.

Helen, T., *Organization of Roman Brick Production*, Annales Academiae Scientiarum Fennicae, Diss. Hum. Litt. 5 (Helsinki 1975).

Hill, H., *The Roman Middle Class in the Republican Period* (Oxford 1952).

Ho, Ping-Ti, *The Ladder of Success in Imperial China* (New York 1962).

Hopkins, K., *Conquerors and Slaves* (Cambridge 1978).

——— "Economic Growth and Towns in Classical Antiquity," in P. Abrams and E. A. Wrigley, eds., *Towns in Societies* (Cambridge 1978), pp. 35–77.

Houston, G. W., "The Administration of Italian Seaports during the First Three Centuries of the Roman Empire," in *Seaborne Commerce*, pp. 157–171.

Jahoda, M., and Warren, N., eds., *Attitudes: Selected Readings* (Baltimore 1966).

Jones, A. H. M., "Ancient Empires and the Economy: Rome," in P. A. Brunt, ed., *The Roman Economy* (Oxford 1974), pp. 114–139.

——— "The Economic Life of the Towns of the Roman Empire," in P. A. Brunt, ed., *The Roman Economy* (Oxford 1974), pp. 35–60.

——— *Studies in Roman Government and Law* (New York 1960).

Jones, C. P., *Plutarch and Rome* (Oxford 1971).

——— *The Roman World of Dio Chrysostom* (Cambridge, Mass. 1978).

————— "A Syrian in Lyon," *AJP* 99 (1978), pp. 336–353.

Juglar, L., *Quomodo per Servos Libertosque Negotiarentur Romani* (Paris 1902).

Kaser, M., "Neue Literatur zur 'Societas,' " *Studia et Documenta Historiae et Juris* 41 (1975), pp. 278–338.

————— *Das römische Privatrecht*, 2nd ed., vol. 1 (Munich 1971).

Kirshner, J., ed., *Raymond de Roover: Business, Banking and Economic Thought* (Chicago 1974).

Kroll, W., "Die Kultur der Ciceronischen Zeit I: Politik und Wirtschaft," *Das Erbe der Alten* 22 (1933).

Lange, D., "Two Financial Maneuvers of Cicero," *CW* 65 (1972), pp. 152–155.

Lepore, E., "Orientamenti per la storia sociale di Pompeii," in *Pompeiana: Raccolta di studi per il secondo centenario degli scavi di Pompei* (Naples 1950).

————— "Per la storia economico-sociale di Neapolis," *PdP* 7 (1952), pp. 300–332.

————— "Neapolis città dell'impero romano," *Storia di Napoli* 1 (Naples 1967), pp. 289–371.

Licordari, A., "Un' iscrizione inedita di Ostia," *Rend. Acc. Linc.* 29 (1974), pp. 313–323.

Litewski, W., "Römisches Seedarlehen," *Iura: rivista internationale di diritto romano e antico* 24 (1973), pp. 112–183.

Loane, H. J., *Industry and Commerce in the City of Rome* (Baltimore 1938).

Lopez, R. S., *The Commercial Revolution of the Middle Ages, 950–1350* (Cambridge 1976).

MacMullen, R., *Roman Social Relations, 50 B.C. to A.D. 284* (New Haven 1974).

Maiuri, A., *La Cena di Trimalchione* (Naples 1945).

————— *La Villa dei Misteri*, 2nd ed. (Rome 1947).

Manacorda, D., "The *Ager Cosanus* and the Production of the Amphorae of Sestius: New Evidence and a Reassessment," *JRS* 68 (1978), pp. 122–131.

Mason, H. J., and Wallace, M. B., "Appius Claudius Pulcher and the Hollows of Euboia," *Hesperia* 41 (1972), pp. 128–140.

McCann, A. M., "The Harbor and Fishery Remains at Cosa, Italy," *Journal of Field Archaeology* 6 (1979), pp. 391–411.

Meiggs, R., *Roman Ostia*, 2nd ed. (Oxford 1973).

Melitz, J., and Winch, D., eds. *Jacob Viner, Religious Thought and Economic Society: Four Chapters of an Unfinished Work* (Durham, N.C. 1978).

Meredith, D., "Annius Plocamus: Two Inscriptions from the Berenice Road," *JRS* 43 (1953), pp. 38–40.

Millar, F., *The Emperor in the Roman World* (London 1977).

Momigliano, A. D., *Studies in Historiography* (New York 1966).

——— "Review of M. I. Finley, *The Ancient Economy*," *Riv. Stor. Ital.* 87 (1975), pp. 167–170.

Mommsen, Th., "Trimalchios Heimath und Grabschrift," *Hermes* 13 (1978), pp. 106–121.

More, J. H., *The Fabri Tignarii of Rome* (Ph.D. diss., Harvard University, 1969).

Moretti, M., and Sgubini Moretti, A. M., *La villa dei Volusii a Lucus Feroniae* (Rome 1977).

Mustilli, D., "La villa pseudourbana ercolanese," *RAAN* n.s. 31 (1956), pp. 77–97.

Nicolet, C., *L'ordre équestre a l'époque républicaine*, vol. 1 (Paris 1966), vol. 2 (Paris 1974).

——— "Institutions politiques de Rome," *Annuaire, École pratique des hautes études*, 4th section, 1976–77 (Paris 1977).

——— *Rome et la conquête du monde mediterranéen*, vol. 1, *Les structures de l'Italie romaine*, 2nd ed. (Paris 1979).

Nock, A. D., "*Seviri* and *Augustales*," *Ann. de l'Institut de Philol. et d'Hist. Orientales* 2 (1933–34), pp. 627–638; reprinted in Z. Stewart, ed., *A. D. Nock, Essays on Religion and the Ancient World* (Oxford 1972).

Noonan, J. T., Jr., "Review of J. Melitz and D. Winch, eds., *Jacob Viner, Religious Thought and Economic Society: Four Chapters of an Unfinished Work*," *Economic Journal* 89 (1979), pp. 482–484.

Origo, I., *The Merchant of Prato* (London 1957).

Ostrow, S. E., "Problems in the Topography of Roman Puteoli," Ph.D. diss., University of Michigan, 1977.

Panciera, S., *Vita economica di Aquileia in età romana* (Aquileia 1957).

Pavis d'Escurac, H., "Aristocratie senatoriale et profits commerciaux," *Ktema* 2 (1977), pp. 339–355.

Percival, J., *The Roman Villa: An Historical Introduction* (London 1976).

Pleket, H. W., "Sociale stratificatie en social mobiliteit in de Romeinse Keizertijd," *Tijdschrift voor Geschiedenis* 84 (1971), pp. 215–251.

——— "Technology in the Greco-Roman World: A General Report," *Talanta* 5 (1973), pp. 6–47.

Ponsich, M. and Tarradell, M., *Garum et industries antiques de salaison dans la Mediterranée*, Bibl. hautes études hisp. 36 (Paris 1965).

Pucci, G., "La produzione della ceramica aretina. Note sull' 'industria' nella prima età imperiale romana," *DdArch.* 7 (1973), pp. 255–293.

——— "Considerazioni sull' articolo di J. Andreau, 'Remarques sur la société pompéienne,' "*DdArch.* 9–10 (1976–77), pp. 631–647.

Rankin, H. D., *Petronius the Artist: Essays on the Satyricon and Its Author* (The Hague 1971).

Raschke, M. G., "New Studies in Roman Commerce with the East," *ANRW* II (Principat) 9.2 (Berlin 1978), pp. 604–1378.

Raskolnikoff, M., "La richesse et les riches chez Ciceron," *Ktema* 2 (1977), pp. 357–365.

Rawson, E., "Architecture and Sculpture: The Activities of the Cossutii," *PBSR* n.s. 43 (1975), pp. 36–47.

——— "The Ciceronian Aristocracy and Its Properties," in Finley, *Property*, pp. 85–102.

Reinhold, M., "Historian of the Classic World: A Critique of Rostovtzeff," *Science and Society* 10 (1946), pp. 361–391.

Rickman, G., *Roman Granaries and Store Buildings* (Cambridge 1971).

——— "The Grain Supply," in *Seaborne Commerce*, pp. 261–275.

Robert, L., "Lettres byzantines," *Journal des Savants* (1962), pp. 1–140.

——— "Trois oracles de la théosophie et un prophête d'Apollon," *CRAI* (1968), pp. 568–599.

Rostovtzeff, M., *The Social and Economic History of the Roman Empire*, 2nd ed., ed. P. M. Fraser (Oxford 1957), 2 vols.

Rougé, J., *Recherches sur l'organisation du commerce maritime en Mediterranée sous l'empire romain* (Paris 1966).

Šašel, J., "Barbii," *Eirene* 5 (1966), pp. 117–137.

Sbordone, F., "Preambolo per l'edizione critica delle tavolette cerate di Pompei," *RAAN* n.s. 51 (1976), pp. 145–168.

Schiller, A. A., "The Business Relations of Patron and Freedman in Classical Roman Law," first published 1935; reprinted in *An American Experience in Roman Law* (Gottingen 1971), pp. 24–31.

Schneider, H., *Wirtschaft und Politik. Untersuchungen zur Geschichte der späten römischen Republik* (Erlangen 1974).

Schnur, H. C., "The Economic Background of the Satyricon," *Latomus* 18 (1959), pp. 790–799.

Seager, R., ed., *The Crisis of the Roman Republic* (Cambridge 1969).

Setälä, P., *Private Domini in Roman Brick Stamps of the Empire*, Annales Academiae Scientiarum Fennicae, Diss. Hum. Lett. 10 (Helsinki 1977).

Shackleton Bailey, D. R., *Cicero: Epistulae ad familiares* (Cambridge 1977), 2 vols.

———— *Cicero's Letters to Atticus* (Cambridge 1965–70), 7 vols.

Shatzman, I., *Senatorial Wealth and Roman Politics*, Collections Latomus 142 (Brussels 1975).

Sherwin-White, A. N., *The Letters of Pliny: A Historical and Social Commentary* (Oxford 1966).

Smith, M. S., *Cena Trimalchionis* (Oxford 1975).

Ste. Croix, G. E. M. de, "Ancient Greek and Roman Maritime Loans," in H. Edey and B. S. Yamey, eds., *Debits, Credits, Finance and Profits, Essays in Honor of W. T. Baxter* (London 1974), pp. 41–59.

Stein, A., *Der römische Ritterstand* (Munich 1927).

Steinby, M., "La cronologia delle figlinae doliare urbane," *Bull. Comm. Arch. Com. Roma* 84 (1974), pp. 7–132.

Stone, L., *The Crisis of the Aristocracy, 1558–1641* (Oxford 1965).

Sullivan, J. P. *The Satyricon of Petronius* (Bloomington, Ind. 1968).

Syme, R., "The Colony of Cornelius Fuscus: An Episode in the *Bellum Neronis*," *AJP* 58 (1937), pp. 7–18.

———— "Pliny the Procurator," *HSCP* 73 (1969), pp. 201–236.

———— *Tacitus* (Oxford 1958), 2 vols.

Taylor, L. R., "Augustales, Seviri Augustales, and Seviri: A Chronological Study," *TAPA* 45 (1914), pp. 231–253.

———— "Horace's Equestrian Career," *AJP* 46 (1925), pp. 161–170.

———— *Voting Districts of the Roman Republic*, MAAR 20 (1960).

Tchernia, A., "Les fouilles sous-marines de Planier (Bouches-du-Rhone)," *CRAI* (1969), pp. 292–309.

——— "Premiers résultats des fouilles de juin 1968 sur l'épave 3 de Planier," *Etudes Classiques* (Aix-en-Provence) 3 (1968–70), pp. 51–82.

———, with Pomey, P., and Hesnard, A., *L'épave romaine de la Madrague de Giens, Gallia*, supp. 34 (Paris 1978).

Testaguzza, O., *Portus* (Rome 1970).

Thiel, J. H., *A History of Roman Sea-Power before the Second Punic War* (Amsterdam 1954).

Thylander, H., *Inscriptions du port d'Ostie* (Lund 1952), 2 vols.

Torelli, M., "Feronia e Lucus Feroniae in due iscrizioni latine," *Archeologia Classica* 25–26 (1973–74), pp. 741–750.

——— "Industria estrattiva, lavoro artigianale, interessi economici: qualche appunto," in *Seaborne Commerce*, pp. 313–323.

Treggiari, S., *Roman Freedmen during the Late Republic* (Oxford 1969).

——— "Lower Class Women in the Roman Economy," *Florilegium* 1 (1979), pp. 65–86.

——— "Sentiment and Property: Some Roman Attitudes," in A. Parel and T. Flanagan, eds., *Theories of Property* (Calgary 1979), pp. 53–85.

Udovitch, A. L., "Formalism and Informalism in the Social and Economic Institutions of the Medieval Islamic World," in A. Banani and S. Vryonis, Jr., eds., *Individualism and Conformity in Classical Islam* (Wiesbaden 1977), pp. 61–81.

Veyne, P., "Vie de Trimalcion," *Annales E.S.C.* 16 (1961), pp. 213–247.

Wallinga, H. T., "Nautika I: The Units of Capacity for Ancient Ships," *Mn.* (1964), pp. 1–40.

Waltzing, J. P., *Étude historique sur les corporations professionelles chez les romains* (Louvain 1895–1900), 4 vols.

Ward-Perkins, J. B., "The Marble Trade and its Organization: Evidence from Nicomedia," in *Seaborne Commerce*, pp. 325–338.

White, K. D., *Roman Farming* (Ithaca, N.Y. 1970).

White, P., "*Amicitia* and the Profession of Poetry in Early Imperial Rome," *JRS* 68 (1978), pp. 74–92.

Will, E. L., "Les amphores de Sestius," *Revue archéologique de l'Est et du Centre-Est* 7 (1956), pp. 224–244.

——— "The Sestius Amphoras: A Reappraisal," *Journal of Field Archaeology* 6 (1979), pp. 339–350.

Wilson, A. J. N., *Emigration from Italy in the Republican Age of Rome* (Manchester 1966).

Wilson, F. W., "Studies in the Social and Economic History of Ostia: Part I," *PBSR* 13 (1935), pp. 41–68.

Wiseman, T. P., "The Potteries of Vibienus and Rufrenus at Arretium," *Mn.* 16 (1963), pp. 275–283.

———— *New Men in the Roman Senate 139 B.C.–14 A.D.* (Oxford 1971).

———— "Senators, Commerce, and Empire," *Liverpool Classical Monthly* 1 (1976), pp. 21–22.

Yavetz, Z., "The Policy of C. Flaminius and the *Plebiscitum Claudianum*," *Athenaeum* 40 (1962), pp. 325–344.

Zeitlin, F., "Petronius as Paradox: Anarchy and Artistic Integrity," *TAPA* 102 (1971), pp. 631–684.

Zevi, F., "Brevi note ostiensi," *Epigraphica* 30 (1968), pp. 89–95.

———— "Nuovi documenti epigrafici sugli Egrili ostiensi," *MEFR* 82 (1970), pp. 279–320.

Index

The index registers persons, places, and principal topics discussed in the text and footnotes. Emperors, members of the imperial house, and well-known persons (for example, Cicero, Pliny the Younger) are listed under their conventional English names; all other Romans are registered by *gentilicia*. Dates, unless otherwise indicated, are A.D.

Adriatic shippers, see *navicularii maris Hadriatici*
L. Aelius Lamia, 42, 44
P. Aelius, 137
M. Aemilius Avianianus, 28
M. Aemilius Lepidus (*cos.* I, 187 B.C.), 36, 44
M. Aemilius Scaurus (*cos.* 115 B.C.), 67
Africa, 4, 24, 26, 29, 42, 84, 102, 123
agriculture, 6, 7, 12, 22, 34, 82, 83, 84, 98, 100, 117, 160
Agrigentum, 27
Alba, 95
Alsium, 95
Altinum, 91
amicitia, economic implications of, 43, 46, 145–146, 150, 154, 157, 165–166, 169, 171
amphorae, 36, 58, 66, 68; names stamped on, 28n, 51–52, 56–58, 68, 68n, 70, 84, 156, 157, 163
Ancona, 158
L. Annaeus Mela, 114
P. Annius Eros, 166
T. Annius Milo (*pr.* 55 B.C.), 62
P. Annius Plocamus, 166
C. Antistius Vetus (*suff.* 30 B.C.), 89
Antium, 33
Antoninus Pius, the Emperor, 125, 160, 165n

L. Antonius Albus (*suff. ann. inc.*), 165n
M. Antonius (*cos.* 44 B.C.), 28
Apani, 52
Aphrodisias, 28n
apparitores, 110
Appian, 160
Apulia, 54, 84
Aquileia, 8, 44, 91, 140, 157, 162, 164
C. Aquillius Proculus (*cos.* 90), 157
Aquinum, 66
M. Aquinus, 65
aratores, 26, 27
architects, 28n, 81n
Arelate, 162
argentarii, 26, 29, 37, 50, 64, 67, 102, 197, 128, 157
Arretium, 16, 65, 164n
Arrianus Maturus, 162
Ateii, 164
Athens, 4, 39, 57, 68
Atilius, 4
Atticus, T. Pomponius, 49, 51, 52, 55, 56, 60, 61, 62, 63, 113, 114, 159
P. Attius Silanus, 135, 136n
Sex. Aufidius, 29, 30
P. Aufidius Fortis, 133
Augustales, 102, 109, 116, 122, 126–148, 162, 166